Westminster College
of
Salt Lake City

_____

Westminster College
of
Salt Lake City

*From Presbyterian Mission School
to Independent College*

R. Douglas Brackenridge

Utah State University Press
Logan, Utah
1998

Utah State University Press
Logan, Utah 84322-7800

Typography by WolfPack
Cover Design by Thomas Cronin

The paper in this book is acid free.

Library of Congress Cataloging-in-Publication Data

Brackenridge, R. Douglas.
    Westminster College of Salt Lake City: from Presbyterian mission school to
    independent college / R. Douglas Brackenridge.
       p. cm.
Includes bibliographical references (p.) and index.
ISBN 0-87421-250-2
1. Westminster College of Salt Lake City—History. I. Title.
LD6031.W568 B73 1998
378.792'258—ddc21   98-19670
                                                                    CIP

Contents

Preface

On numerous occasions, people have inquired how I came to write a history of Westminster College, an institution far removed from San Antonio, Texas, my home for the past thirty-five years. My response invariably brought another query: "When will you complete your work?" To the latter question I can now say, "It is finished." To the former question, I will briefly recount the steps that led to the completion of this narrative.

My educational training and religious background were important factors. My parents, Scottish immigrants who came to the United States in the mid-1920s, imbued their children with a respect for the Reformed tradition and the values it espoused. Holding education in esteem, they fostered learning and urged college education as a means to a more fulfilling life. After graduating from Muskingum College (1954) in New Concord, Ohio, a school very similar in size and religious ethos to Westminster, and Pittsburgh Theological Seminary (1957), I was ordained as a Presbyterian minister. Following a brief period in a parish and the completion of a Ph.D. in ecclesiastical history from the University of Glasgow in Scotland (1962), I accepted an appointment in the Department of Religion at Trinity University in San Antonio, Texas, teaching courses in biblical studies, American religious history, and the Christian tradition.

The immediate impulse for writing this book emerged out of a classroom teaching experience in a course on new religious movements in the United States. Through Thomas O'Day's *The Mormons* and general studies in American religious history by such scholars as Clifton E. Olmstead, Edwin S. Gaustad, and Martin E. Marty, I became familiar with the history and beliefs of Latter-day Saints (the LDS Church). Nevertheless, I remained unacquainted with Mormon scholarship, and my knowledge of the Book of Mormon consisted almost entirely of passages cited in anti-Mormon literature. By incorporating field trips and visiting lecturers into my course, I was brought into contact with representative leaders of the San Antonio religious community, one of whom was Latter-day Saint mission president Thomas Tyler. He spoke to my class on numerous occasions, explaining Mormon principles in the context of dialogue rather than of dogmatism. Tyler also stimulated a reexamination of my assumptions regarding Latter-day Saints. In the process, we became friends both in academic and social settings.

These experiences stirred my curiosity regarding how Presbyterians and Latter-day Saints had interacted over a period of time and led to research at the Presbyterian Historical Society (PHS) in Philadelphia and in the archival collections of the LDS Historical Department, the University of Utah, Utah State University, Brigham Young University, the Utah State Historical Society, Wasatch Academy, and Westminster College. My preliminary research revealed an abundance of primary source materials and a fascinating story of how established religious traditions and new religious movements interrelate. As the importance of Westminster College to the story became evident, I realized that no one had written a comprehensive institutional history. Conversations with college officials led to an agreement that I would write a history to be completed prior to the year 2000, which marks the 125th anniversary of the founding of the Salt Lake Collegiate Institute.

Thanks are due to the many people who have encouraged and supported this project from its inception in 1992. Coordinator and associate for colleges and universities of the Presbyterian Church (U.S.A.) Duncan S. Ferguson introduced me to college officials and provided information regarding church-related colleges. Former Westminster president Charles Dick and his staff provided accommodations on campus and travel expenses between Salt Lake City and San Antonio. Similar support and encouragement has been forthcoming from the incumbent president, Peggy Stock, and her staff. Other administrators who have facilitated my research include Stephen R. Baar, Stephen R. Morgan, and Craig A. Green. The library staff under the direction of Richard Wunder and David Hales have extended every courtesy during my research process. Their assistance in locating materials and arranging ample work space has greatly accelerated the tedious process of examining a widely varied collection of archival documents. I am also indebted to the many faculty, alumni, and friends of Westminster College whose names are listed as interviewees in the bibliography. They contributed anecdotes, insights, and information about Westminster that could not otherwise have been obtained.

Others from the Westminster and Salt Lake City community merit recognition. Claudene Wilcox, administrative secretary to President Dick, advised in the selection of interviewees, scheduled interviews, and initially handled correspondence. Her enthusiasm and expertise helped smooth out rough spots, especially at the beginning of the research project. Anne Mcdonald, director of the Office of Communication, and her staff, especially Dana Tumpowsky, who proofread the manuscript and selected photographs, and Thomas Cronin, who designed the dust jacket, rendered invaluable service. Paula Garfield, administrative assistant to the executive vice president, facilitated travel arrangements and housing and coordinated meetings with various campus administrators. Faculty members, including Carolyn Tucker, Bruce Bemis, and Barry Quinn, have added to my knowledge of college lore and welcomed me into the academic community.

My debt to Professor Keith Wilson of Brigham Young University is enormous. His doctoral dissertation on the process of secularization at Westminster completed in 1995 was informative and insightful. Our extended conversations culminated in a joint lecture and discussion session on Westminster's history during President Stock's inaugural week in 1996. Professor Frederick Buchanan in the Department of Education at the University of Utah, shared his encyclopedic knowledge of Utah and Mormon educational history and introduced me to the Mormon Historical Association. Other scholars who have given me invaluable assistance include Ronald Barney, Davis Bitton, and C. Randall Paul.

Trinity University, the Presbyterian Historical Society, and the Lilly Endowment also played important roles in the completion of this project. The staff of the PHS under the directorship of Frederick J. Heuser showed me every courtesy during my numerous visits to Philadelphia and enabled me to locate important archival materials relating to Westminster College. Trinity University granted me an academic leave during 1996–97 and funded several research trips to Salt Lake City. President Ronald K. Calgaard shared insights gleaned from his long history of involvement in the Presbyterian College Union and pointed me in the direction of fruitful avenues of reflection and research. The Louisville Institute for the Study of Protestantism and American Culture sponsored by the Lilly Endowment awarded a summer stipend in 1992 that enabled me to complete the initial phase of my research in Salt Lake City and Philadelphia.

As always, my colleagues in the Department of Religion were supportive, nudging me through writer's block and applauding even the most minor steps toward completion of the manuscript. Our departmental secretary, Margaret Miksch, listened sympathetically to my litany of computer problems and offered timely and professional assistance in photocopying material, handling correspondence, and protecting me from interruptions. Grant Morrison, administrative secretary of the Office of Academic Affairs, produced the index. I am also grateful to Lois Boyd, my colleague, confidant, and critic, whose intellectual acumen, editorial expertise, and spirited work ethic never cease to amaze me. Finally, I acknowledge the patience and understanding of my wife, Diane Saphire, who more than anyone else has endured the day-to-day agonies of living with a book-in-process.

Although Westminster officials have assisted my research, they have exercised no control over the content of this book. The conclusions reached are solely my own. While attempting to be objective, the author admits a bias of admiration for an institution that has survived chronic fiscal crises and changing institutional missions to become a significant component in the Utah higher education environment. In particular, I acknowledge the contributions of dedicated faculty, administrators, trustees, staff, and students who have shaped the college's distinctive identity. I hope this history will provide a useful narrative for those who wish to recall and understand the origins, growth, and development of Westminster College.

Westminster College
of
Salt Lake City

Introduction

The origins of Westminster College are rooted in Presbyterian and Mormon history, making it one of the truly unique educational institutions in the United States. Westminster began with a purpose unlike its peer institutions. In addition to a commitment to a traditional program of liberal arts education, Westminster's Presbyterian founders endorsed an evangelistic mission to convert and integrate Mormons into mainstream American culture. This institutional purpose would create tension for some time between the college, which represented the minority population, and the Latter-day Saints, who were the dominant culture of Utah, and also would influence the institution's administrative structures, curriculum development, faculty recruitment, and student enrollment.

Westminster College traces its historical roots to the Salt Lake Collegiate Institute, founded by the First Presbyterian Church of Salt Lake City in 1875 as a combination primary and secondary school. Staffed by qualified and experienced teachers, the institute offered graded classes similar to the best eastern public schools and emphasized personalized and progressive education. It acquired a regional reputation as an excellent residential academy. After the introduction of the Utah public school system in 1890, however, the institute phased out grammar school classes. The Woman's Executive Committee of the Presbyterian Board of Home Missions assumed ownership and administrative control of the institute in 1896 and maintained operations until 1910, when it transferred the property to Westminster College.

Endorsed by the Presbytery of Utah in 1892 and chartered as Sheldon Jackson College in 1895, the new institution commenced classes two years later on the Collegiate Institute campus. The college awarded its first baccalaureate degree in 1901 to a sole graduate, Theodore M. Keusseff. Changing its name to Westminster College in 1902, it continued to be housed with the institute, which served as a college preparatory department. In 1911, the institute property was sold, and students moved from the downtown location to a suburban campus developed by Westminster College. From 1909 to 1913 college classes were suspended but in 1914 resumed with first-year and sophomore students. Unable to support a baccalaureate degree program, Westminster functioned for the next two decades as a combination high school and junior college with the bulk of its enrollment coming from high school preparatory students. In 1935 Westminster adopted a four-year junior college format, offering an associate's degree in several fields in addition to a high school diploma. Near the end of World War II, college trustees voted to seek accreditation as a four-year baccalaureate institution, hoping to meet anticipated peacetime needs for higher education, and Westminster awarded its first baccalaureate degree in 1946. Its enrollment increased steadily, bolstered by veterans and state population growth. Over the years, the college expanded its undergraduate curriculum and added graduate programs in a number of specialized fields. Today it offers a liberal arts curriculum complemented by a variety of undergraduate and graduate degree programs.

For much of its early history, Westminster maintained a Presbyterian identity while soliciting support from other Protestant denominations. In addition to long-standing legal connections with the Presbyterian Church U.S.A., Westminster also negotiated less formal agreements with the United Church of Christ (formerly Congregational) and the United Methodist Church (formerly Methodist Episcopal) in the 1950s.[1] The Presbyterian denomination favored regional and local educational institutions rather than ones controlled at the General Assembly, or national, level. It identified Presbyterian colleges by three categories in terms of their relationship to denominational governing bodies. Colleges similar to Westminster, whose boards of trustees were elected or had their appointments ratified by local synods or presbyteries, were deemed "organically connected" to the denomination. Institutions whose charters stipulated that at least two-thirds of their board members must be Presbyterians constituted a second category. Colleges "historically related" to the denomination but not subject to any ecclesiastical control were a third group. Only on rare occasions did denominational governing bodies become involved in day-to-day college operations or in the hiring or dismissal of administrators, faculty, or staff.[2]

Although the denomination maintained legal ties with church colleges through regional synods and presbyteries, it established educational standards and disbursed financial aid through the national Presbyterian Board of College Aid (later through the Board of Christian Education) and the Presbyterian College Union, an auxiliary organization composed of the presidents of church-related colleges. Institutions that failed to maintain the educational standards faced loss of funding and removal from the approved list of institutions of higher education. In 1912, for example, the College Board specified that Presbyterian colleges should have at least six full-time professors, a minimum endowment of $200,000, a library of not fewer than five thousand volumes, and laboratory equipment sufficient for two years of work in physics, chemistry, botany, and zoology. Colleges receiving aid were also expected to have faculty members who were professing Christians and members of some evangelical church, weekly chapel, mandatory Bible classes, and "a positive Christian point of view was to be expressed in the teaching of all subjects laid down in the curriculum."[3]

During the first half of the twentieth century, the Presbyterian Church through its governing bodies and national boards made substantial contributions to church-related colleges for general operating expenses and capital funds. By the early 1960s the annual figure reached $2.5 million, not including donations from individual Presbyterians who contributed outside formal ecclesiastical channels.[4] Because of declining membership and budgetary realignments in the late 1960s, however, the denomination was forced to reduce drastically its financial commitment to higher education. At the same time, Christian educators were engaged in a discussion on whether church-related colleges could enjoy authentic academic freedom while operating under legal obligations to denominational governing bodies.

In this context, the Presbyterian General Assembly reexamined its historical relationship to higher education and agreed that church colleges could more readily achieve academic excellence and maintain academic freedom if they were unfettered. Consequently, it urged its colleges and universities to establish covenant relationships that affirmed historic religious ties with regional governing bodies but involved no legal controls. Westminster entered into a covenant relationship with the Synod of Colorado and Utah in 1970 and with its successor, the Synod of Rocky Mountains, in 1974. During this process, Westminster abolished the distinguishing marks of a church-related college, such as mandatory Sunday worship, compulsory daily chapel, and required Bible classes. When Westminster reorganized in 1983, the covenant relationship was not included in the revised bylaws and has not subsequently been renegotiated. Affiliations with the United Church of Christ and the United Methodist Church ended by mutual agreements in the 1980s and 1990s. While affirming its historic roots in Protestant higher education, Westminster currently identifies itself as a private, independent college.[5]

Other alterations have occurred since mid-century. A number of new buildings, including dormitories, a library, a student center, and a fine arts complex, have been erected to provide Westminster with an attractive, modern, well-equipped campus. Ferry Hall, one of the original college buildings, was condemned as unsafe and razed in 1987. Only Converse and Foster Halls, both newly renovated, remain as visible landmarks of the college's origins. The composition and size of the student body and faculty have changed radically, especially in the last twenty-five years. From a community of approximately 400 students with 25 faculty, Westminster has grown to a student body of 2,200 with 100 full-time and 150 adjunct and affiliated professors. The primarily residential institution with a student body of recent high school graduates now is predominantly composed of second-career, nonresidential students.

Founded in the midst of a decade-long economic depression, Westminster has experienced fiscal instability throughout most of its history. Lacking sufficient endowment and dependable cash flow, the college survived only through the sacrificial service of faculty and staff and timely gifts from religious philanthropists. On numerous occasions even the most sanguine college supporters contemplated closure. These prolonged fiscal problems culminated in an action of considerable economic import in 1983, when Westminster College officially closed and immediately reopened as Westminster College of Salt Lake City. Since that time, with decisive leadership and prudent planning, the college has achieved a balanced budget and increased its institutional endowment. Westminster approaches the twenty-first century more financially secure than at any time in its previous history.

Any comprehensive history of Westminster College must take into account its heritage and environment. The Presbyterian religious tradition informed the intellectual pursuits and ethical conduct of its founders, faculty, benefactors, and students. Prominent figures in the college's history, such as Sheldon Jackson, John M. Coyner, Robert G. McNiece, and Herbert W. Reherd, shared a Presbyterian upbringing that influenced their vision of Westminster College as a religious and educational institution.[6] In fact, Westminster's Presbyterian heritage is reflected in its name, which derives from *The Westminster Confession of Faith*, an exposition of Reformed (Presbyterian) theology produced by English Puritans and Scottish Presbyterians at Westminster, a borough of London, in the seventeenth century. The college is steeped in a theological tradition that traces its roots to the Protestant reformation of the sixteenth century, in particular to John Calvin, whose explication of Christian doctrine captured the hearts and minds of many leading reformers. Calvin's theological system, encapsulated in *The Institutes of the Christian Religion*, provided an intellectual framework for American Protestantism that transcended denominational and national boundaries.[7]

One theme of Calvin's theology had particular importance for American higher education. Believing that only informed Christians could be effective Christians, Calvin prized intellectual acumen as a means of serving God. People who have tasted the liberal arts, he wrote, "penetrate with their aid far more deeply into the secrets of the divine wisdom."[8] In order to foster learning, Calvin established the Geneva Academy in 1559 to train men for the ministry and to provide an educated laity. The academy's curriculum included courses in French, classical languages, music, and Bible studies. As a result, critical writing and learned preaching characterized the work of Presbyterian leaders who shared Calvin's belief that "the tongue without the mind must be highly displeasing to God."[9]

Presbyterians in the United States adopted this high regard for learning, leading efforts to establish academies and universities during the colonial and early national periods. By the time of the Civil War, Presbyterians had founded forty-nine church-related colleges in twenty-three states and were instrumental in establishing a number of other private and state institutions, including Princeton, Hampden-Sydney, Dickinson, Lafayette, Washington and Jefferson, and Wooster.[10] The denomination's highest governing body, the General Assembly, endorsed this establishment of colleges and universities, which became a Presbyterian hallmark as the century progressed. By 1883 the assembly had created a Board of Aid for Colleges and Academies to provide financial assistance and professional advice for fledgling institutions. A representative of that board articulated the denomination's attitude toward higher education: "Among Presbyterians, religion and learning go hand in hand. So colleges and academies are a necessity to the Presbyterian Church. Historically, if not logically, the two go together. The Presbyterian Church does not prosper in ignorance or illiteracy."[11]

In particular, Presbyterians regarded the western frontier as a testing ground in which the future of Protestantism depended on the efficacy of Christian education. As early as 1819 the General Assembly established the Board of Education to assist presbyteries in training young men for the ministry. Later, the General Assembly created a Special Committee on Education charged with the responsibility of promoting the planting of colleges in the West. Religious educators encouraged the proliferation of small colleges in western states and territories by advising that colleges should not be situated more than three-hundred miles from prospective students and that college students in western states would never be concentrated in a few large cities. Presbyterian educator George P. Hays, in advocating small colleges, concluded, "The question for the West to settle is whether an education at a small college is better than none. If the West is to have Christian colleges large enough to shadow the land, they must begin with the mustard seed of faith, and during the day of small things be content to work with small things."[12] Westminster College was founded precisely on the basis of that philosophy.

In their campaign to evangelize and educate western territories, Presbyterian missionaries initially targeted white, Anglo-Saxon Protestants who had no religious backgrounds or who were only nominal church members. This group formed the nucleus of small congregations that were established in towns and villages throughout the West. At the same time, missionaries moving westward evangelized three other groups of people termed "exceptional populations": Native Americans, Hispanics, and Mormons. Attempts toward the conversion and cultural assimilation of these groups required a considerable commitment of financial and human resources with modest results.

As did their contemporaries, Presbyterians held stereotypical, often negative, views of these groups. Many missionaries and pioneers identified American Indians as savages, sorcerers, and pagans and attributed their problems to their use of alcohol. Similarly, some viewed Hispanic Catholics who resided primarily in New Mexico and Colorado as lazy and unreliable and, fueled by a strong anti-Roman Catholic sentiment, considered Hispanic religion to be corrupt and superstitious. Mormons presented a unique situation because they derived largely from the very Anglo-Saxon racial stock that Protestants so highly prized. To account for what they perceived as Anglo-Saxon defections from mainline Protestantism, missionaries and teachers alleged that Mormon converts had been duped or deluded by the mesmerizing message of Joseph Smith and his associates. Presbyterians articulated a belief that Mormonism was a destructive cult that divided families, promoted sexual deviancy, disseminated heretical teachings, and threatened national unity.[13]

The educational environment in Utah affected by the tension between Presbyterians and Mormons can be traced back to the beginnings of the new religious movement. Four members of the Smith family, including Joseph's mother, Lucy, joined the Western Presbyterian Church in Palmyra, New York. Although Joseph and his father remained aloof from denominational affiliation, the son occasionally attended Presbyterian and Methodist revivals and later acknowledged that he "became somewhat partial to the Methodist sect." Smith also was well acquainted with Calvinistic theology, especially the doctrines of election and predestination, which he considered abhorrent. The cacophony of voices among Presbyterians, Methodists, and Baptists, all of whom claimed divine inspiration and scriptural authority, perplexed and unsettled Smith. In desperation, he prayed to God for a revelation that would resolve his spiritual ambivalence. According to Smith, in a series of visions beginning in 1820, God responded to the question "Which of the sects is true?" The heavenly voice replied, "None of them"—that all creeds were an abomination and their adherents hypocritical and corrupt.[14]

These transforming experiences led Smith to establish the Church of Jesus Christ of Latter-day Saints in 1830. Attracting followers from the revivalistic milieu of upper New York state, the adherents were known popularly as Mormons because they accepted revelation believed to have been derived from golden plates published as the Book of Mormon. Under Smith's pragmatic and charismatic leadership the new movement grew rapidly. Claiming to represent primitive Christianity purged from centuries-long encrustations of erroneous beliefs, and labeling all other denominations apostate, the Church of Jesus Christ of Latter-day Saints won converts from disaffected Protestants and unchurched populations throughout the United States and Western Europe. Its rapid growth, absolutist truth claims, secret rituals, and ubiquitous proselytizing evoked jealousy, animosity, and persecution. Presbyterian church sessions routinely excommunicated members who united or associated with Mormons, charging them with immoral behavior and heretical belief in the inspiration of the Book of Mormon.[15]

As a result of concerted opposition, the Latter-day Saints migrated from New York to Ohio to Missouri and finally to Nauvoo, Illinois. There Smith reported a new revelation directing him to restore plural marriage (polygamy) in 1843, and the following year he was assassinated by an angry mob while incarcerated in Carthage, Illinois, on charges of inciting a riot. Smith's death marked the beginning of a new era for Latter-day Saints. His martyrdom precipitated a crisis of succession common to all new religious movements based primarily on the charismatic leadership of their founders. In the ensuing debate over who should lead the Mormon community, no unanimous decision could be reached. The vast majority of Mormons accepted Brigham Young as the legitimate and divinely appointed successor to the Prophet Joseph, although a few splinter groups formed to mark their dissent. Under Young's direction, the Mormons began their historic exodus to the Great Salt Lake Valley where in 1847 they established a religious community that would become a significant force in America's religious landscape.[16]

Some of the earliest anti-Mormon pamphlets and broadsides came from the pens of Presbyterian apologists and were widely distributed through denominational channels. A Presbyterian clergyman, Robert Baird, scorned Mormonism in his *Religion in the United States of America*, published in 1844 and revised and expanded in 1856. Baird termed Mormon theology materialistic and immoral and deemed its communal theocracy a threat to constitutional separation of church and state. He summarily dismissed Mormonism as a religious aberration produced by a combination of cunning leaders and deluded followers and categorized Mormons among non-Christian sects. He described them as "the grossest of all the delusions that Satanic malignity or human ambition ever sought to propagate." He summarized that "the Mormons are a body of ignorant dupes, collected from almost all parts of the United States, and also from the British Isles." Baird believed that like other fanatical sects, the Latter-day Saints would have a short-lived existence after their leader's death, concluding that most Mormons would either revert to traditional Christianity or languish as disillusioned atheists or agnostics.[17]

Other Presbyterian writers held a similar view of Mormonism as a theological system and a religious community. In particular, they focused on the controversial Mormon practice of plural marriage and called for federal intervention in Utah to end polygamous relationships. Denominational newspapers and magazines regularly featured polemical anti-Mormon editorials and articles that reached audiences throughout the United States. Titles such as "Mormon Deviltry," "The Mormon Prayer: Treason and Irreligion," and "Heathenism at Home" typified the Presbyterian assault on Mormon beliefs and practices. One prominent Presbyterian minister offered the following as a satisfactory solution to the "Mormon problem": "Gather all the leading Mormons into their big tabernacle and turn the U.S. artillery loose upon them."[18] Such language created an atmosphere which made cordial relationships between Presbyterians and Mormons virtually impossible to sustain.

Mormons responded in kind to the Presbyterian rhetoric. Because of harsh treatment by Protestant clergymen and parishioners in New York, Ohio, Illinois, and Missouri, Mormon leaders denigrated Protestantism as theologically defective and ethically moribund. George Q. Cannon, editor of the *Deseret Evening News*, believed that non-Mormon churches needed purification. "They are in a far worse fix that those mentioned in the New Testament. The latter were threatened with the loss of their candlesticks, but if present day churches ever had any, they have lost them completely, for their light has become gross darkness."[19] Others painted portraits of greedy, amoral, pretentious, and dogmatic sectarians determined to exterminate Mormonism. Presbyterian clergymen were depicted as licentious power mongers obsessed with seducing Mormon women and acquiring personal fortunes. One writer called Protestant ministers "miserable hirelings who, in spite and anger, fulminate their 'Christian' diatribes against our leaders and our institutions."[20]

Mormon apologists also caricatured Presbyterian doctrines of the Trinity, predestination, and eternal punishment and ridiculed the belief in a God who lacked "body, parts, and passions." One writer referred to the doctrine of the Trinity as an absurdity. Such a god, he said, "is a footless stocking without a leg, sitting upon the top of a topless throne, far beyond the bounds of time and space; and we are asked to believe, render obedience to, and worship this being?"[21] Another editorialist concluded his remarks on trinitarian Christianity with this comment: "Viewed without sectarian, colored spectacles, the scriptures proclaim modern 'Christian' theology a delusion and a mass of contradictory nonsense."[22]

In this context, relationships between Presbyterians and Mormons in nineteenth-century Utah were frequently abrasive, especially in the more isolated Mormon towns and villages. Presbyterian missionaries leveled charges against Mormons ranging from disruption of worship and destruction of church property to threatened or actual physical abuse. The Presbytery of Utah complained to Mormon authorities that in towns like Logan, American Fork, Springville, and Payson religious meetings were "frequently disturbed by hootings through the windows, cursing against the teachers, and by boisterous singing and shouting round the doors." Presbyterians further charged that buildings had been "defiled in unmentionable ways, our property injured by stoning, and our books cut to pieces and scattered under the seats by those attending our services."[23] In response, Mormon leaders claimed that Presbyterian accounts either exaggerated or misrepresented actual situations. In most instances they provided affidavits from respected citizens, both Mormons and non-Mormons, containing testimonies that contradicted or modified Presbyterian accusations. Mormons also argued that Presbyterians circulated such stories in order to gain financial support for missions from eastern Protestants who were emotionally stirred by stories of hostile and degenerate Mormons. Affronted by persistent attacks on their character, most Mormons viewed Presbyterian missionaries as outsiders whose message should be either politely ignored or publicly opposed.[24]

Over the years, relationships between Westminster College and the local Mormon community have ranged from hostility to ambivalence to cordiality, reflecting in microcosm attitudes expressed in the wider American scene. The anti-Mormonism that gave the college its founding impulse had largely disappeared by the 1930s and by mid-century no longer informed institutional policies and procedures. Instead, Westminster espoused an inclusive ecumenical stance on theological issues and cultivated positive relationships with Mormon authorities. The Church of Jesus Christ of Latter-day Saints also changed. Beginning in 1890 with its refusal to sanction plural marriages, the church made other doctrinal redefinitions that reduced tensions and ameliorated relationships with mainline Protestantism. LDS Church leaders eschewed the pejorative language that dominated nineteenth century theological debates and supported interfaith discussions and community projects. Since the 1950s, Latter-day Saints have given substantial financial support to the college and have served on the Westminster Board of Trustees since 1967.[25]

Previous narratives about Westminster have been organized around the tenure of individual presidents, marking each administration as the beginning and the end of a distinct period of institutional history. Rather than follow a similar pattern, which has inherent historical limitations, this study identifies time periods during which significant developments occurred. Period one, from the Civil War to the end of the nineteenth century, describes Presbyterian beginnings in Utah and the organization and expansion of Westminster's forerunner, the Salt Lake Collegiate Institute. This phase, in which the institute provided the foundation on which the college was built, has never been critically examined. Period two recounts the origins of Sheldon Jackson College and the formation of its successor institution, Westminster College; the construction of a permanent campus; and the integration of the Collegiate Institute and Westminster College into one corporate entity. It also traces the development of Westminster from a two-year to a four-year junior college. Period three begins with the onset of World War II and focuses on Westminster College as a four-year baccalaureate-granting college from its evolution as a small, church-related institution to a modern, private, independent college, and describes curricular, fiscal, social, and religious changes. The epilogue discusses current institutional goals and projections as Westminster College enters the twenty-first century.

The approach of this narrative precludes biographical sketches of the many individuals who devoted much of their active careers to

Westminster College. Only the presidents, a few key administrators, some of the early founders and instructors, and various trustees are mentioned in an overview of more than 125 years of history. Yet the heart of any educational institution is its faculty members and their day-to-day contact with students in classes, conferences, advising, and social situations. Many of the faculty of Westminster have influenced a number of student generations. One notes Stephen Baar, Bruce Bemis, Patricia Aikins Coleman, C. Don Doxey, Shirley Knox, Catherine Kuzminski, Tom Steinke, Barry G. Quinn, Robert G. Warnock, and Richard Wunder. From farther back are names such as Alice and James Boyack, Viola Evans Chapman, Lottie Felkner, Kenneth Kuchler, Jack J. Gifford, Janet Palmer, May Marie Schewender, John S. Telecky, Martha (Monroe) Tiller, Lloyd Wilcox, and Myra Yancey.

More than any other individual during the last half century, Professor Jay W. Lees epitomizes Westminster College's commitment to classroom teaching. For thirty-seven years, longer than anyone in the history of the college, Lees energized, inspired, and challenged Westminster students. A Salt Lake City native and graduate of the University of Utah, Lees joined the faculty of Westminster as an instructor in speech and drama following a Latter-day Saint mission in France and Canada and a stint in the U.S. Army. In the script of one of his first plays, "Outward Bound," Lees used the word *hell* several times. President Emeritus Reherd expressed displeasure about his using the word, but President Robert Steele told him not to worry about it. In 1964 Lees organized the Westminster Players, who performed in a multipurpose area in Converse Hall, later designated Courage Theater by Lees after he returned from England and a visit to the John Courage Brewery. In 1983 the Courage Theater was dedicated to Lees, and later a part of the new fine arts building was named in his honor.[26]

Stories regarding Lees abound in Westminster folklore. Lees insisted that students be prompt for rehearsals and inform him in advance if they were detained. One student called the Lees's residence with a message for his drama teacher at 2 A.M. "Couldn't it wait?" asked Lees's daughter who answered the telephone. The student replied, "No, I'm in jail and can make only one call. I want to let him know that I won't be at rehearsal." Another story concerned a student who was frequently absent. Lees took the entire class to this student's dorm room and conducted the session there with the offending student lying in bed with a sheet over his head.[27] On numerous occasions Lees was recognized by students for his teaching ability and his willingness to spend time with students. John Young, class of 1952, described Lees as a man who could draw out latent abilities in his students and stimulate them to be productive and creative. "He encouraged us to come out of ourselves and be someone different."[28] Westminster has been fortunate to have had a loyal group of dedicated and competent classroom teachers who never lost sight of the institution's primary task of educating men and women. In the narrative that follows, their presence is often overshadowed by institutional crises, campus activities, and curricular changes, but invariably they have personalized the educational experience and provided a historical continuity that has enhanced Westminster's reputation as a caring institution.

NOTES

1. The Presbyterian Church in the United States of America (PCUSA) was organized at the national level in 1789 with the creation of a General Assembly in Philadelphia, Pennsylvania. At the end of the Civil War, southern Presbyterians formed their own denomination, the Presbyterian Church in the United States (PCUS). In 1958 the PCUSA united with the United Presbyterian Church of North America to form the United Presbyterian Church in the United States of America (UPCUSA). In 1983 the southern and northern branches reunited to form the present-day Presbyterian Church (U.S.A.).

2. C. Harve Geiger, *The Program of Higher Education of the Presbyterian Church in the United States of America* (Cedar Rapids, Iowa, 1940), 83–89.

3. Ibid., 91–101. For a concise history of church-related colleges in the twentieth century, see Bradley J. Longfield and George M. Marsden, "Presbyterian Colleges in Twentieth-Century America," in Milton J. Coalter, John M. Mulder, and Louis B. Weeks, *The Pluralistic Vision: Presbyterians and Mainstream Protestant Education and Leadership* (Louisville, Kentucky, 1992), 99–124.

4. Manning M. Pattillo, Jr. and Donald M. Mackenzie, *Church-Sponsored Higher Education in the United States* (Washington, D.C., 1966), 264–65. Many colleges received substantial financial support from regional synods and presbyteries. Because of its mission status, the Synod of Utah was unable to provide Westminster any funding.

5. *Westminster College 1994–1995 Academic Catalog*, 9–10. Westminster is still on the annual list of institutions officially related to the denomination issued by the General Assembly of the Presbyterian Church (U.S.A.). See *Minutes of the General Assembly of the Presbyterian Church (U.S.A.)*, 1996, I:369–70.

6. For a study of Calvin's impact on American culture, see W. Fred Graham, *John Calvin: The Constructive Revolutionary* (Lansing, Michigan, 1987).

7. For an introduction to Calvin's life and thought, see T. H. L. Parker, *John Calvin: A Biography* (Philadelphia, 1975); and John T. McNeil, *The History and Character of Calvinism* (Philadelphia, 1967). For a survey of American Presbyterian history, see Randall Balmer and J. Fitzmier, *The Presbyterians* (Westport, Connecticut, 1994).

8. Cited in John Leith, *Introduction to the Reformed Tradition* (Atlanta, 1977), 8.

9. Ibid., 78–79.

10. Donald G. Tewksbury, *The Founding of American Colleges and Universities before the Civil War* (New York, 1865), 91.

11. *Minutes of the General Assembly of the Presbyterian Church in the United States of America* (Philadelphia, 1886), 184, hereafter cited as *GAMPCUSA*. The Board of

Aid for Colleges and Academies was reorganized in 1904 as the College Board and in 1916 merged into the General Board of Education. This continued until 1923 when a denominational reorganization resulted in the formation of the Board of Christian Education. A subcommittee, the Department of Colleges, Theological Seminaries and Training Schools, had responsibility for colleges and universities. Its administrative supervision remained with the Board of Christian Education until 1972 when it was merged into a new structure called the Program Agency. For a summary of these developments, see Frances L. Hollis, "The Task Force on the Church and Higher Education," *Journal of Presbyterian History* 59 (fall 1981): 440–65.

12. George P. Hays, "Higher Education," *Presbyterian Home Missionary* 12 (January 1883): 10.

13. Mark T. Banker, *Presbyterian Missions and Cultural Interaction in the Far Southwest* (Urbana and Chicago, 1993), 24–35.

14. Richard L. Bushman, *Joseph Smith and the Beginnings of Mormonism* (Urbana and Chicago, 1988), 55–59.

15. Marianne Perciaccante, "Backlash against Formalism: Early Mormonism's Appeal in Jefferson County," *Journal of Mormon History* 19 (fall 1993): 40–45. For an overview of Mormon history, see Leonard J. Arrington and Davis Bitton, *The Mormon Experience: A History of Latter-day Saints* (New York, 1980); and Jan Shipps, *Mormonism: The Story of a New Religious Tradition* (Urbana and Chicago, 1985).

16. Arrington and Bitton, *The Mormon Experience*, chaps. 4–7.

17. Robert Baird, *Religion in the United States of America* (Glasgow and Edinburgh, 1844), 647–49; and 1856 edition, critical abridgment, ed. Henry Bowden (New York and London, 1970), 271–74.

18. "A Representative Anti-'Mormon' Radical," *Deseret Evening News*, 14 August 1880; and *Salt Lake Tribune*, "Talmadge on Mormonism," 8 October 1880.

19. George Q. Cannon, "Editorial," *Deseret Evening News,* 3 May 1871.

20. "Remarks by Elder C. W. Penrose," *Deseret Evening News*, 5 July 1879. Another writer referred to clergy as "peripatetic plate-passers who come among us with their stale and hackneyed 'cock-and-bull,' raw-head and bloody-bones romances about the Mormons" and urged his readers to avoid contact with such people. "For Prudential Reasons," *Deseret Evening News*, 13 August 1880.

21. Ibid.

22. "The Deity of Mormon Theology," *Deseret Evening News*, 4 December 1880.

23. Minutes of the Presbytery of Utah, Presbyterian Church U.S.A., 12 March1880, Presbyterian Historical Society Archives, hereafter cited as PHS Archives. For other accounts, see George K. Davies, "History of the Presbyterian Church in Utah," *Journal of Presbyterian History* 24 (September 1946): 147–51.

24. For Mormon responses to Presbyterian charges, see "Rev. (?) R. G. McNiece Self-Convicted," *Deseret Evening News*, 21 June 1884, and "More Proof of McNiece's Falsehood," *Deseret Evening News*, 23 June 1884.

25. *Westminster College 1994–1995 Academic Catalog*, 9–10. In spite of Westminster's proclamation of independence, the General Assembly of the Presbyterian Church (U.S.A.) continues to include Westminster in its annual list of church-related colleges and universities. See *Minutes of the General Assembly of the Presbyterian Church (U.S.A.)*, 1997, I:426; and *Presbyterian Outlook*, 27 October 1997, 32.

26. "Jay Touched Us All," *Westminster Review* (summer 1991): 7. Lees wrote and annually produced "What Wilbur Wrought," a melodrama that allowed for audience

participation. Numerous student generations recall the play as one of the highlights of their Westminster careers and a tradition that never seemed to become inappropriate or outdated.

27. Pat Lees, interview by author, 26 April 1994, Westminster College Archives, hereafter cited as WC Archives. Lees was the first, and for many years the only, LDS member on the Westminster faculty.

28. John Young, interview by author, 23 May 1994, WC Archives.

Part One ~

Grade School and High School

New Salt Lake Collegiate Institute Building, 1895.

Previous page: Salt Lake Collegiate Institute student body with John Coyner at front door, c. 1881.

Assembly room, Salt Lake Collegiate Institute, c. 1895.

Women's dormitory room, Salt Lake Collegiate Institute, c. 1895.

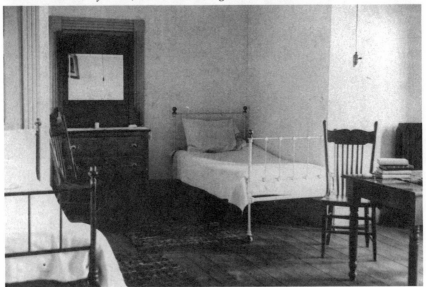

College outing into the canyon, early twentieth century.

Mary Coyner, first elementary school teacher, Salt Lake Collegiate Institute.

John M. Coyner, founder and first principal, Salt Lake Collegiate Institute.

Josiah Welch, pastor of First Presbyterian Church (1871–76) and trustee, Salt Lake Collegiate Institute.

Robert G. McNiece, pastor of First Presbyterian Church (1877–96) and first professor, Sheldon Jackson College.

Collegiate Institute boarding students in the Octagon House with matron and teacher, Mary E. Moore, seated center, c. 1895.

Collegiate Institute Primary Department with teacher, Miss Haines, 1889.

The Octagon House at left and the First Presbyterian Church manse at right, c. 1900.

First Presbyterian Church, Octagon House and manse, c. 1900.

Collegiate Institute student body and faculty, early twentieth century.

Collegiate Institute graduating class, c. 1896.

AN APPEAL
TO
EVERY TRUE PRESBYTERIAN
Interested in Higher Christian Education.

The Proposed Sheldon Jackson Presbyterian College
AT SALT LAKE CITY, UTAH.

Officers:

General JOHN EATON, LL.D., President.   Rev. JOSIAH McCLAIN, Secretary.
ROBERT G. McNIECE, D.D., Dean of Faculty.   GILL S. PEYTON, Treasurer.

Trustees of the College:

Rev. S. E. Wishard, D.D.; Rev. Geo. W. Martin, Seth H. Tolles, Gill S. Peyton, Henry G. McMillan, Rev. Wm. M. Paden, D.D.; Rev. Sheldon Jackson, D.D.; Rev. C. M. Shepherd, W. I. Brown, Edward B. Critchlow, Joseph R. Walker, Rev. N. E. Clemenson, Robert G. McNiece, D.D.; Rev. Josiah McClain, Col. Wm. M. Ferry, Walter Murphy (deceased), Albert S. Martin, Rev. Hugh H. McCreery, George Bailey, LL.B.

THE SHELDON JACKSON COLLEGE,
SALT LAKE CITY, UTAH,

Solicits the aid of the entire Presbyterian Church in the U. S. of America, and proposes a novel plan for raising $250,000 and giving the donors full and valuable return for these subscriptions in home building sites in Salt Lake City.

Like "Bread cast upon the waters," your charity is likely to return a hundredfold

We want all true Presbyterians to give us not only their prayers and moral support but their financial assistance to build this college and aid in rooting out Mormonism, which all Presbyterians must feel is a menace to our Church in Utah, besides being a blot on the bright escutcheon of our enlightened civilization.

Advertisement for Sheldon Jackson College with illustration of proposed Eaton Hall, 1898.

Sheldon Jackson, Presbyterian missionary and college benefactor. Photograph courtesy of Presbyterian Historical Society.

1

Mission to Mormons

Education and the Gospel go hand in hand and it is our desire and aim to bring these powerful ameliorations to bear upon the ignorance, superstition, and fanaticism of the poor dupes of Brigham Young and his unscrupulous assistants.
—Edward E. Bayliss, Rocky Mountain Academy, 1871.

Driving the golden spike on Promontory Summit in 1869 marked the completion of the first transcontinental railroad and triggered a dramatic increase of gentile immigration into Utah Territory. Although most outsiders sought wealth, some came to save souls. Included in the missionary enterprise was a contingent of Presbyterian male clergy and female schoolteachers. Their goals were to draw Mormons back into traditional Protestantism and to win nonbelievers for Christ. Convinced that education was a powerful force in moral and spiritual regeneration, these missionaries established a network of grade schools and academies to supplement church ministries during the last three decades of the nineteenth century. Out of this zeal emerged the vision of a Presbyterian college, located in the Mormon heartland, that would stand as a model of Christian higher education and as an instrument of evangelistic outreach.[1]

The first Presbyterian clergymen who traveled to Utah Territory remained only long enough to survey missionary prospects. In 1862 John Anderson, a minister from the First Presbyterian Church of San Francisco, served as chaplain to the Third California Volunteers under the command of Colonel Patrick Edward Conner, who established Camp Douglas in Salt Lake City. In a series of columns for the *San Francisco Bulletin* Anderson described the army's long march and its entry into Salt

Lake City during which the soldiers were received in silence by residents who lined the wide streets.[2] Anderson used a large tent and a pulpit Bible given him by his San Francisco parishioners to accommodate religious services when the regiment made camp in Utah Territory. This tent may well have been the first non-Mormon religious edifice in Utah. When Anderson was transferred to another assignment in 1863, he was not replaced, and services were temporarily discontinued.[3]

Following Anderson's brief tenure, Henry Kendall, general secretary of the New School Presbyterian Church Board of Domestic Missions, traversed Utah Territory in 1864 en route to California.[4] Reaching Salt Lake City on July 1 after a 600-mile day and night ride from Denver on the Overland Stage, Kendall spent a week investigating the Mormon capital and its inhabitants. Granted an interview with Brigham Young, Kendall found the Mormon president an animated and affable conversationalist. Young extolled the resources and prospects of Utah, particularly the anticipated completion of a transcontinental railroad that would link the territory with the two coasts. Kendall inquired if Young had any objections to the establishment of Protestant churches in Utah. Young replied, "No objection whatever on our part, or to sending missionaries to the Mormons either, if you like." Young even invited him to speak on Sunday morning at the Tabernacle because he desired to have his parishioners know what other denominations believed. Kendall reported that he preached to "a large, respectful, and attentive audience."[5]

Although Young later changed his attitude toward Protestant missionaries when they built churches, attacked polygamy, and opposed statehood, Kendall took the Mormon leader at his word that he welcomed diversity in Utah Territory. When Old School and New School Presbyterians reunited in 1870, the General Assembly of the Presbyterian Church in the U.S.A. selected Kendall to coordinate its extensive home missionary enterprise. His enthusiastic endorsement of Utah missions carried considerable weight in denominational councils in which budgetary decisions often defined the success or failure of missionary operations. Indeed, without Kendall's support, the Presbyterian missionary enterprise in Utah would have had difficulty competing with more productive evangelistic ventures in other western territories.[6]

A year after Kendall's visit, Norman McLeod, a Presbyterian clergyman serving under the auspices of the interdenominational American Home Missionary Society, was commissioned to organize a Congregational Church in Salt Lake City. He achieved this goal in February 1865 but simultaneously gained notoriety as a vitriolic opponent of Mormonism. His fiery speeches at political gatherings and scathing articles in the *Union Vedette*, a local gentile newspaper, led Mormon authorities to reexamine their open-door policy to Protestants. In his sermons and addresses, McLeod invariably singled out polygamy as a threat to the Christian home and an impediment to national unity. Polygamy as taught by Brigham Young, he once contended, "is a doctrine, for the dark, fierce, remorseless, far-sweeping purpose of humiliation and crushing-out of hope and utter ruin to woman and through woman to her children, that would do credit to the archfiend and enemy of mankind."[7] Late in 1865 McLeod went east to raise funds and appear before a congressional committee concerning the state of affairs in Utah. Stopping in Fort Leavenworth, Kansas, on his way back, McLeod received a letter from friends in Utah warning him not to return. During his absence, the Sunday school superintendent, J. King Robinson, had been assassinated under mysterious circumstances, and threats on McLeod's life had been circulated. McLeod returned to the East, where he continued his assault on Mormonism through lectures and newspaper articles. McLeod returned to Salt Lake City as an army chaplain in 1872 but stayed only a little over a year. The Congregational Church he had founded languished until 1874 when a new pastor reorganized it.[8]

McLeod's most lasting impact on Salt Lake City, however, was neither pastoral nor polemical, but in the area of education. Recognizing the poor quality of Mormon district schools and the paucity of Mormon Sunday schools, McLeod advised administrators in the American Home Missionary Society that the surest way to convert Mormons lay not in establishing churches but Sunday schools and day schools in which children were taught biblical truths and American values. In time, McLeod argued, they would abandon the faith of their parents and unite with evangelical Protestant denominations. Following McLeod's recommendation, Congregationalists eventually opened the Salt Lake Academy and established day schools in Utah under the sponsorship of the New West Education Commission.[9]

The impetus for Presbyterian missionary activity in Utah originated in 1869 more than a thousand miles east in Sioux City, Iowa. In that year, three Presbyterian clergymen knelt in prayer on Prospect Hill, a high bluff overlooking the Missouri River. Gazing westward, Sheldon Jackson and two ministerial colleagues envisioned a vast territory unclaimed by Christianity. No Presbyterian congregations had been established along the new Union and Central Pacific railways stretching between Omaha, Nebraska, and Sacramento, California. The three men prayed that God would give them faith and strength as Christian missionaries to evangelize the western territories.[10] Subsequently the Presbytery of Missouri appointed Jackson "Superintendent of Missions for Western Iowa, Nebraska, Dakota, Idaho, Montana, Wyoming, and Utah, or as far as our jurisdiction extends." With that open-ended commission, Jackson directed the spread of Presbyterian churches and schools throughout the western territories and as far north as Alaska. Jackson also was pivotal in founding a college named in his honor, Sheldon Jackson College, the forerunner of Westminster College.[11]

Sheldon Jackson (1834–1909) received his religious training in a devout Presbyterian household in Esparance, New York, a predominantly Huguenot settlement just south of the so-called burned-over district, a hotbed of revivalistic activity that spawned numerous new religious movements including Joseph Smith and the Latter-day Saints. Locally educated, Jackson chose a ministerial career and was graduated from Princeton Theological Seminary in 1858 with a bachelor of divinity degree. Offering his services to the Board of Foreign Missions, Jackson taught one year among the Choctaws at Spencer Academy in Arkansas until health problems forced his removal.[12] For the next ten years, except for a brief tenure as Civil War chaplain, he was an itinerant missionary in Minnesota and Wisconsin for the Board of Domestic Missions of the New School Presbyterian Church, founding churches and recruiting missionaries. During one eighteen-month period Jackson traveled 1,080 miles, 400 of them on foot and the remainder by sleigh or horseback. He organized twenty-three churches and recruited twenty-eight ministers. Jackson raised money from private sources through a variety of promotional techniques, among which was the establishment of a Raven Fund patterned after the prophet Elijah. By such unorthodox methods, he achieved a degree of independence from national church officials, accumulating more than $20,000 for frontier evangelism.[13]

In the spring of 1869, Jackson came to Iowa and there received an appointment to extend the Presbyterian home mission frontier westward. Under his assertive leadership as superintendent of missions, the enterprise west of the Mississippi flourished during the last three decades of the nineteenth century. From 1869 to 1883 Jackson divided his time between on-site supervision in western territories and promotional tours in the East. During these fourteen years, Jackson averaged about thirty thousand miles per year on the road, utilizing virtually every means of transportation, including stagecoach, horse and muleback, buckboard, lumber wagon, and oxcart. He preached wherever he could gather an audience: in barrooms, cabins, tents, mining camps, and fields. When he located Presbyterian families, he organized them into a congregation and moved on to the next town or village.[14] Jackson edited the *Rocky*

Mountain Presbyterian, a monthly newspaper that promoted Presbyterian missions in the West.[15] Featuring eyewitness accounts of missionary exploits, Jackson's periodical had readership from coast to coast, generated recruits for his expanding missionary enterprise, and enlisted the financial support of Presbyterian women who played a prominent role in establishing and maintaining educational missions in Utah.[16]

Within one week of his appointment in 1869, Jackson dispatched three clergymen to establish churches at important points on the Union Pacific transcontinental railway. Melancthon Hughes arrived in Corinne, Utah, a gentile railroad community, on June 11, 1869, to be greeted by Jackson, who had arrived a few days earlier. Experiencing an economic boom, Corinne and its more than a thousand inhabitants had no provision for religious services. Hughes began holding public worship in the local courthouse with only two Presbyterians in his original congregation, and the group encountered opposition from local rowdies who disrupted services and ridiculed the need for religion in a wide-open town like Corinne. After only two months, Hughes left Utah, purportedly to bring back his wife, but instead accepted a pastorate in Atlantic, Iowa.[17]

The Board of Home Missions replaced Hughes with Edward E. Bayliss, who arrived in Corinne on April 13, 1870, and reconstituted the small number of Presbyterian adherents. Before attempting to establish a church, Bayliss formed a Sunday school within a week of his arrival. With forty-one scholars, three teachers, and a superintendent, it was the first Presbyterian Sunday school in Utah Territory. Bayliss later erected the first Presbyterian church building in Utah and, with Sheldon Jackson at his side, formally organized a congregation with nine charter members.[18] Having an interest in higher education, Bayliss expressed the need for a first-class college that would both train men and women to assume positions of leadership in Utah Territory and evangelize Mormons through its commitment to Protestant principles and biblical truths.[19] Bayliss called a meeting of interested people who elected him president and Sheldon Jackson chairman of the board of directors.

To raise $25,000 for initial capital, Bayliss planned a lecture tour of eastern cities to feature the "evils of Mormonism." At this point, executives of the Board of Home Missions objected to his plans on two counts: that the infant congregation would suffer from his absence and that such educational ventures were premature and potentially disruptive of church growth. Secretary Kendall instructed Bayliss to abandon the university project, and shortly thereafter Bayliss resigned and left Utah Territory.[20] While searching for a replacement for Bayliss, Sheldon Jackson served as pulpit supply to the feeble congregation. During one three-month period,

Jackson made four round trips of thirteen hundred miles to keep his engagements.[21] Even with Jackson's efforts and denominational support of missionaries in Corinne, the Presbyterian Church eventually closed its doors. Construction of the Utah Northern Railroad, begun in 1871, diverted the Montana trade from Corinne towards Ogden and through Logan and other Mormon settlements to the north. By the end of the 1870s, Corinne had lost much of its population and was becoming a small Mormon town similar to most others in Utah Territory.[22]

Presbyterians were active in another mining town in the Wasatch Mountain range at the head of Little Cottonwood Canyon, not far from Salt Lake City. In 1873 J. P. Schell, a recent graduate of Union Theological Seminary in New York, organized a congregation and erected a church building in Alta. After opening his work in the Alta courthouse, which he described as "an unpainted, unplastered, unpaneled shanty," Schell succeeded in both ventures.[23] On October 5, 1873, with Sheldon Jackson in attendance, the congregation dedicated its white frame building which doubled as a schoolhouse and reading room. Hiring a woman teacher, Schell opened a day school which quickly had a full class of students. He optimistically reported to Jackson that he was gaining acceptance among the Mormon families and a number of Mormons were attending his meetings.[24] On August 4, 1878, however, a fire swept through Alta, destroying the entire town with the exception of the depot, the courthouse, and a few stables. The town was never rebuilt.[25]

The Presbyterian missions in Corinne and Alta were located in predominantly gentile communities. Visiting Salt Lake City in 1871, Sheldon Jackson decided that a Presbyterian foothold in the heart of Mormon Zion was needed. He requested Henry Kendall to dispatch a missionary to Salt Lake City at the earliest opportunity. Within a month, Kendall had persuaded a young ministerial graduate, Josiah Welch, to accept the challenge.[26] Welch disembarked in Salt Lake City on the evening of September 28, 1871, confident that his preaching and administrative abilities would produce results even among a population of committed Mormons and nominal gentiles.[27] His arrival coincided with a period of economic, political, and social change in the territorial capital. With a population of 12,900 in 1870, Salt Lake City was rapidly becoming a thriving commercial center, especially after the completion of the Utah Central Railway, linking Salt Lake City with the Union Pacific-Central Pacific junction in Ogden in that same year. The mining boom in the canyons surrounding Salt Lake City attracted non-Mormon immigrants, many of whom settled and built homes in the central city.[28]

Tensions between Mormons and newcomers escalated in 1870 when President Ulysses S. Grant appointed a set of federal officials mandated to assert their political authority over territorial residents. Mormons and their opponents formed opposing political parties and engaged in heated public debate which occasionally changed into physical confrontations. In October 1871 U.S. marshals arrested Brigham Young and Mayor Daniel H. Wells, charging them with cohabitation and adultery for living with plural wives, marking the beginning of extended efforts by federal authorities to suppress polygamy in Utah Territory.[29] Under such circumstances, Welch had difficulty recruiting prospective members and locating a suitable meeting place. He held the first meeting of a small group of Protestants in Faust's Hall, a refurbished hayloft above a livery stable on Second South on October 8, 1871. Later, on November 12, he organized the First Presbyterian Church with ten charter members, all of whom joined by transfer of letter from various Protestant denominations. After meeting in several locations, including a skating rink, the small group settled into the Liberal Institute, a gentile meetinghouse, which became their extended ecclesiastical home.[30]

Seeking visibility in a predominantly Mormon environment, Welch laid plans to erect a substantial Presbyterian edifice in the heart of Salt Lake City. He became controversial, however, when he published a plea to Presbyterian women in eastern papers, requesting their financial support of his Utah ministry. Welch luridly described polygamous relationships, portrayed Mormon women as "poor, deluded, and downtrodden," and referred to Mormonism as "a heathen system." Editorials in the *Deseret Evening News* chastised Welch and described Presbyterians as money-grabbing, hypocritical, zealots. C. C. Goodwin, editor of the anti-Mormon *Salt Lake Tribune*, responded in kind. The resulting diatribe generated considerable publicity for Welch's congregation and eventually attracted the interest of eastern readers who contributed generously to Welch's financial campaign.[31]

In spring 1874 church trustees secured several lots at the corner of Second South and Second East Streets, known as the Octagon corner because of a distinctive eight-sided polygamous homestead, once occupied by William S. Godbe and his plural wives. On that site, only a few city squares from the Mormon Temple then in an early phase of construction, Welch's constituents erected an attractive brick edifice costing $18,500. Financed largely by money raised by Welch on several trips to Pennsylvania and New York, the new building was dedicated on October 11, 1875, and Welch was formally installed the following week as pastor. Membership soon reached sixty with attendance averaging nearly three times that number. In addition, prior to morning worship a Sunday school attracted more than 150 scholars. Prospects looked promising, especially with a steady stream of gentiles arriving in Salt Lake City to swell the ranks of potential members.[32] Welch predicted the imminent end of Brigham Young's empire and the disaffection of his followers. "The scales are falling from scores of eyes. The seeds of skepticism are springing into a luxuriant growth. A few years, unless there is a great reaction, will see the spiritual power of this hierarchy broken and humbled, just as its civil and political power is today."[33]

Other Presbyterian clergymen arrived in Utah Territory to commence new ministries. Consequently, on March 1, 1875, a small band of ministers and elders gathered at First Presbyterian Church in Salt Lake City to organize the Presbytery of Utah, a body in Presbyterian polity that is responsible for its ministers, congregations, and sessions in a defined area and supervises the ordination of all ministers. Attending was one of Jackson's most colorful recruits, Duncan J. McMillan, an ambitious clergyman who had left his family home in Illinois in 1874 searching for a moderate climate for his bronchial condition and an opportunity to test his evangelistic skills. He met Jackson, who persuaded him to explore the possibilities of either Utah or Montana Territories. McMillan finally opted for southern Utah, where no Protestant missionary had ever ventured to proselytize Mormons. He would figure prominently in establishing a network of Presbyterian day schools in Utah and would later play a crucial role in the founding of Westminster College.[34]

Although having been warned of bloodthirsty Danites and primitive living conditions, McMillan selected Mt. Pleasant, Sanpete County, where some dissident Scandinavians reportedly had formed a small Liberal Club. Using these apostates as a nucleus, McMillan planned to organize a Presbyterian Church and convert Mormons to evangelical Christianity. After an arduous 150-mile trip by rail, stagecoach, and mail wagon, McMillan arrived in Mt. Pleasant on March 3, 1875. To his surprise, Mormon Church authorities and townspeople with few exceptions treated him cordially and respectfully. The local bishop invited him to speak at several Mormon meetings and placed the meetinghouse at his disposal. He had little success in his preaching efforts, however, and turned to education as an evangelistic wedge to reach adults through their children. Because the Board of Home Missions refused to underwrite the expense of schoolwork, McMillan initially financed the operation with money out of his own pocket and by signing promissory notes. Apostate Mormons offered to sell their newly constructed hall below cost if McMillan promised to renovate it for educational purposes. Relying on his limited skills, McMillan borrowed hand tools and carved benches from rough lumber to build desks. On April 19, 1875, with thirty-five students he commenced classes, the beginning of what later would become Wasatch Academy, an institution that continues to provide college preparatory education for students in Utah and surrounding states.[35]

McMillan had a notable encounter with Brigham Young, who visited Mt. Pleasant in June 1875 while on a promotional tour to encourage support for the erection of temples in Salt Lake City, Manti, and St. George. Young denounced McMillan's efforts to establish sectarian schools and called him "a wolf in sheep's clothing, a serpent that charms only to devour." Young rebuked local church authorities for allowing McMillan to beguile people with promises of free education and advised residents to avoid the school altogether. This caused attendance to drop and adversely affected McMillan's relationships with local church leaders, but he maintained the school and subsequently established a chain of small schools and churches in southern Utah.[36]

Another incident gave McMillan a reputation in denominational circles. As reported in the *Rocky Mountain Presbyterian*, McMillan was to fill a preaching date in a city, later identified as Ephraim, but was warned that he would be killed by angry Mormons if he entered the pulpit. Rejecting advice to leave town immediately, McMillan proceeded to his preaching engagement bearing both a gun and a Bible. According to Sheldon Jackson, McMillan "read the scriptures, poured out his soul in prayer, and then preached such a loving gospel that enmity for the time being was disarmed." Accounts of this incident were reproduced in a variety of newspapers and magazines, including the widely read *Harpers Weekly*. McMillan subsequently toured eastern states describing his encounter with Brigham Young and retelling the Bible and pistol story to receptive audiences. Mormons vehemently denied McMillan's claim to have displayed a pistol in order to control an audience, but the story persisted and was embellished in its retelling.[37]

Even before McMillan's venture into the Sanpete Valley, Josiah Welch had begun to reexamine the effectiveness of his ministry in Salt Lake City. He had been successful as a fund raiser and church builder, but Welch's mandate from Jackson had been to convert Mormons as well as to shepherd Protestants. Yet three years later, even as he dedicated his new church building, the Latter-day Saint empire was rapidly expanding. Only a handful of dissident Mormon families displayed any interest in First Presbyterian Church and even fewer inquired about church membership. While they listened to Protestant sermons and accepted Bibles and tracts, Mormons were essentially untouched by calls for conversion.

Their allegiance to Mormon community and theology transcended any interest they might have in denominational Christianity.[38] Impressed by the success of day schools recently established in Salt Lake City by Episcopalians and Methodists, Welch became convinced that traditional evangelistic strategies—building churches, holding revivals, and organizing Sunday schools—would not topple Mormonism in Utah; on the contrary, it seemed only to stiffen resistance, especially among Latter-day Saint authorities. With no free public school system in Utah Territory, Welch reasoned that denominational schools would bridge cultural gaps and attract Mormon children who in turn would draw their siblings and parents.[39]

This strategy met strong resistance in denominational headquarters. In spite of their historic commitment to education, Presbyterians questioned the propriety of denominational parochial schools, believing that the responsibility for education belonged in the public domain, especially at the elementary and high school level. Official missions policy mandated the establishment of churches with resident pastors, not the erection of schools with missionary teachers. Although sympathetic to difficulties in dealing with exceptional populations, especially their need for education, denominational officials refused to authorize funds to employ mission teachers in the southwest even when Sheldon Jackson implored the Presbyterian Board of Home Missions, "They won't come to hear preachers; send us a teacher."[40] Jackson was never deterred by policies from following his own course of action. He encouraged Welch and McMillan to seek private funding and to open schools on an experimental basis. Welch had anticipated utilizing First Presbyterian Church's large open basement area for day school classes. Although substandard by eastern educational criteria, the church basement bettered or equaled most Utah classrooms. If successful, the school might stimulate interest in building new facilities; they envisioned that in time it would serve as a model for public education and an instrument of evangelistic outreach.[41]

Demands of a growing congregation and failing health precluded Welch from taking on the assignment of teacher and superintendent. After several months of unsuccessful negotiations, Welch reached a verbal agreement with an experienced teacher in Ogden who promised to open a Presbyterian school in Salt Lake City in time for the 1874–75 school year. At the last moment, however, she declined the appointment, citing unsatisfactory financial arrangements. Discouraged but resolute, Welch continued to search for a teacher.[42] About this same time, a thousand miles away in Illinois, John McCutcheon Coyner, a distinguished public school-teacher and administrator, faced health and financial problems that would link him with Welch and Mormon missions in Utah. A graduate of Hanover College (1852) in Indiana with a major in mathematics, Coyner became director of Waveland Collegiate Institute, a feeder school for Hanover College. In 1860, Coyner assumed a similar position at a new academy in Lebanon, Indiana, and remained there during the Civil War. Later, Coyner served as principal or superintendent of schools in Centreville, Knightstown, Cambridge City, Indiana, and Rushville, Illinois. In 1873 his alma mater honored him with a Ph.D. degree in mathematics in recognition of his educational accomplishments.[43]

Outwardly Coyner had achieved status and security as a professional public school administrator. In midwestern educational circles, he had a reputation as an energetic and progressive superintendent, someone destined for higher responsibilities, perhaps even at a national level. Coyner's personal life, however, belied his confident, assertive demeanor as an educational executive. Early in life he experienced periodic depression, a condition that became exacerbated with demanding career and family pressures. When he finally consulted physicians, they advised an immediate reduction of stress, warning him in medical language of the day that continued pressure would result in one of three things— apoplexy, brain fever, or insanity. Faced with these possibilities, Coyner resigned his administrative post and returned to Indianapolis, where he owned some private and commercial property.[44]

During his tenure in Rushville, Illinois, Coyner invested heavily in speculative land purchases through an Indianapolis agent. By the early 1870s, he had accumulated about $20,000, a substantial sum for that time period. When he resigned in the spring of 1873, Coyner planned to live at least temporarily on the largesse of his profitable real estate portfolio. His financial advisor, however, persuaded him to reinvest accrued earnings in a highly volatile land market, assuring him that land would double in value in a matter of months. On the contrary, Black Friday initiated the Panic of 1873 and real estate values plummeted almost overnight. In the process, Coyner lost virtually everything. Devoid of steady income and physically unfit for administrative duties, Coyner, an active elder in the Presbyterian Church, turned to his denomination for employment. At that time Protestant denominations received federal funding to operate and staff schools for Native Americans. The Presbyterian Board of Foreign Missions in New York offered him a principalship at the Lapwai school in the Nez Perce nation in northern Idaho, a position which he gratefully accepted.[45] Leaving his wife and daughter in Indianapolis, Coyner headed west in January 1874, concerned whether he could survive the rigors of primitive reservation living conditions. On the way to Idaho, Coyner broke his journey in Salt Lake City, where he had a letter of introduction to Josiah Welch from a former parishioner. After a tour of the city which included visits to Methodist and Episcopalian day schools, Coyner and Welch discussed the possibility of erecting a church building and opening a day school. As they parted, Coyner told Welch, "Whenever you get ready to start the school let me know, and if I am footloose I will come and help you."[46]

After a stay in San Francisco where he had been promised an administrative position in the public school system if the mission work proved too demanding, Coyner reached Lapwai, Idaho, early in February and began his work as principal at the Native American school. The relaxed pace of school activities and the Idaho climate improved his mental and physical health. When the school year ended in June, Coyner decided to resume his administrative career in San Francisco and to summon his wife and daughter to meet him there.[47] Several letters to his wife requesting her to meet him in San Francisco never reached their destination, however, and Coyner missed the mule team freight wagon that would transport his belongings to San Francisco to meet a steamship connection. Awaiting the next monthly steamship, Coyner was persuaded by the Lapwai government agent, John Monteith, to remain at the mission school and prepare a set of readers and spellers in both Nez Perce and English. He offered to employ Mary Coyner, his wife, as matron and his daughter, Emma, as an assistant teacher. Coyner accepted and asked his family to move from Indianapolis to Idaho.[48] Shortly after their reunion in August 1874, the government curtailed funds, which reduced salaries and cancelled the translation project. Coyner decided to leave the mission school at the end of the spring term in 1875 and relocate in San Francisco as he had previously planned.[49]

Sometime during November 1874, Coyner wrote to Josiah Welch inquiring about the status of the proposed Presbyterian academy in Salt Lake City. Welch informed Coyner that a house of worship had been erected with a basement set aside for school facilities and that he was anxious to open the school in the fall of 1875. He reminded Coyner of his promise to return to Salt Lake City if circumstances permitted and urged him to begin a new educational ministry in the Mormon capital. Convinced that the offer was another link in an inexplicable chain of providential occurrences, Coyner notified Welch in December 1874 that he would accept the Salt Lake City assignment.[50] Overjoyed, Welch wrote Sheldon Jackson, "I tell you, we have a prize in them [the Coyners]. I predict that he will sweep everything before him."[51]

Having made a decision, the impetuous Coyner pressed Welch to open the new school on a ten-week trial basis beginning in April 1875, rather than wait until September. Initially Welch demurred, arguing that it would be best to commence with a full academic year, but because he feared that Coyner might change his mind during the interim, he accepted the early opening date. Gathering their belongings, the Coyners left Lapwai early in March heading for their new assignment in Utah. After a perilous overland journey by stage and train which was delayed by a blinding snowstorm, they arrived in Salt Lake City on April 2, 1875, exhausted but optimistic that their new venture would be successful.[52] Coyner rose early the next day, anxious to promote the new school. He went directly to the *Salt Lake Tribune* office where editor Goodwin welcomed him to Zion and promised editorial support for the Presbyterian school. At the post office, Coyner received news from Indiana that hopes to recoup even a small portion of his investments had not materialized. On the way to his boarding house, Coyner met a local businessman who asked if he was the professor who planned to open a new school in the Presbyterian Church. Receiving an affirmative response, the man continued, "One of three things is true. You have a fortune to sink, you have wealthy friends to back you, or you have come here to starve." Coyner replied that while he had neither private income nor wealthy friends, he had not come to Salt Lake City to starve. Looking back on the interchange, Coyner observed, "His remarks were not, under the circumstances, very inspiring."[53]

Financial problems loomed large initially. Neither Coyner nor Welch had sufficient cash with which to commence operations. First Presbyterian Church, already burdened with debt, could do no more than grant free use of its facilities for school purposes. Coyner's $1,500 salary was contingent on sufficient cash receipts, and he contracted to assume responsibility for any incurred debt. Through Welch's connections with local bankers, however, Coyner established credit and borrowed start-up money. Small personal loans secured from Welch and other First Presbyterian constituents also helped Coyner meet daily needs.[54]

On this precarious financial base, Coyner purchased $12 worth of lumber and hired a carpenter willing to work on the promise of anticipated income from tuition payments. Together they built and painted forty-five roughly hewn desks in the basement of First Presbyterian Church. At the same time, Coyner obtained some used textbooks and procured other necessary school supplies. In cramped quarters, on borrowed money, and with rudimentary equipment, the history of Salt Lake Collegiate Institute was about to begin. It would enhance the educational development of Salt Lake City and provide the foundation on which Westminster College would be built.[55]

NOTES

1. Banker, *Presbyterian Missions and Cultural Interaction*, 35–41.

2. Edward W. Tullidge, *History of Salt Lake City* (Salt Lake City, 1886), 277–79, citing the *San Francisco Bulletin*.

3. Robert J. Dwyer, *The Gentile Comes to Utah: A Study of Religion and Social Conflict*, 2d ed. (Salt Lake City, 1971), 30–31; and Edgar T. Lyon, *Evangelical Protestant Missionary Activities in Mormon Dominated Areas 1865–1900* (Ph.D. diss., University of Utah, 1962), 33.

4. Presbyterians divided in 1837 into Old School and New School denominations over issues relating to church government, doctrine, and slavery. The two sides operated independently until 1870, when they reunited to form the Presbyterian Church in the United States of America.

5. Henry Kendall, "A Week in 'Great Salt Lake City,'" *Hours at Home* 1 (May 1865): 63–66.

6. For a profile of Kendall, see Thomas S. Goslin II, "Henry Kendall: Missionary Statesman," *Journal of Presbyterian History* 27 (June 1949): 70–73.

7. Norman McLeod, "The Complicity of the Republic," *Salt Lake Tribune*, 13 November 1872. On another occasion, he publicly stated that "Brigham Young was a sham and his theocracy of crime and blood a miserable scare-crow." See "Rev. McLeod's Lecture," *Salt Lake Tribune*, 9 September 1872.

8. Lyon, *Evangelical Protestant Missionary Activities*, 38–44.

9. Ibid., 176–87.

10. Robert Laird Stewart, *Sheldon Jackson: Pathfinder and Prospector of the Missionary Vanguard in the Rocky Mountains and Alaska* (New York, 1908), 100–102. The other two men were T. H. Cleland and J. C. Elliott.

11. For a critical analysis of Jackson's career, refer to Norman J. Bender, *Winning the West for Christ: Sheldon Jackson and Presbyterianism on the Rocky Mountain Frontier, 1869–1880* (Albuquerque, 1996). See also Ted C. Hinckley, "Sheldon Jackson: Gilded Age Apostle," *Journal of the West* 23 (January 1984): 16–25; and Norman J. Bender, "Sheldon Jackson's Crusade," *Midwest Review* 4 (spring 1982): 1–12.

12. Clifford M. Drury, *Presbyterian Panorama* (Philadelphia, 1950), 186–87.

13. Ibid., 187.

14. Alvin K. Bailey, "Sheldon Jackson, Planter of Churches," *Journal of Presbyterian History* 26 (September 1948): 129–30.

15. The only Presbyterian publication of its kind, the *Rocky Mountain Presbyterian*, reached a wide audience. Presbyterian ministers received a free copy and were urged to seek subscribers from their local congregations. Every Presbyterian emigrant passing through Denver whose address could be secured also received complimentary copies. Files of the *Rocky Mountain Presbyterian* are located in the PHS Archives.

16. Presbyterian women organized as the Woman's Executive Committee in 1878, which changed its name to the Woman's Board of Home Missions in 1897. For an overview of their contributions to Presbyterian missions, see Lois A. Boyd and R. Douglas Brackenridge, *Presbyterian Women in America: Two Centuries of a Quest for Status*, 2d ed. (Westport, Connecticut, 1996).

17. George K. Davies, "A History of the Presbyterian Church in Utah," *Journal of Presbyterian History* 23 (December 1945): 240.

18. Ibid., 241.

19. Edward Bayliss, "Corinne Utah" (4 August 1870), in *Sheldon Jackson Scrapbook* 58:100, PHS Archives, hereafter cited as Jackson Scrapbook.

20. Davies, "A History of the Presbyterian Church in Utah," 243–44; and Lyon, *Evangelical Protestant Missionary Activities*, 79–80. Bayliss also proposed the formation of another school, the Rocky Mountain Female Academy, in Corinne, but financial support never materialized.

21. "Sheldon Jackson Goes to Reward," *Salt Lake Tribune*, 9 May 1909.

22. Dean L. May, "Towards a Dependent Commonwealth," in Richard D. Poll et al., eds., *Utah's History* (Logan, Utah, 1989), 217–41.

23. Davies, "A History of the Presbyterian Church in Utah," 247.

24. Ibid., 248.

25. Ibid., 247–48.

26. Born in Virginia in 1841, Welch was reared in southern Ohio and received his early education in that state. Following academic studies at Washington and Jefferson College in Pennsylvania, Princeton Seminary in New Jersey, and Union Theological Seminary in New York, Welch was ordained by the Presbytery of Steubenville on April 26, 1870. Although Welch initially was commissioned to serve as a missionary in Montana Territory, Kendall intervened and changed his assignment to Utah Territory. See "The Late Josiah Welch," *Herald and Presbyter*, 11 April 1877; and *Addresses at the Tenth Anniversary of the First Presbyterian Church of Salt Lake City, November 13, 1882* (Salt Lake City, 1882), 4–5, WC Archives.

27. Minutes of First Presbyterian Church, 1872–1902, Historical Statement, University of Utah Special Collections, 1049, box 3, hereafter cited as UU Spec. Colls.

28. Thomas G. Alexander and James B. Allen, *Mormons and Gentiles: A History of Salt Lake City* (Boulder, Colorado, 1984), 87–88.

29. Ibid., 89–100.

30. "Presbyterian Church," *Salt Lake Tribune*, 1 January 1875; and "Presbyterian Church," 1 January 1877.

31. "Insult to Gentile Ladies," *Salt Lake Tribune*, 15 December 1871; and "The Heathen System," 8 March 1872. See also "Editorial," *Deseret Evening News*, 13 and 19 December 1871.

32. "The Heathen System," *Salt Lake Tribune*, 8 March 1872.

33. "Presbyterian Church," *Salt Lake Tribune*, 1 January 1875.

34. Davies, "A History of the Presbyterian Church in Utah," *Journal of Presbyterian History* 24 (March 1946): 44–45.

35. Florence McMillan, *The Reverend Duncan J. McMillan: A Tribute* (New York, 1939), 25–26.

36. Davies, "A History of the Presbyterian Church in Utah," 47–49.

37. R. Douglas Brackenridge, "The Evolution of an Anti-Mormon Story," *Journal of Mormon History* 21 (Spring 1995): 80–105.

38. "Discourse of Orson Pratt," *Deseret Evening News*, 17 December 1871. Referring to Mormon reluctance to return to the folds of traditional Protestantism, the writer queried, "Who would exchange a bell for a whistle?"

39. *Addresses at the Tenth Anniversary of the First Presbyterian Church of Salt Lake City*, 4–5, WC Archives.

40. Stewart, *Sheldon Jackson*, 277.

41. *Addresses at the Tenth Anniversary of the First Presbyterian Church of Salt Lake City*, 4–5.

42. Ibid.

43. "Obituary, John McCutcheon Coyner," *Herald and Presbyter*, 1 July 1908.

44. John Coyner to Mrs. F. E. Haines, 18 November and 10 December 1880, RG 305-15-31, PHS Archives.

45. John M. Coyner, "History of the Salt Lake Collegiate Institute from Its Organization April 12, 1875 to May 5, 1885," typescript, 16 December 1897, 3, WC Archives.

46. Coyner, "History of the Salt Lake Collegiate Institute," 4.

47. Ibid., 5.

48. Ibid., 5–7.

49. Ibid., 8.

50. Ibid., 9.

51. Josiah Welch to Sheldon Jackson, 9 April 1875, Jackson Correspondence, RG 239, PHS Archives, hereafter referred to as Jackson Corr.

52. Coyner, "History of the Salt Lake Collegiate Institute," 7–10.

53. Ibid., 10.

54. Minutes of the Board of Directors of the Salt Lake Collegiate Institute, in Minutes of the Session of First Presbyterian Church, Salt Lake City, 15 November 1878, UU Spec. Colls., 1049, box 1. These minutes overlap with Board of Directors' Minutes but are recorded in a separate location to reflect an accurate history of the Collegiate Institute.

55. Coyner, "History of the Salt Lake Collegiate Institute," 10. For an overview of Presbyterian precollegiate educational institutions, see John H. Fisher, "Primary and Secondary Education and the Presbyterian Church in the United States of America," *Journal of Presbyterian History* 24 (March 1946): 13–43.

2

Professor Coyner's New School

From a human standpoint, the outlook was not encouraging. Two basement rooms, bare of everything like school furniture, poorly lighted and illy [sic] ventilated, no desk, no maps, no endowment, no money, and no positive assurance of students, was all there was.
                                        —John Coyner, October 1883.

Temperament, conviction, and experience motivated John Coyner to undertake the organization of a Presbyterian day school in Salt Lake City. Although he periodically suffered severe episodes of depression, Coyner possessed an all-consuming work ethic and a dedication to academic excellence that inspired colleagues to seek higher levels of achievement. A contemporary characterized Coyner as "a steam engine in trousers," whose work day began early and ended late. Standing six-foot-two, wearing a dark suit and bowler hat, and sporting a prematurely gray beard, Coyner was an imposing presence.[1]

He maintained a high profile in Salt Lake City both as a churchman and a professional educator. His innovative teaching methods resulted in articles about the Collegiate Institute. A strict disciplinarian, his booming voice captured the attention of students who deviated from educational protocol, but he could also be gentle, caring, and understanding. Townspeople recognized him as "the Presbyterian professor," especially when he donned a long white duster (overcoat) and traversed the city streets in a carriage pulled by his white horse, Charlie, on what he termed "begging missions" for funds to support the Collegiate Institute.[2]

John Coyner was born in Augusta County, Virginia, on December 16, 1827. Coyner's middle name, McCutcheon, derived from a temperance preacher who reportedly saved his father from a life of alcoholism and poverty. Coyner remembered his parents as devout, Sabbath-keeping Presbyterians whose abolitionist convictions led them to separate from slave-holding friends and relatives and move in 1837 from Virginia to South Salem County, Ohio. As a child, Coyner studied the *Westminster Confession of Faith* and absorbed a stern Calvinistic theology and moral principles through parental example and teaching. Coyner eventually applied these convictions to the antipolygamy crusade then gaining momentum among non-Mormon residents in Utah. Frequently comparing abolitionism with the struggle to suppress polygamy, he viewed the latter as the foremost threat to national morality in his generation.[3]

Coyner and Josiah Welch devised a three-fold purpose for the Collegiate Institute: provide a comprehensive Christian education for Utah youth that combined Biblical learning with academic excellence; train a corps of teachers in anticipation of free public schools in Utah Territory; and make educational opportunities available to children with no means who otherwise would receive no formal instruction. In publications directed at local audiences, Coyner and Welch did not refer to Mormonism either in contextual or evangelistic terms but by emphasizing the institute's missionary mandate. Writing in the *Rocky Mountain Presbyterian*, Welch described the institute's mission to resolve "the Mormon problem." In fulfilling its objectives, the faculty hoped to surround Utah children with Christian influences and lead them into Presbyterian Sunday schools. The children in turn would draw parents and other family members into the orbit of evangelical Christianity. By training teachers and educating children, Welch concluded that "we will plant a leaven in this Mormon lump which will rend it in pieces."[4]

To encourage parents to send their children to the institute, trustees advertised low tuition and high standards for student behavior. Quarter-term rates included primary, $6, intermediate, $8, academic, $10, and collegiate, $12. Out-of-town students paid $5–$7 per week to live with families who met Coyner's moral standards. Students had to adhere to a strict moral code articulated in the institute's prospectus, and entering students signed a pledge and became members of the Abstainer's League, an association formed as an auxiliary to the Collegiate Institute. They promised to abstain from use of alcohol, tobacco, gambling with playing cards, profane languages, and to "endeavor by all proper means to influence others to do the same."[5]

On Monday morning, April 12, 1875, at 9 A.M., twenty-seven students assembled in the basement of First Presbyterian Church to mark the opening of the Salt Lake Collegiate Institute. They ranged in age from young beginners learning their ABCs to a twenty-year-old man. Unlike the traditional one-room schoolhouse, the institute was graded by departments with individualized instruction. Mary Coyner handled primary children, Emma Coyner guided intermediates, and John Coyner directed precollegiate students. The two-year primary curriculum consisted of reading, writing on slates, oral and written sentences, arithmetic, geography, spelling, declamation, singing, and light gymnastics. In a three-year course, intermediates covered reading, arithmetic, geography, grammar, spelling, penmanship, composition, declamation, and language lessons. The primary and intermediate students provided the core of institute enrollment.[6] Advanced classes offered three different tracks: a "normal school course," combining basic humanities and sciences classes with educational theory and practice teaching; a "scientific course," traditional natural and physical sciences supplemented with geometry, history, geography, and mental and moral science; and a "classical course," emphasizing Latin and Greek studies with related history, English, and science courses.[7]

In addition to courses normally included in public school curricula, the institute had a daily Bible study, a classroom exercise portrayed as nonsectarian or Christian rather than reflecting any particular denomination. Coyner affirmed in his educational creed that "the broad fundamental truths of morality and correct living as set forth in the Bible are the foundation of all true education."[8] Biblical studies were conducted informally in lower grades but were required courses at high school and precollegiate levels.[9] A series of courses on Old Testament and New Testament history, Christian ethics, and moral philosophy provided a broad Protestant approach to interpreting Scripture and developing Christian values.[10]

Within a few weeks, with sixty-three tuition-paying students attending classes, concerns about attaining sufficient enrollment vanished. In fact, Welch informed Sheldon Jackson that the school was so successful that they would not be able to accommodate everyone who applied.[11] When a Mormon woman separated from her polygamous husband attempted to enroll her two children and informed Coyner that she had no money to pay tuition, however, Coyner admitted the children and with Welch's assistance canvassed Presbyterian Sunday schools in the east to provide thirty-dollar scholarships for needy students. Before the abbreviated term ended in June, they had secured six scholarships. Coyner continued to accept indigent students, especially those from Mormon families, often taking out personal loans to cover operating expenses.[12] At the end of its first full academic year, September 1875 to June 1876, attendance reached nearly 150. Coyner feared that the institute could not be sustained indefinitely without additional scholarships and dependable salary support for teachers. He estimated that at least sixty scholarships ($1,800) and salaries for three teachers were necessary to keep the school functioning. In correspondence with Sheldon Jackson, Coyner pleaded for additional funding and stressed the evangelistic opportunities available through educational ministries in Utah.[13]

Coyner maintained a monthly budget by a combination of imaginative bookkeeping and providential intervention. He related how at the end of one month he needed fifty dollars to balance his account. Coyner claimed he slept soundly in anticipation of God's deliverance, but morning came and no money appeared. In a storage room, he noticed a small roll of paper in a cup that had been empty a month previous. Undoing the roll, Coyner found three new twenty-dollar greenbacks. No one could account for their presence, but Coyner attributed the find to the power of a providential God. Whatever their source, they paid the bills and kept the institute afloat for another month.[14] Although praising God for such financial deliverance, the Coyners pondered the Deity's providential purposes in other areas. Their daughter Emma had married Josiah Welch in 1875, and the couple intended to serve First Presbyterian Church and assist with the work of the institute. When her husband became ill in 1876 and went to the eastern U.S. for medical treatment, Emma accompanied him; neither she nor Josiah Welch ever returned to Utah, for both died within a few months of each other.[15] Devastated, John and Mary Coyner considered relinquishing responsibility for the institute. On her death bed, however, Emma Coyner had enjoined her father to persevere with his educational venture. "Papa, live for your school," was one of her last messages to him. The Coyners decided to stay in Utah until they felt the Collegiate Institute was on a permanent basis.[16]

Despite occasional donations and pledges, Salt Lake Collegiate Institute neared the end of its second full academic year with no stable fiscal resources. At a meeting of the Presbytery of Utah held in Ogden early in 1877, Coyner, Duncan McMillan, and several elders met with Sheldon Jackson, who was passing through Utah on one of his many missionary junkets. The meeting began at 7:30 P.M. and ended at 4:00 A.M. so that Jackson could catch a morning train to Denver. About 1 A.M. Coyner reported on the Collegiate Institute and again raised the question of denominational support for educational missions, to which Jackson responded negatively. Coyner then asked, "Who gives the Foreign Board authority to send out teachers to the foreign field?" When Jackson responded, "The General Assembly," Coyner queried, "Then why not give the Home Board the same authority?" This conversation resulted in the

Presbytery of Utah requesting the forthcoming General Assembly of the Presbyterian Church in the U.S.A. to empower the Board of Home Missions to commission teachers to the exceptional populations of Utah (Mormon), New Mexico (Hispanic), and Alaska (Native Americans).[17]

Following ardent speeches by Duncan McMillan and Henry Kendall at the 1877 General Assembly meeting in Chicago, commissioners approved the overture with the proviso that funds for such schools would be raised primarily by churchwomen. This decision was shortly followed by the creation of the Woman's Executive Committee and the commencement of organized financial support for educational missions in the states and territories of the United States.[18] As soon as the General Assembly approved the appointment of women as missionary teachers, Coyner applied for assistance. As a result, the Home Mission Board subsidized three woman teachers at the institute. Mary Coyner received the first commission that was ever issued to a woman, marked number "1" and dated July 1, 1877.[19]

With financial assistance from the Woman's Executive Committee, Coyner cultivated other religious organizations and individual church members. During the 1878–79 school year, however, the Board of Home Missions ruled that all funds raised by missionaries in the field should revert to a general account administered by the board in return for its support of teachers' salaries. Coyner contended that removing private funding would undercut his ability to subsidize needy students, most of whom were from Mormon families. Unless the board rescinded its action, Coyner threatened to withdraw from board sponsorship and pay teachers' salaries from his own accounts. After intense negotiations, board officials compromised with Coyner. Since previously he had raised funds for his own salary, they now agreed to contribute $600 per year towards his compensation and to support three teachers at the rate of $1,500 per year. Funds received by Coyner from other sources were to be sent to the Board of Home Missions for general distribution, an arrangement that was followed throughout most of the Collegiate Institute's history.[20]

With a continuity of teachers assured through Home Missions assistance, Coyner addressed a second problem of space. Students were having to be turned away, because the Collegiate Institute had outgrown its basement facilities in First Presbyterian Church. By presenting sketches of a proposed modern schoolhouse, Coyner persuaded First Presbyterian Church trustees to put a mortgage of $1,000 on a 40-by-120-foot adjacent lot they owned and promised that he would raise an estimated balance of $3,000 with a national appeal for funds.[21] Assisted by his teachers, Coyner mailed three thousand letters to Presbyterian churches throughout the United States and sought support as well from local businesses for the new building. Assuming success, Coyner set the dedication of a four-room schoolhouse on August 22, 1877, with the territorial governor as guest speaker. When the day arrived, and nearly $1,500 short of his goal, Coyner drove around in his buggy soliciting additional gifts from local donors. Lacking $800 when the ceremony began in the afternoon, he made one last plea before the dedicatory prayer so that they might open the building debt-free. Coyner himself made a personal contribution in the name of his deceased daughter Emma, and called for $100, $50, and $25 subscriptions from the audience; he secured the balance in less than fifteen minutes. The school now had its own furnished building free of financial encumbrance.[22]

In an editorial, the *Salt Lake Tribune* commended Salt Lake Collegiate Institute, describing it as "one of the neatest school houses to be found in the Territory, one that presents a cozy, comfortable appearance." An adobe structure thirty-three feet wide by sixty-four feet long, it was divided into four main rooms with fifteen-foot ceilings, amply lighted, ventilated, and fitted with stoves for winter weather. Equipment included a large sliding blackboard, charts, maps, and a variety of textbooks.[23] Continued growth necessitated a second building, a brick structure costing $10,500, to be erected during the summer of 1880 by contributions from the Woman's Executive Committee and local businessmen. As the project neared completion, Coyner received word that a shortfall in national receipts would delay the churchwomen's donation. Coyner forged ahead with construction, and, writing to a half-dozen Presbyterian benefactors, he requested and received loans secured only by his signature. By the time final bills were presented, he had sufficient funds to pay off contractors and suppliers.[24]

At the dedication on August 30, 1880, speaker Robert McNiece applauded the principal's fiscal daring. McNiece said the new building stood for three things: a Christian home—"one family with one father and mother who journey through life together"; a Christian state—"where everyone may think for himself without direction from others"; and Christian education—"life is a preparatory school, and hence we are in favor of training [children] for this life and the life to come." After McNiece's address, as he had done in 1877, Coyner made an emotional appeal for aid and raised $2,000 in less than ten minutes to make the building debt-free.[25]

In subsequent years, Coyner upgraded and expanded facilities. In 1883 the institute opened a female boarding department in the Octagon House adjacent to campus, a building which had recently been purchased by the First Presbyterian Church.[26] One of his institute faculty members, Mary E. Moore (from 1879 to 1895), served as matron in addition to her teaching responsibilities. Under her supervision, some fifteen young women had access to inexpensive accommodations and received training in practical housekeeping.[27] Other campus additions helped to accommodate a student body that by 1880 had grown to 225 students in primary, intermediate, grammar, high school, and music departments. To provide space for music and art students, Coyner added a second story to the original school building in 1881. About the same time, the Coyners donated $1,000 to build a parsonage on campus for the minister of First Presbyterian Church with a proviso that no rent be charged to the pastor or his successors. With funds from the Woman's Executive Committee in 1884, institute trustees purchased the Liberal Institute building for a gymnasium and a temporary dormitory. After this, there were no further changes to the institute campus during the next decade.[28]

The institute was eligible for grants from the newly formed Presbyterian Board of Aid for Colleges and Academies and Coyner's request for funds was in the mail even before grants had been announced. That board's first allocation of $1,000 went to the Collegiate Institute. With tuition income and support from the Woman's Executive Committee, institute trustees could now pay Coyner's entire salary, cover basic operating expenses, and hire a principal for the high school in 1883, Professor J. F. Millspaugh, who eventually became Coyner's successor.[29]

The Collegiate Institute's growing reputation as an academic institution was based on more than its physical plant and modern equipment. Publications extolled its academic excellence as marked by student deportment, qualified faculty, and innovative teaching methods.[30] Reporters from the *Salt Lake Tribune* and *Salt Lake Herald* termed the institute "Professor Coyner's New School." One account emphasized how students changed classes quietly and orderly at the tap of a bell. Coyner asserted to his visitor, "You can come here and sit for two hours, and I'll give you $50 if you see a student whisper to another student." The observer doubted that anyone would ever collect on that wager.[31]

On another occasion, a reporter paid an unannounced visit to institute classrooms. Taking a seat in Mary Coyner's primary class, he heard students recite from their first reader. Every word had to be spelled out and pronounced accurately, often requiring prompting from the instructor. Noting that this appeared to be a tiring chore, the reporter complimented Coyner for her careful oversight and discipline of the little children under her care. In Emma Coyner's class, he observed students reciting an arithmetic lesson under "a competent, painstaking teacher, [who] preserves excellent order, and is perfectly en rapport with her class." He watched John Coyner guide his advanced students through a rigorous writing drill. Coyner conducted the exercise in time to the tapping of a bell. First tap, "Position!" The class sat erect, elbows on desks, eyes forward. Second tap, "Take out books and pen holders!" Third tap, "Uncover ink-wells!" Fourth tap, "Open copy-book, assume position for writing!" Fifth tap, "Take up pens!" Then at the command "Ready!" they began writing. Coyner repeated the drill several times until students acquired military precision in its performance.[32]

Faculty guided every aspect of student deportment under the rubric of Christian discipline. Coyner prohibited profanity on or off campus, reminding students that habitual offenders would be dismissed from school and their money refunded. In the presence of a *Tribune* reporter, Coyner demonstrated how he enforced discipline on violators of the Second Commandment. Addressing the boys (female students apparently were not habitual offenders), he asked any guilty parties to rise. All rose except two. Coyner gave them one week to break their habit. On the following Friday when six acknowledged their culpability, they were placed on probation and their behavior carefully monitored.[33] Strict moral discipline did not preclude sensitivity to students' needs nor commitment to their intellectual growth. For its time and location, the institute under Coyner's supervision displayed progressive educational philosophy. Teachers acknowledged that discipline was not an end in itself to be arbitrarily imposed on submissive students. Rather they viewed it primarily as a means to develop moral character. Mary Moore said, "Discipline does not attain its end when it secures mere outward obedience to law, but only when such obedience is rendered willingly with regard to the rightness of the thing demanded."[34]

Coyner encouraged parental involvement in the educational process. "Parents, come and visit us. Your children will be glad to see you. The teachers will be glad to see you. The superintendent will be glad to see you. Come at any time and come often."[35] Coyner kept out-of-town parents regularly informed of student progress by quarterly reports that detailed both academic and social accomplishments. He also organized the Presbyterian Teachers' Association in 1883 in order to promote better teaching methods in denominational day schools. Among other things, teachers were encouraged to visit students in home settings on a regular basis so that they could encourage better parent-child relationships.[36]

Not bound to sequential courses and prescribed time frames, students could bypass courses and skip grades on the basis of comprehensive monthly examinations. Failing in two successive months resulted in a loss of class standing. These comprehensive exams taxed both memory and communication skills.[37] His questions on American history included "Write thirty important dates, State the causes of the Revolution, Write a brief memoir of Washington, and Give an analysis of the work of the term." The spelling quiz asked, "What is the alphabet?, What are the inconsistencies of our alphabet?, Give a tabular analysis of the elementary sounds, and Spell the following words: vicissitude, panegyric, metaphysics, symphonious, erroneous, spontaneous, equestrian, Deuteronomy, entomology." The advanced arithmetic class was required to "Write the definitions of sixty-three terms used in arithmetic, multiply 38,468 by 238, and give analysis, Write tabular analysis of denominate tables, and Change 3m. 4 fur. 20 rds., 2 yds., 1 ft., 6 in. to meters." Tutorials offered talented students the opportunity to explore certain topics in depth, and advanced students could do supervised independent study and laboratory work.[38]

Despite heavy emphasis on memorization, Coyner encouraged his teachers to undertake interactive teaching. As a model, he conducted assemblies for the student body that provided opportunities for intermingling graded departments and personalized learning experiences. Every other Friday afternoon, the uniquely designed partitions that separated the various departments were raised to permit a unified auditorium. Rather than use prescribed lectures or recitations, Coyner designated three scholars to prepare questions from any subject area of the curriculum. He then responded to the questions at length. Following his response, Coyner encouraged the entire student body to submit queries on any topic and "to free his or her mind of any dark doubt which haunts it and receive the solution then and there." An adult who attended an assembly concluded that it was "an exceedingly pleasant and profitable incidental feature of the school."[39]

Coyner edited the *Utah Educational Journal,* a nonsectarian monthly periodical designed to improve educational theory and practice throughout the territory. Believing the Bible to be the foundation of all true education, he permitted nothing in the *Journal* that opposed "what are regarded by all Christian people as its sacred teachings."[40] Yet Coyner also convened educational conventions for Protestants, Mormons, Catholics, and Jews, at which the agendas consisted of papers and discussions on current educational philosophy and workshops on practical pedagogy.[41] Mormon officials published appreciative accounts of the institute and its ecumenical approach to education and praised Coyner as an exemplary principal and teacher. The *Salt Lake Daily Herald* described the Collegiate Institute as "a model school, useful and ornamental to Salt Lake City," commending Coyner for "imparting to the rising generation knowledge which will befit them for honorable and responsible positions in life."[42] A subsequent story noted the institute's remarkable progress during its first three years in Salt Lake City.[43]

Coyner's cordial relationships with Mormon authorities ended when he joined forces with opponents of plural marriage and Utah statehood. Upon his arrival in Utah, Coyner assumed that improved education and increased contact with non-Mormon immigrants would bring about the gradual demise of polygamy and other objectionable practices. "Being an educator by profession," he said, "my only purpose was to establish the Salt Lake Collegiate Institute and quietly as a Christian teacher to train the rising generation in the way of right living." By 1878, however, he had rejected gradualism as an effective solution to Mormon expansionism. Convinced that Mormon leaders intended to control the nation, Coyner considered it his Christian duty to do all he could to oppose the rapidly growing religious movement.[44] An 1879 landmark Supreme Court decision (*Reynolds v. the United States*) provided impetus for opponents of polygamy by ruling that the free exercise clause in the Constitution applied to religious beliefs, but not necessarily to actions arising from those beliefs. This decision led to passage of the Edmunds Act in 1882 that disenfranchised polygamous Mormons by enlarging the scope of "unlawful cohabitation" and to the more severe Edmunds-Tucker Act of 1887 that broadened federal authority to abolish polygamy.[45]

Coyner's new attitude was greatly influenced by his close association with his neighbor, Robert McNiece, pastor of First Presbyterian Church and chairman of the board of trustees of the Collegiate Institute. A graduate of Dartmouth and Princeton Seminary and former editor of the Fort Wayne *Daily Gazette*, McNiece came to Salt Lake City in 1877 to fill the vacancy left by the death of Josiah Welch. Feisty, combative, articulate, and uncompromising, McNiece became an antagonist of Mormonism, contributing frequently to the *Salt Lake Tribune* and publishing in eastern newspapers and journals. McNiece once turned his back and refused to be seated next to visiting dignitary Joseph Smith III during a civic celebration with the territorial governor as the speaker.[46] With impetus from McNiece, Coyner gained notoriety as one of the most outspoken anti-Mormons in Utah.

Although Coyner distinguished between Mormon theology and the Mormon people, whom he regarded as "brothers and sisters in common humanity," reporters often ignored that qualification.[47] In a widely circulated series of *Letters on Mormonism* that first appeared in the *Boston Journal of Education* and was later reprinted in *The Handbook on Mormonism*, Coyner attacked Mormon theology and its practice of plural wives. The popular press frequently cited one of his statements: "The question has been asked whether I find any good in Mormonism. In regard to the Mormon religion, I answer most emphatically, none. The more I examine it, the more I am convinced that the whole thing is conceived in sin and begotten in iniquity. It truly may be said to be the conception of him who is the Father of lies."[48] Coyner repeated these accusations while raising funds for the Collegiate Institute in the eastern states. Addressing the Presbyterian General Assembly in Saratoga, New York, in 1879, Coyner stated, "Mormonism is made up of twenty parts. Take eight parts diabolism, three parts animalism, from the Mohammedan system, one part bigotry from old Judaism, four parts cunning and treachery from Jesuitism, two parts Thugism from India, and two parts Arnoldism, and then shake the mixture over the fires of animal passion and throw in the forms and ceremonies of the Christian religion, and you will have the system in its true component parts."[49]

Coyner also objected to Mormonism on political grounds, charging that Latter-day Saints made poor citizens because of their unquestioning obedience to the church hierarchy. He told a national gathering of Christian educators in 1883 that Mormonism was a form of slavery and that there would be continued strife in the nation as long as it existed. Mormonism was not a religion, Coyner insisted, but a despotic political system that under the cloak of religion is "vampyre-like [sic] sucking the life-blood of the nation." He proposed stripping the Mormon hierarchy of all territorial and municipal power and replacing it with an authoritative legislative commission that would give non-Mormons an opportunity to participate fully in local government. Coyner also advocated federal intervention into Utah's educational system by organizing a territorial school board composed of "loyal citizens" with authority to compel Mormon children to attend a public school system with a curriculum designed to make them loyal American citizens. Admitting that these were radical proposals, Coyner concluded, "Nothing but radical measures will cure this disease."[50]

Coyner's anti-Mormonism generated a response in the Mormon press, particularly in editorials in the *Deseret Evening News*. Various contributors condemned Coyner as a "hypocritical pedagogue" and a "Presbyterian bigot" who courted Mormon families in Salt Lake City but condemned them in other states. One writer advised Mormons against sending their children to denominational schools and particularly suggested they avoid Coyner: "But we specially object to placing 'Mormon' children under the daily and prolonged influence of a bigoted, libelous and unprincipled defamer, and therefore take this method of warning the 'Mormon' public against Coyner and his Institute."[51] An editor accused Presbyterians of misrepresenting conditions in Utah in order to raise "Coins for Coyner" and establish schools in all the principal towns of the territory. The writer charged that Presbyterians were attempting to gain control of Mormon children and "pervert them from the truths taught by their parents, provide situations and salaries for impecunious Presbyterian preachers, and bring in a handsome revenue for the head academy in Salt Lake City, of which Coyner is the Principal."

While reaffirming Presbyterian rights to worship and establish schools, the editor reminded Mormons that they had the freedom not to attend denominational schools.[52] The institute's enrollment, however, steadily increased. Attracted by quality education and generous scholarships, apostate Mormons ignored church authorities' warnings to avoid denominational schools. Continuing gentile immigration to Utah Territory bolstered enrollment. At least half of the student body came from non-Mormon families, prosperous miners, merchants, and professionals, most of whom had sufficient financial resources to afford private education. These paying students provided a steady source of income to supplement the often erratic and limited grants from the denominational boards.[53]

Presbyterian women's organizations were troubled regarding the high percentage of Protestant students enrolled at the institute. They based their support for the institute on its effectiveness in evangelizing Mormons and not on its fiscal stability or innovative curriculum. On numerous occasions Coyner defended the institute's status as a mission school, justifying Protestant enrollment on two grounds: first, the institute was training future teachers and leaders for Utah Territory, looking forward to statehood. Graduates of the institute, Mormon or non-Mormon, would stimulate higher moral and educational standards which would promote the downfall of Mormonism. Second, by admitting Protestant students, particularly those from wealthy families, the institute established links with people who were capable of providing the institution with a sizable endowment, an essential ingredient for any successful educational academy.[54]

Many easterners remained skeptical. Even some of Coyner's Utah colleagues denigrated the institute's alleged missionary status in their periodic reports to the Woman's Executive Committee. Duncan McMillan, synodical missionary and rival for denominational funding, praised the institute as a first-rate educational institution, but he argued that outlying mission day schools in isolated Mormon villages were the most effective agents of evangelization in Utah Territory. "The Mormons are not half so much afraid of courts of justice and government officials and colleges and fine buildings away off at Salt Lake City, as they are of the Christian woman with the Bible in her hand and Christ in her heart. The leaders don't care a fig how many *Salt Lake Collegiate Institutes* & *St. Mark's Academies* & *Rocky Mountain Seminaries and St. Mary's Institutes* the various denominations establish there, but *how* they squirm wherever a devoted 'school marm' goes with the Bible in her hand to one of their towns."[55]

In spite of the criticisms, Coyner and McNiece envisaged the Collegiate Institute as a four-year college, thus establishing the first Protestant institution of higher learning in the Great Western Basin. That dream appeared to be on the threshold of fulfillment in 1883 when the Synod of Colorado, which then embraced Utah Territory, held its annual meeting in Salt Lake City. Commissioners approved a recommendation to secure a charter for a four-year college that would initially occupy institute buildings and eventually develop a more modern and expanded campus. "The present institution [Salt Lake Collegiate Institute] is exactly fitted for this purpose and future enlargement," wrote trustees McNiece and Coyner, who set a goal to raise $120,000 to create four endowed chairs: President, Languages, Mathematics, and Natural Science. In appealing for funds, the trustees affirmed that the college would attack "the priestly and odious union of church and state [that] is pushing out its tyrannical and blighting power into Wyoming, Idaho, and Arizona." They also assured supporters that the college would frame its charter so that the institution would be permanently controlled by the Presbyterian Church in the United States of America.[56]

These ambitious projections for a Presbyterian College in Salt Lake City never materialized. Colorado Presbyterians established a college in Denver and diverted their resources to that institution. At the same time, the General Assembly approved new synodical boundaries in 1883, creating the Synod of Utah, composed almost entirely of small, non-self-supporting congregations. With virtually no financial base outside of Salt Lake City, institute trustees came up empty handed in their quest for $120,000. An advertisement challenging wealthy Presbyterian benefactors to underwrite the proposed college received no responses. Hampered by these difficulties and entangled in government red tape to secure a charter, Coyner and McNiece reluctantly abandoned the project.[57]

As early as 1881, Coyner had seriously contemplated leaving Salt Lake City and retiring to live in California.[58] He confided to the Woman's Executive Committee secretary that despite success with the institute, he was experiencing chronic stress and mental fatigue. "For the last ten days I have been threatened with the return of my old trouble softening of the brain owing largely to loss of sleep and anxiety. I fight against it but cannot always conquer."[59] In addition, Mary Coyner, who suffered from debilitating rheumatism, had great difficulty fulfilling her obligations as the primary teacher. Her prolonged depression, stemming back to the untimely death of their daughter Emma, was compounded by her fear that her husband would be assassinated because of his anti-Mormon activities. When hopes of expanding the institute into a full-fledged college evaporated, Coyner announced that the 1884–85 school year would be his last.[60]

Concurrent with his retirement, Coyner issued an Educational Creed setting forth the philosophical principles of inclusivism, equality, and integrity on which the Collegiate Institute would continue to operate. Included in the creed were statements affirming nondiscriminatory educational policies, equal employment opportunities and salaries for women, and rejection of union of church and state in educational matters. Because Coyner and his successors adhered to this creed, the Salt Lake Collegiate Institute continued to be one of the most progressive educational institutions in the intermountain area.[61]

As Coyner neared the end of a decade in Salt Lake City, his accomplishments exceeded the expectations of even the most sanguine institutional supporters. Enrollment stood at 245 students. The faculty, composed of three men and five women, all held degrees from respected colleges and had previous teaching experience in eastern school systems. Library holdings, scientific equipment, and music and art facilities had few equals in Utah Territory. Property and buildings belonging to the institute were appraised at approximately $31,000, and the only outstanding debt was one of $3,000 secured by mortgage. In 1883 the institute opened a branch school on Fourth West between First and Second South Streets to accommodate students in that growing area of the city. Known as the Camp Mission School, it employed two additional teachers who conducted classes for approximately a hundred students.[62]

Following an emotional farewell convocation attended by a large number of students and friends, the Coyners left Salt Lake City in April 1885 for Pasadena, California, where they hoped that a warmer climate would rejuvenate their bodies and revive their spirits.[63] Mary Coyner lived only a few years, but John remarried and flourished as a rancher in southern California, where he remained active in civic and church affairs. He returned only once to Salt Lake City, in June 1900, while traveling to a meeting of the Presbyterian General Assembly. At a reception held in his honor, Coyner reminisced about experiences in Utah and the founding of the Collegiate Institute. Friends had hoped to use the occasion to name one of the campus buildings Coyner Hall in gratitude for his labors, but the Board of Home Missions, now owners of the property, turned down the request, citing a policy of naming buildings only as memorials.[64] Coyner died on May 17, 1908, at the home of a younger brother in Hopkinsville, Kentucky, at the age of eighty. His obituary aptly concluded, "Whatever he did, he did with all his might, for he was the very embodiment of energy."[65]

NOTES

1. "Dedicated," *Salt Lake Tribune*, 31 August 1880.
2. "Obituary, John McCutcheon Coyner," *Herald and Presbyter*, 1 July 1908, 7. An institute student described Coyner as an imposing presence at the school and "a man of tremendous earnestness of purpose and perhaps appeared sterner than he really was. At any rate, he was respected and obeyed by his pupils." Ethel Paul, "An Address at the Fiftieth Anniversary of The Collegiate Institute," 17 April 1925, WC Archives.
3. "Obituary, John McCutcheon Coyner," 7. See also "Death of the Founder of the Collegiate Institute," *Utah Westminster* 1 (July 1908): 2–3.
4. "From Salt Lake City," *Rocky Mountain Presbyterian* (June 1875): 2; "Salt Lake Collegiate Institute," *Rocky Mountain Presbyterian* (September 1875): 3. Hoping to attain national recognition and support, Welch and Coyner formed a twenty-five member Board of Trustees composed of prominent Presbyterian clergy and laymen (including Sheldon Jackson), the majority of whom were nonresidents of Utah. After a few years of operation, however, they enlisted the session of First Presbyterian Church as trustees.
5. *First Annual Circular of the Salt Lake Collegiate Institute for the Year Ending June 8, 1875*, 4, WC Archives, hereafter cited as *CSLCI*, with appropriate date and page.
6. Ibid., 2–3. For a good overview of the early years of the Collegiate Institute, see Joseph A. Vinatieri, "The Growing Years: Westminster College from Birth to Adolescence," *Utah Historical Quarterly* 43 (fall 1975): 344–51.
7. *CSLCI*, 1975, 3.
8. "Our Educational Creed," *Earnest Worker* 1 (September 1883): 3, WC Archives.
9. *CSLCI*, 1887–88, 2.
10. *CSLCI*, 1875, 3.
11. Josiah Welch to Sheldon Jackson, 3 May 1875, Jackson Corr., PHS Archives.
12. Coyner, "History of the Salt Lake Collegiate Institute," 11–12. During his tenure as institute principal, Coyner subsidized as much as sixty-five percent of the student body by scholarship funds.
13. Ibid., 15.
14. Ibid., 20.
15. "Hymeneal," *Salt Lake Tribune*, 15 October 1875.
16. Coyner, "History of the Salt Lake Collegiate Institute," 3–14. See also *Our Mission Field* (August 1877): 4.
17. Ibid., 20–21.
18. Ibid., 15–16. See also *Seventh Annual Report of the Presbyterian Board of Home Missions*, 1877, 7–10, PHS Archives.
19. Coyner, "A History of the Salt Lake Collegiate Institute," 15–16. A copy of this document is in the archives of the Presbyterian Historical Society.
20. Ibid., 22.

21. Ibid., 17.

22. Ibid., 19–20.

23. "School Work," *Salt Lake Tribune*, 7 August 1877.

24. Coyner, "History of the Salt Lake Collegiate Institute," 25.

25. "Dedicated," *Salt Lake Tribune*, 31 August 1880.

26. *CSLCI*, 1893–94, 6; and Minutes of the First Presbyterian Church of Salt Lake City, 3 September 1883, UU Spec. Colls., 1049.

27. *CSLCI*, 1892–93, 4. Moore nurtured many students who went on to distinguished careers as educators, physicians, and businesswomen. When asked once what she treasured most among her belongings, Moore said, "My students are my most loved possessions." Lydia Burchard to Robert J. Caskey, n.d., WC Archives. Following her death in 1895, the Woman's Executive Committee named the home Mary E. Moore Hall in her honor. Minutes of the Board of Directors of the Church Corporation of First Presbyterian Church of Salt Lake City, 25 July 1881, UU Spec. Colls., 1049, box 1.

28. "Collegiate Institute," *Salt Lake Tribune*, 10 September 1881.

29. Coyner, "History of the Salt Lake Collegiate Institute," 27–28.

30. *Presbyterian Home Missions* 1 (November 1882): 259–60.

31. "Professor Coyner's New School," *Salt Lake Herald*, 22 June 1877; and "Our Schools," *Salt Lake Tribune*, 20 November 1879.

32. "Presbyterian School," *Salt Lake Tribune*, 29 April 1875. The reporter stated that this highly structured regimen contrasted with Mormon territorial schools where scholars were "slovenly and dilatory" and "slouching through everything."

33. "Presbyterian School," *Salt Lake Tribune*, 29 April 1875.

34. "Utah Presbytery," *Salt Lake Tribune*, 16 August 1883.

35. *Earnest Worker* 1 (September 1883): 1.

36. "The Teachers' Association," *Salt Lake Tribune*, 17 August 1883. The association met annually until 1911. Minutes of the meetings are preserved in the archives of Wasatch Academy, Mt. Pleasant, Utah.

37. "School Examination," *Salt Lake Tribune*, 19 June 1875.

38. "The Collegiate Institute," *Salt Lake Tribune*, 5 December 1878.

39. "Collegiate Institute," *Salt Lake Tribune*, 10 September 1881.

40. John M. Coyner, "Editorial," *Utah Educational Journal* 1 (July 1875): 1.

41. "Salt Lake Collegiate Institute," *Rocky Mountain Presbyterian* (October 1875): 1.

42. "Professor Coyner's New School," *Salt Lake Daily Herald*, 22 June 1877.

43. "The Collegiate Institute," *Salt Lake Daily Herald*, 5 December 1878. "This fact is an encomium on the energy and ability of the professor," the editor concluded, "and on the character of the Collegiate Institute, to which words could add but little."

44. John M. Coyner, *Letters on Mormonism* (Salt Lake City, 1879), 3.

45. B. Carmon Hardy, *Solemn Covenant: The Mormon Polygamous Passage* (Urbana and Chicago, 1992), 39–60.

46. For information on McNiece, see Emil Nyman, "A Short History of Westminster College," mimeographed, 1975, Appendix J, WC Archives. A description of the encounter with Joseph Smith III, president of the reorganized Latter-day Saints, is in Roger D. Launius, *Joseph Smith III, Pragmatic Prophet* (Urbana and Chicago, 1988), 296.

47. Coyner frequently affirmed that his critique of Mormonism was directed at the hierarchy of the church not the people in general. See Coyner's letter in *Salt Lake Tribune*, "Utah Mission Field," 6 June 1879.

48. Coyner, *Letters on Mormonism*, preface and 11. See also *Handbook on Mormonism* (Salt Lake City, Chicago, and Cincinnati, 1882), 5–22, 95; and "Extracts from an Address [by John M. Coyner] before the National Teacher's Convention, Madison, Wisconsin," *Utah Evangelist* 2 (August 1884): 4.

49. "The General Assembly," *Interior* (29 May 1879): 3. This was frequently cited in anti-Mormon sources. See Dwyer, *The Gentile Comes to Utah*, 184–85.

50. John M. Coyner, "Disloyalty of Mormons, and Education in Utah," in J. C. Hartzell, ed., *Christian Educators in Council: The National Education Assembly Held at Ocean Grove, New Jersey, August 9–12, 1883* (New York and Cincinnati, 1883), 137–38.

51. "To 'Mormon' Parents and Guardians," *Deseret Evening News*, 21 August 1879. The editorial assault on Coyner continued until he left Salt Lake City. See "Two Modes of Attack," *Deseret Evening News*, 2 June 1881; "Coyner: Again After Coin," 8 November 1883; and "More Falsehood Refuted," 30 January 1884.

52. "Insatiable Clerical Sponges," *Deseret Evening News*, 26 December 1879; and "'Christian' Cunning and 'Mormon' Duty," 6 June 1879. "The Presbyterians may build, but who shall inhabit? They may open schools, but who will attend them?"

53. John M. Coyner to Mrs. F. E. Haines, 29 December 1880, RG 305-15-31, PHS Archives.

54. Minutes of the Woman's Executive Committee of the Presbyterian Church U.S.A. (17 May 1881, typescript): 158–159, PHS Archives, hereafter cited as WEC Minutes.

55. Duncan J. McMillan to Mrs. Haines, 30 July 1880, RG 305-15-52, PHS Archives. The rivalry between Coyner and McMillan is also reflected in their correspondence with Sheldon Jackson.

56. "An Appeal in Behalf of Salt Lake Collegiate Institute," 11 May 1883, 1–3. William Paden Collection, WC Archives.

57. John M. Coyner, "A Millionaire Wanted," *Earnest Worker* 2 (May 1884): 5. See also Andrew E. Murray, *The Skyline Synod: Presbyterianism in Colorado and Utah* (Denver, 1981), 38–39.

58. John M. Coyner to Mrs. F. E. Haines, 1 October 1880, 16 March and 3 December 1881, RG 305-15-31, PHS Archives.

59. John M. Coyner to Mrs. F. E. Haines, 28 November 1880 and 10 December 1881, RG 305-15-31, PHS Archives.

60. Minutes of the Board of Directors of the Salt Lake Collegiate Institute, 1 December 1884, UU Spec. Colls., 1049.

61. *Utah Evangelist* 1 (April 1884): 3.

62. "A Prosperous School," *Salt Lake Tribune,* 12 April 1884; and "Commencement Exercises," *Utah Evangelist* 2 (June 1884): 3.

63. Coyner, "History of the Salt Lake Collegiate Institute," 25–30; and "Taking Leave," *Salt Lake Tribune*, 1 May 1885.

64. Robert J. Caskey to George F. McAfee, 14 June 1897, RG 111-4-11, PHS Archives. On October 15, 1914, during a meeting of the Synod of Utah, trustees of Westminster College dedicated entrance pillars to the campus in honor of John and Mary Coyner, called the Coyner Memorial Gateway.

65. "Obituary, John McCutcheon Coyner," *Herald and Presbyter*, 1 July 1908.

3

Old Collegiate

The Collegiate Institute will continue to be what it has ever been, a thorough Christian school where the Bible is used as a text book of morals, and where the truths and principles of Christian morality are taught by faithful Christian teachers apart from all sectarian views.
—Circular of the Salt Lake Collegiate Institute, 1892–93.

John Coyner's dominant personality shaped virtually every facet of the Collegiate Institute during its first decade of operation. He also extended his influence by selecting a successor, Jesse F. Millspaugh, whom he had hired as principal in 1883. Unlike the charismatic and controversial Coyner, however, Millspaugh preferred a traditional, managerial style of operation, one better suited to Utah's volatile political environment during the antipolygamy crusade of the 1880s. Millspaugh, who served 1885–1890, and his successors, Robert J. Caskey (from 1892 to 1904) and George B. Sweazey (from 1904 to 1914), guided the Collegiate Institute through ambivalent relationships with the Presbyterian mission boards, Mormon church authorities, and trustees of Sheldon Jackson (later Westminster) College. In addition, the three men enhanced the school's reputation for quality Christian instruction and developed a loyal following of students, alumni, and friends in the intermountain region.[1]

Only twenty-eight years old when he arrived in Salt Lake City, Jesse Fonda Millspaugh brought a balance of academic and administrative skills to his position of superintendent of the Collegiate Institute. Millspaugh attended the University of Michigan, graduating with honors in 1879. After serving two years as high school principal in Frankfort, Indiana (a position previously occupied by Coyner), Millspaugh obtained a medical degree from the University of Pennsylvania in 1883. Weakened by a heart condition induced by inflammatory rheumatism, he never practiced as a physician but instead pursued a career in collegiate education.[2]

Millspaugh viewed the institutional mission of the Collegiate Institute in much the same terms as had the school's founder. Advertisements emphasized the demanding curriculum and rigid discipline, promoting admission to those determined to lay a strong foundation for a university education and professional careers.[3] Although Millspaugh accepted systematic drill and memorization as tools in the learning process, he urged students to challenge sources and form independent judgments based on observation and inquiry. Institute catalogs affirmed, "No textbook statement is received for a fact which can not be demonstrated by an experiment."[4] His educational philosophy centered on what he called "the triune nature of the pupil"—the physical, the mental, and the spiritual. By combining these three approaches, he hoped to produce a well-rounded student whose goal was not simply the acquisition of knowledge but the development of character.[5] In particular, Millspaugh believed that Utah youth needed to cultivate principles of patriotism, citizenship, and respect for law to counteract the example of Mormon opposition to federal rules forbidding polygamy. Like many of his peers, Millspaugh held Mormon doctrines in low esteem, once noting that Latter-day Saints were as "unfamiliar with genuine Biblical insight as the Hill dwellers of Siam."[6]

Millspaugh was a decisive administrator who on the one hand valued innovation and experimentation but on the other hand prized consistency and order. He established bookkeeping procedures to correct previous intermingling of accounts and also introduced an auditing system, so that annual reports accurately reflected the institute's financial status. Convinced that an attractive physical plant stimulated learning and projected a positive community image, Millspaugh inaugurated a campus improvement project. Photographs of the institute taken during his tenure portray a well-manicured and shady campus with ample recreational facilities.[7] Millspaugh solicited donations to increase library holdings and upgrade laboratory equipment. Through his efforts the institute acquired one of the best collections of reference works in Salt Lake City and obtained scientific instrumentation including "an elegant compound microscope." Although modest by contemporary standards, the Collegiate Institute's learning environment compared favorably with that offered by other high schools in Utah Territory.[8]

Curriculum during his tenure reflected new educational trends. Millspaugh instituted a kindergarten department in 1884 directed by Elizabeth Dickey, whose salary was provided by the national Presbyterian

Woman's Executive Committee. Instruction focused on three areas: gifts, which stressed color, motion, construction of geometrical forms, and conceptualizing number, size, position, and dimensions; occupation, which provided hands-on experiences in such activities as sewing, drawing, weaving, pasting, and modeling in clay; and circle games and singing, designed to provide a "healthy moral sentiment" and to develop the student's powers of observation "and a deeper love for nature and its Divine author."[9] An expanded normal school curriculum in 1886 anticipated a demand for trained teachers when Utah legislators implemented a territorial free public school system. This curriculum included lectures and assigned readings on educational topics, analyses of various teaching methods and school management, and a practicum for supervised teaching in classroom situations.[10] Millspaugh also established a truncated three-year academic course that included business courses, such as bookkeeping and finance, designed to prepare students for post-Collegiate Institute entry into the growing Utah economy.[11]

Like his predecessor, Millspaugh supported equity for women in access to educational and professional opportunities. In several handwritten essays, he criticized prevailing cultural attitudes that narrowly defined "woman's sphere" to exclude her participation in public life. "One of the disgraces of history is the position which has been accorded women. In no age but the present, and now but in slight degree, has she been permitted to enter upon her true sphere—one which is equal to man's."[12] Millspaugh encouraged female students to explore the wide range of subjects included in the institute curriculum that was, unlike some secondary schools, open to women. Woman students directed their own literary society that held weekly meetings to review classical literature and to discuss contemporary issues. Parents and local dignitaries frequently attended their gatherings to hear questions debated such as "Is Woman More Useful in a Public or Private Life?" or "Is It Honorable for Women to be Independent?"[13]

Many woman graduates attended college or other professional schools. One example was Margaret Freece, class of 1892, who was admitted to the Woman's Medical College in Chicago in 1892 and upon graduation received a commission from the Presbyterian Board of Foreign Missions to serve in China. Electing to stay near family, Freece applied for a license to practice medicine in Utah and became one of the first woman physicians in the state.[14] Maude Adams, one of America's best-known actresses in the early twentieth century, was another of Millspaugh's protégées. After several years of traveling as a child actress, Maude was sent to live with her grandmother in Salt Lake City, at which time she enrolled in the Collegiate Institute. Although Maude did well in classes, she disliked the school discipline and missed the excitement of stage life. After four years at the institute, she persuaded her parents to let her resume her acting career.[15]

Disavowing Coyner's anti-Mormonism, Millspaugh attempted to improve relationships with Mormon officials and church members in Salt Lake City and sought avenues of cooperation with Latter-day Saints in their quest for an improved educational system in Utah Territory. He saw that institute catalogs avoided references to Mormons, downplayed denominational ties, and emphasized curricular diversity and faculty credentials. Active in Salt Lake City local organizations that included both Mormon and non-Mormon educators, his reputation as a progressive administrator and ecumenical Christian enhanced the institute's regional image as an outstanding college preparatory school.[16] In his zeal to tap the generosity of Presbyterians in the eastern United States, however, Millspaugh angered Mormon authorities when writing in a Presbyterian women's organization periodical about efforts of early missionaries "to carry the truth to the deluded people of Mormonism." Although conceding that relationships had improved in recent years, he charged that Utah was still controlled by the Mormon priesthood. He ended the article with a plea for funds to expand the work of the Collegiate Institute so that "this Territory which has been a blot upon our national escutcheon, and a menace to our Christian institution, will be transformed into the fairest of our States."[17]

Such isolated disagreements with Mormon authorities apparently had little negative impact on the institute's enrollment. Between 1885 and 1890, attendance averaged about 325 students, some of whom lived on campus or in nearby homes. The religious composition of institute students was 14 percent Mormon, 26 percent apostate Mormon, 30 percent Evangelical Protestant, and the remainder Roman Catholic, Spiritualist, and Jewish. Only a handful identified their family tradition as atheist or "nothing."[18] Applications for admission soon exceeded space available, which mandated creating new classroom, laboratory, and boarding facilities on the already overcrowded campus. Supported by school trustees, Millspaugh drew up plans in 1889 for a modern physical plant that would make the Collegiate Institute the best-equipped high school in Salt Lake City and began a financial campaign to underwrite the cost of modernizing the campus. Concentrating on Salt Lake City businessmen and Presbyterian mission officials in New York, he received nominal sums from the local people, but sufficient funds from the denomination to construct a foundation for the building. Although six years would pass before blueprints became a reality, Millspaugh's initial leadership featured prominently in the project's ultimate success.[19]

Even with record enrollments and the foundation for a new building in place, the Collegiate Institute's accomplishments were overshadowed by financial crises that had plagued the school since its opening session. Millspaugh confided to colleagues, "During the five years of my work here there has been no time when we have not been hampered, and harassed, and almost in despair over our financial matters."[20] Operating cost shortfalls, which averaged $2,000 annually, resulted in salary reductions and a growing debt. He kept up a steady flow of correspondence to various denominational officers pleading for funds. On several occasions, institute trustees threatened to close down the school unless money was immediately forthcoming, a tactic that did not resonate well with harried board officials.[21]

Millspaugh welcomed with some ambivalence the introduction of free public schools into Utah in 1890. On the one hand, they represented a victory for non-Mormons like himself who had for decades sought the end of Mormon hegemony in territorial schools. On the other hand, they called into question the future of Protestant parochial schools like the Collegiate Institute, founded because there was no free school system in place. "The effects of this revolution upon Christian work in the territory is not precisely to be predicted. It is for the Christian churches to say whether they will continue mission school work after the inauguration of an American school system."[22] On that note, Millspaugh relinquished his leadership of the Collegiate Institute to become the first superintendent of schools in Salt Lake City, a position he held for eight years. Historians credit Millspaugh with laying the foundation of Utah's modern school system both by his curricular reforms and by his evenhanded management of Mormon and gentile factions in Salt Lake City.[23]

Millspaugh's departure from the Collegiate Institute in 1890 left a leadership void not immediately filled. Charles S. Richardson, a graduate of Colby University in Maine, directed the institute for one year. Robert J. Caskey, an alumnus of Knox College in Illinois who had been principal of the high school department since 1887, succeeded Richardson. His mandate from the Presbyterian Board of Home Missions was unequivocal: "The main point, including almost all others, is that the work which the Board has offered you and you have accepted is strictly a mission work. It is *education*, but it is only and always *religious* education."[24] Caskey inherited an institution on the verge of collapse. As public schools provided a quality education free from sectarian religious agendas, enrollment in Utah Presbyterian, Methodist, Episcopal, and Congregational schools plummeted. Despite its excellent reputation, the Collegiate Institute experienced a fifty percent reduction between 1890 and 1893, with the largest drop in the lower grades. By 1895, when the institute eliminated its primary and intermediate programs, only sixty-three students were matriculated, about the same number as when the school opened twenty years earlier.[25]

The onset of a prolonged economic depression marked by the Panic of 1893 compounded financial woes by depleting already inadequate denominational revenues and plunging mission boards into debt for the first time in history. The Presbyterian Board of Home Missions had budget deficits for five straight years from 1889 to 1894, noting in annual reports that the costs of school work had outrun the means to support it.[26] In 1893–94 the board reported the largest operating deficit of its history of more than $250,000. Board executives attributed the deficit to "the financial troubles in the country which have disturbed every kind of business and affected to a greater or less extent all contributors."[27] Although the financial condition gradually improved, Utah missions never regained their previous levels of support, resulting in a policy of retrenchment throughout the entire Presbyterian home missionary enterprise. Downsizing that began in the 1890s eventually closed all denominational elementary schools in Utah and consolidated high school work into one location, Wasatch Academy in Mt. Pleasant, Utah.[28]

Collegiate Institute teachers bore the brunt of denominational retrenchment and financial exigency. Traditionally teachers received only half-salary monthly until December, when they were paid the balance due in time for Christmas holidays. A similar process was followed during the spring term. In 1891–92 salaries could not be met either in December or June, and local banks considered the institute a poor risk for short-term loans. Furthermore, the Board of Home Missions requested teachers to return ten percent of their salaries as a "voluntary tithe" to compensate for the reduction of receipts at the national level. Caskey protested vigorously against such patently unfair policies and complained that even at full salary ($600), which was twenty percent below what a public school-teacher made, faculty retention was a significant problem.[29]

Salt Lake Collegiate Institute faced other problems in its relationship to the Board of Home Missions, which considered the school an anomaly. Located in a prosperous urban environment, functioning under an autonomous board of trustees, and following its own unique curricular path, the institute projected the image of an eastern preparatory school rather than a frontier mission station. For a number of years, Mission Board officials had been working behind the scenes to transfer the

Collegiate Institute to the Board of Aid for Colleges and Academies. In one confidential communication, an official noted that "the work of the Institute, while most excellent, has no distinctive missionary character, and is really not within the province of our Board."[30] The College Board, already overburdened with destitute colleges and academies, procrastinated on making a decision to assume responsibility for another fragile institution.[31] The Woman's Executive Committee also questioned its relationship to the Collegiate Institute because the high school program did not fit the women's traditional emphasis on grammar school education.[32] Many thought that repeated requests by institute administrators for additional staff and modern facilities seemed inappropriate especially when other Utah missionaries operated out of one-room schoolhouses. One committee member commented that "At present [1894] all our connection with the Institute seems to be to raise money and pay the bills."[33] Others complained that too many appeals had been made for the Collegiate Institute and noted that synodical societies wanted to assist a variety of educational missions in Utah.[34]

Instead of retrenchment, institute trustees and staff argued for the continuation and expansion of mission schools in Utah. They insisted that rural public schools were inadequate and ill-staffed, leaving denominational schools as the only model for quality education. Moreover, they claimed that public schools, except for schools in Salt Lake City and Ogden, were controlled by the Mormon teachers and administrators who excluded outsiders from staff positions. Various Presbyterian missionaries also contended that many human and financial resources had been invested in Utah, and to abandon twenty-five years of dedicated work appeared unconscionable.[35] Nevertheless, the Board of Home Missions continued to phase out mission schools in Utah and heightened efforts to transfer the Collegiate Institute to the College Board. During this period, trustee McNiece implored Sheldon Jackson to use his influence in denominational circles to secure an appropriation of $30,000 to construct a new academy building and bolster faculty salaries.[36] Largely through Jackson's intervention, Home Mission officials and institute trustees worked out a compromise that rescued the school from closure. With Presbyterian women providing major funding, the Board of Home Missions underwrote construction costs of a new institute building and the salary of the matron of the Girls' Home. All property and assets were to be turned over to a local board of trustees composed primarily of ruling elders from First Presbyterian Church, chaired by McNiece. Essentially the institute would have to become self-supporting, relying on tuition and income from boarding students along with small annual grants from the College Board.[37]

In a ceremony attended by Salt Lake City dignitaries, church officials, and the campus community, Collegiate Institute trustees dedicated the new academy building on June 5, 1895. A reporter for the *Salt Lake Tribune* observed that "a happy feeling seemed to pervade the atmosphere" as McNiece presided and introduced various guests. McNiece singled out Pennsylvania women's synodical groups and Nettie McCormick, wife of Chicago industrialist Cyrus McCormick, for their significant financial contributions to the building fund. Principal Caskey briefly recounted the institute's history and predicted its role as a feeder school for the proposed Sheldon Jackson College. The program concluded with a flourish of patriotism designed to impress the Mormon populace of Salt Lake City with the institute's distinctly "American" orientation. "A bright flag of the loved colors of the United States was hoisted on the staff from the top most pinnacle of the handsome structure."[38]

Optimism diminished when projected enrollments failed to materialize and tuition and board income did not cover operating expenses. In addition, loans for furnishing the new building were coming due, and trustees could not meet the next payments. Desperate for cash, the institute advertised for boarders to occupy rooms on the top floor of the institute building at low weekly rates.[39] Even with a reduced staff consisting only of Caskey and three teachers, faculty salaries were in arrears and accounts with local merchants went unpaid. Institute trustees admitted that they were unable to run a viable educational program solely with resources available to them in Utah and that, without outside help, the institute would have to suspend classes, vacate the new building, and sell school property at a public auction.[40] Desiring to keep ownership in Utah, trustees petitioned the Presbytery of Utah to take control of the institute, but Presbyters declined, citing paucity of funds.[41] The institute turned again to the Board of Home Missions and the Woman's Executive Committee. Writing on behalf of the trustees, McNiece offered to relinquish all property and assets and to grant the Home Mission Board full administrative oversight and fiscal control of the institute.[42]

This appeal received a mixed response. A substantial minority doubted the wisdom of assuming such a financial burden especially during a period of economic recession. Others thought that the institute rightfully belonged under the care of the Board of Aid for Colleges and Academies. Ultimately, however, rather than abandon a project in which they had invested so much time, money, and prayer, Presbyterian women accepted responsibility for the Collegiate Institute beginning September 1, 1896. The new agreement made no provision for a Utah-based board of trustees; henceforth all curricular, staffing, and financial decisions would be made in New York rather than in Salt Lake City.[43]

Because of this arrangement, Caskey was hampered by bureaucratic procedures that necessitated securing permission from New York before making routine decisions. Caskey expressed his frustration by sending caustic notes to New York administrators from whom he received similar replies. When he asked to have a telephone installed in 1899, Caskey received a note stating, "A request from the Salt Lake Collegiate Institute, Utah for a telephone connection was upon motion refused."[44] Directed by the Board of Home Missions to use a Presbyterian hymnal for worship services at the institute, Caskey demurred. An irate Home Mission Board secretary ordered Caskey to purchase denominational hymnals.[45] Such disagreements finally took their toll. Pessimistic about the institute's future and frustrated by denominational red tape, Caskey submitted a terse letter of resignation to the Board of Home Missions effective at the end of the 1903–4 academic year after seventeen years of service to the institute.[46] McNiece publicly praised Caskey for his devoted service to the Collegiate Institute but privately acknowledged that the college trustees were relieved that the principal was leaving Utah.[47]

Caskey's replacement, George Beaty Sweazey, brought impressive academic credentials to his new position as principal of the Collegiate Institute. Appointed the second faculty member of Sheldon Jackson College in 1897, Sweazey through the years taught a variety of courses at the college and the institute, including physics, surveying, chemistry, Bible, Greek, Latin, German, mathematics, mechanical drawing, and civics. He also taught a popular Sunday school class at First Presbyterian Church attended by high school and college age students.[48] Like his predecessors, Sweazey managed the institute on very limited resources, relying on annual contributions from the Board of Home Missions and revenue from tuition and boarding students.

Many families could not make tuition payments in cash, and it was not uncommon for Sweazey to accept students with only a promise of future payment. One parent sent his son with $75 owed on the previous year's tuition and said, "If you can take the boy on fair promises, we will stand good for another year."[49] A female student from Spanish Fork wrote, "My father will bring up fifty bushels of potatoes Monday. I am writing for him as he is so busy digging beets that he cannot write."[50] Having borrowed money from the principal to pay for shipping her trunk to Salt Lake City and still short of finances, a student promised that "when our lavender bush blossoms, I'll try to make glad the housekeeper's heart."[51] A young man who planned to work his way through high school by delivering newspapers requested deferment of tuition payment because his employer was unable to pay him at the present time. "Could I enter school and pay you when Mr. Ward pays me? I expect to take up my paper route as soon as I enter school." In bright blue ink Sweazey wrote across the top of the letter "accepted."[52]

Under Sweazey, upon entering the institute each student received a Bible and was required to participate in daily morning devotional exercises consisting of scripture reading, singing, and prayer. Parents who wished to exempt their children from this requirement could do so by expressing their wishes in writing to the principal. Because services were carefully scripted to be nonsectarian, it appeared that few parents did so. In addition to daily worship, students had an extended prayer meeting each Thursday at the close of school and participated in Christian Endeavor societies associated with First Presbyterian Church.[53] The institute's curriculum also required two credit hours of Bible during each year of high school.[54] By emphasizing religion in the classroom, institute instructors hoped to stimulate religious inquiry, promote church membership, and produce Christian commitment. They also exhibited respect for the Christian Sabbath (Sunday) by devoting the day to public worship and spiritual edification, ceasing all secular activities.[55] Although nonresidents were only encouraged to attend Sunday school and church, boarding school students had no option. On Sundays they were escorted across campus by their teachers to First Presbyterian Church for church school classes and morning worship and attended additional afternoon and evening Bible study groups.[56]

Rules on student behavior included strictures against profanity and the use of alcoholic beverages and tobacco, the latter singled out as "detrimental to both physical and mental development of boys during their period of growth." A student who smoked and refused to reform was subject to immediate expulsion.[57] The activities of boarding students were monitored twenty-four hours a day, with regulations prohibiting card playing and games of chance on school premises. Attendance at the theater, matinee, or opera, all of which were deemed "hostile to health, to study and to morals," was forbidden. In fact, school officials specified that "In no case are [students] permitted unnecessarily to be on the streets at night." Violators of this rule risked restriction to their rooms or expulsion from campus. Later, appearances at off-campus dances or card parties were added to the list of forbidden activities.[58]

Sweazey's extensive correspondence indicates that most parents endorsed the institute's emphasis on religion and morality. When one male student was issued a one-month suspension for attending a theater matinee, his parents complimented Sweazey for the institute's strict standards.[59] Another student caught using tobacco received a similar punishment, and his mother upheld the administration of discipline without complaint.[60] A father responded to a letter from principal Sweazey informing him that his son had been disruptive and inattentive in class: "Any measure you may take to waken him to a sense of responsibility and earnestness has the approval of his mother and myself and we hope shortly to hear of a decided improvement in George both in his conduct and school work."[61]

The effectiveness of such a religious and moral regimen is difficult to assess. Annual statistical reports submitted by the institute to the Board of Aid for Colleges and Academies indicate that some students were converted and a few decided to enter the ministry. Between 1875 and 1884, fifty-seven students reportedly had made a profession of faith in Christ. Four woman graduates were teaching in denominational schools and four men were studying for the ministry. Reportedly "a large proportion [were] of Mormon origin."[62] In subsequent annual statistical reports during the nineteenth and early twentieth centuries, the institute averaged about eight to twelve conversions and thirty-five new church members.[63] Articles featuring the Collegiate Institute published in the *Home Mission Monthly* emphasized evangelistic rather than pedagogical accomplishments. Standard fare were stories of young men and women who had abandoned their Mormon heritage for mainstream Christian denominations. Instructor Mary E. Moore noted the difficulty of doing mission work in Utah but expressed her "deepest gratitude that of over twenty-three graduates all but five professed Christ before leaving the school." Particularly encouraging, she noted, was the fact that some of these graduates, raised in Mormon households, were now teaching in Presbyterian mission schools.[64]

While cultivating a spiritual environment at the Collegiate Institute, faculty and staff also encouraged secular extracurricular activities. Completion of the new building in 1895 had added additional space for boarding students and recreational facilities and opened the way for a more structured athletic program. The institute curriculum had traditionally featured some form of physical education consisting primarily of gymnastics and informal games for both men and women. By the early 1900s, however, the institute was fielding boys' football and baseball teams that occasionally played games with local and regional high schools. Because football had an exceptionally high injury rate due to lack of protective equipment and rules that permitted offensive strategies such as the flying wedge, institute officials published a disclaimer in their annual catalogs regarding responsibility for athletic participants.[65] Due to a small male enrollment, Collegiate Institute teams found it difficult to compete with local high schools. In 1899, they canceled a football game with Salt Lake High, noting that they needed more practice because their opponent was so strong.[66] Two years later, a reporter for the *Salt Lake Tribune* described a contest with Salt Lake High as "probably the worst exhibition of football that ever drew a crowd at Walker field. There was some good individual work, but the lack of co-operation was distressing and the fumbling something to make one weep. Perhaps the ball was made from the skin of a greased pig."[67]

Women were limited to intramural and recreational activities. Early catalogs specified that because women were required to take daily exercise in the open air, they should bring umbrellas and rubber overshoes.[68] Gradually, a few women's sports became part of the institute's athletic program. In 1905, Sweazey noted that women had taken up tennis with great enthusiasm, and a few years later women formed a tennis club and received an appropriation of $2.75 for tennis balls.[69] Basketball also became popular with institute women. As early as 1911 women had formed two teams for intramural competition, and by 1916 they had acquired a female coach and were scheduling games with local and area teams.[70]

Under Sweazey's supervision, the Collegiate Institute formed a Student Association to coordinate athletic events and raise money for equipment and travel. An annual fee of one dollar admitted members to entertainments, athletic games, and contests in which institute students participated. At its first meeting, association members appropriated $3.50 for one ankle brace and for one pair of shoes.[71] At subsequent meetings, students allotted small sums, such as "twenty-five cents for pumping up a football, $3.00 for baseballs, $1.00 for bats, $6.00 for a basketball, and $1.00 to pay for repairs necessary for two old basketballs and to settle a debt of 15 cents made for sewing up the football last fall." Other actions included selecting purple and gold as school colors and making small appropriations to put numbers on basketball uniforms and to pay travel expenses for various athletic teams.[72]

Distinctions between male and female sports persisted, however. When women requested indoor practice space for basketball, they were informed that the only room available was one smaller than required by the rules for indoor practice, but that it would be adequate for their needs.[73] Only reluctantly did the Student Association agree to cover their travel expenses. The question of awarding letters to woman basketball players generated considerable discussion, resulting in a compromise by the Student Association. Women would be given rings instead of traditional letters.[74] Other extracurricular activities captured student interest. The institute sponsored a debating society "for securing practices in extemporaneous discussion and familiarity with parliamentary usages."[75] Competition among schools in the Salt Lake City area was keen, and students raised money to cover travel expenses for regional debates. When Otto Hauerbach won an interstate oratorical contest in 1895, institute teachers and students recessed classes, cheered and shouted, and rang the school bell in honor of the popular student.[76]

A highlight of the school year was the annual collegiate class day held on the evening prior to graduation. Songs, speeches, and humorous skits performed by students provided an opportunity to settle accounts with the teachers in return for hard discipline. One performance entitled "Funeral Rites" featured orations in English, German, and Latin, and arranged "hog Latin" over their books, teachers, and studies. Another part of the program consisted of presentations to the faculty. The principal received a pair of rubber heels for his shoes, "by the aid of which he is expected to move around quietly and arrive unexpectedly."[77] In addition to student performances, class day provided the setting for three traditions long associated with the Collegiate Institute. First, the graduating class presented the new senior class with a large robe adorned with colored patches representing previous classes, accompanied by appropriate speeches from the retiring and rising senior class presidents. Second, the brightest rising senior, decided by vote of the graduating class, received an old-fashioned tin lantern to symbolize his or her intellectual acumen. Third, the "spooniest senior," the one with the most voracious appetite, was awarded possession of a large tin spoon by its previous owner.[78]

Institute faculty took great pride in their graduates, many of whom successfully matriculated in colleges such as Princeton, Dartmouth, Wabash, and Knox. A survey of graduates conducted in 1912 indicated that 125 women and 60 men had completed the academic course since the first diplomas had been issued in 1882. Ninety-three of the graduates continued their education at the college level. Of the professions followed by the alumni, teachers far outnumbered all others combined, with eighty-eight graduates employed in educational work ranging from kindergarten to college. Two of that number were country superintendents and two were high school principals. Other professions included mining and business (thirty-one), physicians (seven), lawyers (three), librarians (two), social workers (two), authors (two), electricians (two), and one singer in grand opera.[79]

The Collegiate Institute might have continued as a private secondary school had Presbyterians not moved to establish a college in Salt Lake

City. Viewing the institute and its assets as essential to the attainments of their goals, the college trustees obtained ownership of the institute in 1910 and designated it "the preparatory department of Westminster College." Although college officials assured the public that "the character of the work and the individuality of 'Old Collegiate' [would] remain unchanged," the high school's distinctive ethos gradually diminished and then ended as Westminster attained baccalaureate status.[80]

NOTES

1. *CSLCI*, 1913–14.

2. D. H. Christensen, "Jesse Fonda Millspaugh," *Utah Educational Review* 25 (March 1932): 300–301; and Minutes of the Board of Directors of the Salt Lake Collegiate Institute, 8 August 1883, UU Spec. Colls., 1049, box 1, hereafter cited as MBDSLCI. Born in Orange County, New York, on June 18, 1855, Millspaugh shortly after moved with his family to a farm near Battle Creek, Michigan. At age four, he and his four brothers were orphaned and raised by an aunt and uncle whose religious values and high regard for education significantly impacted his career decisions.

3. *CSLCI*, 1897–98, 4.

4. *CSLCI*, 1888–89, 4 and 1891–92, 11.

5. *CSLCI*, 1888–89, 3. For a clear exposition of Millspaugh's educational philosophy, see "The Education Which Utah Needs," in *The Situation in Utah: Discussions of the Christian Convention Held in Salt Lake City, Utah, April 1888* (Salt Lake City, 1888). Paden Papers, WC Archives.

6. Jesse F. Millspaugh, Institute Notebook, 93, WC Archives. The notebook is a rich source of statistical information regarding the institute and contains drafts of papers and addresses in Millspaugh's handwriting.

7. MBDSLCI, 27 August 1884. Even Coyner was subject to Millspaugh's penchant for neatness. While Coyner was east on a money-raising trip, Millspaugh directed that "the manure and debris on Prof. Coyner's premises and contiguous to the School be removed and the bill of expense therefore be presented to Prof. Coyner on his return for settlement." Ibid., 6 and 27 August 1884.

8. *CSLCI*, 1887–88, 2. See also Jesse F. Millspaugh, "Present Condition and Future Prospects of the Salt Lake Collegiate Institute," *Presbyterian Home Missionary* 4 (December 1885): 281.

9. MBDSLCI, 6 August 1884; "Salt Lake Collegiate Institute," *Church Review* (29 December 1895): 70–71; *CSLCI*, 1886–87, 8. Due to limited classroom space, the kindergarten program was discontinued in 1889, but classes later resumed in the First Presbyterian Church under congregational supervision.

10. *CSLCI*, 1886–87, 13. A number of the initial teachers in the Salt Lake City Public School System were graduates of the Collegiate Institute, and others served with distinction in towns and villages throughout the state.

11. *CSLCI*, 1888–89, 9; and 1891–92, 12–14.

12. Millspaugh, Institute Notebook, 130, WC Archives.

13. "Salt Lake Collegiate Institute," *Utah Evangelist* 1 (May 1884): 6; and *CSLCI*, 1887–88, 2.

14. Born into a polygamous Mormon family, Freece and other family members converted to Presbyterianism under the influence of mission schoolteachers. Freece's outstanding academic work merited a scholarship to the Collegiate Institute where instructors encouraged her to pursue advanced degrees. After becoming a doctor, she resided in Salina, Utah, where she devoted her life to a family practice that included urban and rural, rich and poor, Mormon and gentile. An ardent feminist, she frequently gave lectures on women of the Bible in which she described females as being the "trail blazers for that large freedom of thought and actions." Freece continued to support Westminster College, providing scholarships for needy students and donating real estate. Freece's notebooks and other biographical data can be found in the Peter Freece Collection, vol. 16, Brigham Young University Archives, and in a Freece folder in the WC Archives.

15. John A. Garraty, ed., *Dictionary of American Biography* (New York, 1977) Supplement Five, 7–8; and Phyllis Robbins, *Maude Adams, An Intimate Portrait* (New York, 1956), 18–21; and *The Young Maude Adams* (Francetown, New Hampshire), 15–28. Born Maude Ewing Adams Kiskadden, her mother was a leading player in Brigham Young's Deseret Stock Company, and "Little Maudie" made her debut at nine months in *The Lost Child*. After leaving the institute, she had a succession of juvenile roles and caught the attention of James Barrie, who in 1897 featured her in a dramatization of his successful novel, *The Little Minister*. Her career skyrocketed with leading roles in other Barrie productions, including that of Peter Pan, perhaps her most memorable and well-received performance.

16. Frederick S. Buchanan, *Culture Clash and Accommodation: Public Schooling in Salt Lake City, 1890–1904* (San Francisco and Salt Lake City, 1996), 49–51.

17. J. F. Millspaugh, "Progress of the Work among the Mormons," *Home Mission Monthly* 3 (May 1889): 152–55. For a Mormon response, see "Religious Slanderers," *Deseret Evening News*, 10 September 1891.

18. Millspaugh, Institute Notebook, 90. For budget-minded parents, annual expenses were reasonable: high school students, $70.80; grammar school students, $24.60; and intermediate and primary students, $17.10. About half the student body paid no fees or were awarded work grants in lieu of tuition.

19. Ibid., 90, 92.

20. Ibid., 80.

21. Annual Report of Salt Lake Collegiate Institute to Board of Home Missions, (1888–90, typescript), RG 32-32-13, PHS Archives. For a typical protest, see Robert G. McNiece to H. D. Ganse, 19 January 1887, RG 32-26-3, PHS Archives.

22. Millspaugh, Institute Notebook, 131.

23. Buchanan, *Culture Clash and Accommodation*, 24–56. In 1898 he accepted a position as president of Winona State Normal School in Minnesota, and in 1904 he became president of Los Angeles State Normal School (later the University of California, Los Angeles), where he served with distinction for thirteen years until his retirement and death in 1919. D. S. Christensen, "Jesse Fonda Millspaugh," *Utah Educational Review* 25 (March 1932): 300–301; and "Dr. Jess F. Millspaugh, Former Salt Laker Dies," *Deseret News*, 13 December 1919.

24. Henry Kendall to Robert J. Caskey, n.d. [c. 1892], WC Archives.

25. Enrollment figures for the Collegiate Institute can be found in annual reports to the Board of Aid for Colleges and Academies, published in *GAMPCUSA*, 1893, 345; 1896, 330; and in reports to Board of Home Missions, RG 32-16-4, PHS Archives.

26. *Annual Report of the Presbyterian Board of Home Missions, 1890–1891*, 24, 27, PHS Archives.

27. *Annual Report of the Presbyterian Board of Home Missions, 1893–1894*, 16, PHS Archives.

28. WEC Minutes, 12 December 1894, 1–2, RG 305, PHS Archives.

29. Charles Richardson to H. D. Ganse, 20 January 1891; and Robert Caskey to E. C. Ray, 13 November 1891, RG 32-26-4, PHS Archives.

30. William Irvin to H. D. Ganse, 6 August 1891, RG 32-26-4, PHS Archives. A roll book of institute students in the Westminster College Archives covering the period 1888–1920 indicates that only a small percentage of students came from Mormon families. Most were Presbyterians, Methodists, Episcopalians, or other Protestant denomination. Many students list no religious preference.

31. William Irvin to H. D. Ganse, 6 August 1891, RG 32-26-4, PHS Archives.

32. Mrs. D. E. Finks to E. C. Ray, 2 February 1892, RG 32-26-4, PHS Archives.

33. WEC Minutes, 5 June 1894, 1, RG 305, PHS Archives.

34. Mrs. William B. Holmes to Robert Caskey, 22 March 1895, WC Archives.

35. Samuel E. Wishard to George F. McAfee, 3 January 1895, RG 111-4-10, PHS Archives.

36. Robert G. McNiece to George F. McAfee, 4 March and 2 April 1894, RG lll-4-10, PHS Archives. By securing local control of the Collegiate Institute, McNiece planned to use its campus as a preparatory department for the proposed Presbyterian college in Salt Lake City. Please refer to chapter 4.

37. These arrangements, incidentally, were made without input from Principal Caskey, who learned of the new relationship only after the fact. George F. McAfee to Robert J. Caskey, 5 and 25 April 1895, RG 111-4-11, PHS Archives.

38. The new four-story brick and sandstone structure fronting on Second East Street was eighty feet long and sixty-four feet wide. In addition to offices, classrooms, and dining facilities, the building had twenty-seven dormitory rooms that could accommodate up to fifty students. Boasting such amenities as steam heat, electric lights, and marble lavatories and bathrooms on each floor, and marked by a distinctive bell tower that proclaimed in bold letters "Collegiate Institute," the edifice received rave reviews in local newspapers. See, "New Collegiate Building," *Salt Lake Tribune,* 6 June 1895, and "The Salt Lake Collegiate Institute," *Church Review* 4 (29 December 1895): 61.

39. Robert G. McNiece to Sheldon Jackson, 10 September 1895, Jackson Corres.

40. Robert G. McNiece to Sheldon Jackson, 28 March 1896, WC Archives; and George F. McAfee to E. C. Ray, 5 August 1896, RG 32-26-5, PHS Archives.

41. MBDSLCI, 30 March 1896.

42. MBDSLCI, 4 June and 28 July 1896; and WEC Minutes, Ways and Means Committee, 16 June 1896, RG 305-14-8, PHS Archives.

43. MBDSLCI, 18 May and 4 June 1896; WEC Minutes, 3 December 1895, 1–2; and 28 April 1896, 48, RG 305-14-8, PHS Archives; Robert J. Caskey to E. C. Ray, 4 May 1897, RG 32-22-5, PHS Archives.

44. WEC Minutes, Ways and Means Committee, 26 November 1899, RG 305-14-68, PHS Archives. The first mention of telephone service at the institute appears in the *Annual Circular* of 1904–5. The number was 1107. Another time Caskey requested $25 to purchase a scientific reference book for the institute library. He was informed that money could not be appropriated from the General Fund for such purposes. WEC Minutes, Ways and Means Committee, 17 September 1898, RG 305-14-8. PHS Archives.

45. He argued that the adjective *Presbyterian* might alienate some people who would not be afraid of the name Christian. In Utah, Caskey explained, "We conceal the denominational and put forward the Christian phase." Robert J. Caskey to George F. McAfee, 14 June 1897, RG 111-4-10, PHS Archives. The response, in a handwritten addendum, emphasized, "Let it be known far and wide that the Collegiate Institute is a Presbyterian school!" George F. McAfee to Robert J. Caskey, 6 June 1897, RG 111-4-10, PHS Archives; and 2 May 1904, WC Archives.

46. S. F. Lincoln to Robert J. Caskey, 2 September 1903; and George F. McAfee to Robert J. Caskey, 15 October 1903. Caskey recommended George B. Sweazey to be his successor (Robert J. Caskey to George F. McAfee, 28 April 1904, WC Archives).

47. Robert G. McNiece to George B. Sweazey, 6 August 1903, WC Archives. McNiece and Caskey had frequently clashed over the relationship between the Salt Lake Collegiate Institute and Sheldon Jackson College. See chapter 4.

48. Emil Nyman, "Deans of Westminster College" (1975, typescript), WC Archives. Born in Switzerland County, Indiana, on April 12, 1875, the same day that John Coyner opened institute classes in the basement of First Presbyterian Church, Sweazey received the B.A. and M.A. from Wabash College and later did one year of graduate work in chemistry at the University of Bonn in Germany.

49. George W. Martin to George B. Sweazey, 6 September 1904, WC Archives.

50. Mary Thomas to George Sweazey, 2 October 1904, Sweazey Papers, WC Archives.

51. Lina Briggs to George Sweazey, 18 May 1908, Sweazey Papers, WC Archives.

52. Gilbert Nance to George Sweazey, 27 August 1904, Sweazey Papers, WC Archives.

53. Presbyterian Board of Aid for Colleges and Academies, Application for Aid Form, 1890, Collegiate Institute, 2, RG 32-26-3, PHS Archives.

54. *CSLCI*, 1902–3, 21. Beginning with an examination of the Pentateuch, the course of study provided an introduction to Old Testament history, the life of Christ, and early church history, including Acts and the Pauline letters. For years the institute utilized the King James Version of the Bible, but replaced it with the new American Revised Version shortly after the latter appeared in 1901.

55. Pupils were not permitted to bring or remove baggage on Sunday, and parents were requested not to schedule their child's arrival or departure on Sunday. When advertisements for the Collegiate Institute appeared in Sunday editions of the *Salt Lake Tribune*, Sweazey received a letter from the Woman's Board of Home Missions requesting that the practice cease. See S. F. Lincoln to George B. Sweazey, 11 October 1905, WC Archives.

56. *CSLCI*, 1904–5, 14.

57. *CSLCI*, 1877, 12.

58. As a concession to changing times, these restrictions were modified early in the twentieth century to permit attendance with written parental consent. *CSLCI*, 1876, 4–5; 1886–87, 6–7; 1899–1900, 8–9; and 1902–3, 22.

59. Thomas Snedden to George Sweazey, 2 May 1906, Sweazey Papers, WC Archives.

60. Mrs. Fields to George Sweazey, 28 November 1908, Sweazey Papers, WC Archives.

61. George W. Martin to George Sweazey, 12 October 1904, Sweazey Papers, WC Archives. Notified of his son's accumulation of demerits and resultant punishment, a father responded, "Enforce your rules. All his privileges must be cut off and he must

comply. I ask no favors, but demand that the rule be followed." J. W. Sammon to George Sweazey, 21 February 1908, Sweazey Papers, WC Archives.

62. "Annual Report of the Board of Aid for Colleges and Academies," in *GAMP-CUSA*, 1884, 219.

63. In 1894 the institute listed "114 students, 40 in academic courses, 3 in classical studies, 22 church members, 5 credibly converted, none in the ministry." "Annual Report of Board for Aid of Colleges and Academies," in *GAMPCUSA*, 1894, 322.

64. "Utah," *Home Mission Monthly* 2 (May 1888): 149, 158.

65. *CSLCI*, 1902–3, 22–23. "The school assumes no responsibility for accidents in football or other hazardous sports in which its students may engage. Pupils engaging in such sport do so at their own risk."

66. George B. Felt, *A Century of Utah High School Football 1893–1993* (Salt Lake City, 1993), 25.

67. "Neither Side Scored," *Salt Lake Tribune*, 24 November 1901. Another season consisted of only one game. Lacking experienced players and a coach, the team reportedly disbanded after receiving rough treatment from the opposing team. "Athletics," *Collegiate Life* 2 (May–June 1912): 27, WC Archives.

68. No such provision was made for boys. *CSLCI*, 1896–97, 11.

69. *CSLCI*, 1905–6, 11; and Minutes of the Student Association of the Salt Lake Collegiate Institute, 14 April 1911, WC Archives, hereafter cited as MSASLCI.

70. "Girls' Athletics," *Collegiate Life* 2 (October 1911): 11. See also MSASLCI, 13 October 1916, WC Archives.

71. MSASLCI, 10 September 1910, WC Archives.

72. MSASLCI, 27 October 1910, 10 February and 5 March 1911, 3 February 1915, 20 October 1916, and 8 February 1917.

73. MSASLCI, 25 September and 23 November 1913.

74. MSASLCI, 5 March 1911, 22 March 1912, and 28 March 1917.

75. *CSLCI*, 1909–10, 12.

76. Hauerbach later became a renowned lyricist for such songs as "Rose Marie," "Indian Love Call," and "Smoke Gets in Your Eyes" and collaborated with Victor Herbert, Oscar Hammerstein II, and Jerome Kern on some of the most memorable musicals in American history. See "Salt Lake City Lyricist," *Deseret News*, 19 October 1957.

77. "Collegiate Class Day," *Salt Lake Tribune*, 5 June 1901; and "Graduates at the Institute," *Salt Lake Tribune*, 7 June 1895. Deemed one of the most comical events was a funeral procession for a casket filled with books led by a student dressed in a traditional long clerical coat.

78. At one stage of the tradition the spoon had been accompanied by a large wooden porridge bowl, but it had disappeared and not been replaced. The spoon tradition, however, continued to be observed by several generations of Westminster College students. "The Presentation of Honor," *Collegiate Life* 2 (May–June 1912): 25, WC Archives.

79. "The Alumni," *Collegiate Life* 2 (May–June 1912): 9, WC Archives.

80. *CSLCI*, 1913–14, 7.

Part Two ~

High School and Junior College

Westminster student body in front of Ferry Hall, 1921.

Previous page: Westminster students and faculty with Robert G. McNiece seated far right, 1904.

Third Presbyterian Church, originally Gunton Memorial Chapel, with pastor and Westminster trustee Josiah McClain in foreground.

Ferry Hall, named in honor of William and Jeannette Ferry, erected in 1908.

Campus barn and haystack, 1913.

Boys' dormitory, called "the cracker box," 1918.

Ferry Hall in the early 1920s.

Converse Hall with new barn on left and Coyner Gate in right foreground, 1926.

Westminster classes of 1926, 1927, 1928, and 1929, with Ferry Hall in background.

Converse Hall after the fire, March 1926.

Cushman Cottage, president's home on 1300 East, early 1920s.

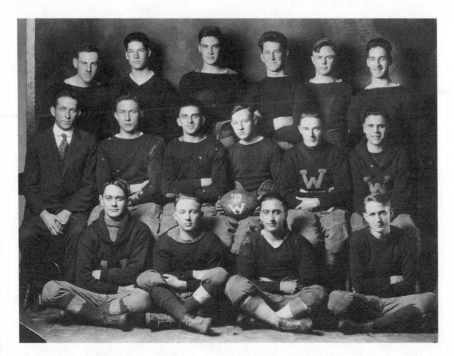

Westminster football team, 1919.

Women's tennis team, 1920s.

Herbert W. Reherd, fourth president of Westminster, at his retirement, 1939.

Ferry Hall in the winter, 1940s.

Westminster students, faculty, and staff, 1935.

Westminster faculty on holiday at Saltair, 1920s.

St. Mark's student nurses, 1952.

Converse Hall, viewed from Hansen Stadium, early 1950s.

4

Pro Christo et Libertati

Sheldon Jackson College stands for all that a Christian College stands for under common circumstances; but in addition to that, it stands specifically for a great cause, the cause of Christianity against Mormonism at the very headquarters of this delusion.
—John Eaton to Robert G. McNiece, 1898.

When Presbyterian missionaries first entered Utah in 1869, they envisioned the development of a network of elementary and secondary schools covering every major valley in Utah and a four-year college in Salt Lake City. By 1890 the Presbyterian Board of Home Missions sponsored thirty-three day schools and four academies in Utah stretching from St. George in the south to the Idaho border in the north. The secondary schools—Salt Lake Collegiate Institute, Wasatch Academy in Mt. Pleasant, Hungerford Academy in Springville, and New Jersey Academy in Logan—graduated students who wished to continue their education at the college level. The establishment of a college required a substantial commitment, including start-up money, however, and the Synod of Utah, little more than a missionary outpost, lacked such resources. The Presbyterian Board of College Aid would consider financial assistance only after local trustees had secured a sizable endowment, erected buildings, and commenced operations.[1]

With public higher education more readily available in the territory, Utah Presbyterians realized that their window of opportunity for establishing a private college was closing. Their hopes that the Collegiate Institute could be transformed into a four-year college seemed unrealistic because the campus property did not allow for expansion and the cost of real estate in the city center was prohibitive. Moreover, by continuing as a secondary school, the institute was seen as providing a steady supply of candidates for Presbyterian higher education. Although they lacked finances and property, Utah Presbyterians had a forceful leader in the person of Robert McNiece. The senior pastor in the Presbytery of Utah and president of the board of trustees of the Collegiate Institute, McNiece was highly regarded locally as an eloquent preacher and adept administrator and had acquired national recognition for his essays and articles on Mormonism in newspapers and denominational publications. He possessed enthusiasm, determination, and optimism concerning Presbyterian higher education in Utah and would dedicate the remainder of his life to that cause.[2]

From the time he came to Utah in 1877, McNiece foresaw a Presbyterian college that would rival and exceed Mormon institutions of higher learning. He and John Coyner tried to elevate the Collegiate Institute to baccalaureate status in 1883 but abandoned the project when they were unable to attract financial backing. Nearly a decade later, McNiece undertook again to arouse interest in the college venture. After meeting informally with prominent laymen and fellow clergy who assured him of their commitment to Presbyterian higher education, he drew up a proposal to establish a college "that shall furnish a classical and scientific course of education equal to any institution in the East" and presented it to the Presbytery of Utah at its meeting March 28, 1892.[3]

McNiece offered a number of reasons why the presbytery should support the project. Utah needed a viable alternative to territorial institutions of higher learning which he alleged were controlled by Mormons. The new institution would serve the entire intermountain region from Colorado to California, attracting students who desired quality, private education other than expensive eastern universities. When statehood was achieved and Protestants no longer had the protection of federal territorial laws, the college would function as a means of combating Mormon influence. McNiece also appealed to Presbyterian self-interest, suggesting that other denominations might step in and establish a college.[4] Presbyters appointed a standing committee to study the proposal and report later in the day. The committee responded favorably and nominated a board of trustees composed of five clergy and four laymen: McNiece as chairman, clergy members Samuel E. Wishard, Josiah McClain, George W. Martin, and C. M. Shephard, and laymen William M. Ferry, Frank Pierce, F. E. Gregg, and W. I. Brown.

The presbytery unanimously approved the recommendations and instructed the trustees to secure incorporation, locate a suitable campus site, and seek financial support necessary to accomplish such an undertaking.[5] Public announcement of the proposed college coincided with the visit on May 14 of some seven hundred Presbyterians en route to a meeting of the 1892 General Assembly in Portland, Oregon, who would be breaking their journey in Salt Lake City to avoid Sabbath travel. The delegation would include commissioners, denominational executives, and prominent clergymen whose influence could be crucial in acquiring support for the college project. As host pastor of First Presbyterian Church, McNiece arranged a schedule of meetings and sightseeing excursions designed to generate national publicity and impress the eastern visitors, some of whom were potential donors.[6]

The group arrived in the early hours of Sunday morning, May 15, their avoidance of Sabbath travel thwarted by heavy rail traffic. Nevertheless, they rose early, ready for a busy day of Sunday meetings—worship at eleven in various Protestant churches, attendance at the Mormon Tabernacle at two in the afternoon, and participation in a mass interdenominational rally held in the Salt Lake Theater at eight in the evening. Mormon President Woodruff warmly welcomed the Presbyterian tourists, and Charles H. Penrose, a high-ranking church official, devoted the Tabernacle service to an exposition of Mormon doctrine for a Presbyterian audience. Although Presbyterians officially distanced themselves from Mormon ecumenical gestures, many were impressed with the religious ethos of Salt Lake City and the work ethic of its populace. McNiece and his friends later claimed that Penrose and associates had "pulled the wool over their eyes during the visit."[7]

At the evening meeting, McNiece marshaled an impressive slate of speakers that included one of the secretaries of the Board of Home Missions, William C. Roberts, and several prominent pastors of large eastern churches. Each applauded Presbyterian missions in Utah and pledged continuing support for evangelization. McNiece and synodical superintendent Samuel Wishard utilized their platform moments to urge vigilance against the Latter-day Saints and their antidemocratic theocracy. Wishard stressed the importance of education, noting that a college in Salt Lake City would be a major step in reforming Utah. At one point during the meeting, word came that Mormon President Woodruff had offered Presbyterians free use of the Salt Lake Theater. As chairman, McNiece accepted the gesture but with sardonic thanks, noting that he would welcome Woodruff into the Presbyterian Church "when he gives tangible evidence of being a good orthodox Christian." Someone "seconded the motion," which was enthusiastically endorsed by the overflow audience.[8] McNiece later apologized to Woodruff, claiming that his jest intended no character defamation, but he refused to acknowledge Mormonism as a legitimate expression of the Christian faith.[9]

After a day of sightseeing in Salt Lake City on Monday, including a tour of the magnificent new temple then nearing completion, and an excursion to the Great Salt Lake, the Presbyterian contingent prepared to resume its journey to Portland. Their comments indicated that McNiece and his fellow presbytery representatives had made an effective case for educational missions. Before departing, however, some commissioners from New Jersey were approached by a gentile real estate investor, John Middlemiss, who proposed to develop a large tract on the northwest side of town, which he alleged to own, and to provide without charge sufficient acreage for a college. His only requirement was written confirmation that college buildings would be erected on his tract, thus increasing its residual value.[10]

Impressed by this generous offer, the New Jersey delegation took Middlemiss's proposition before the Portland General Assembly, which accepted it without a dissenting vote. Amid considerable fanfare, denominational leaders heralded the unexpected gift as a providential omen for the future of Westminster College of Salt Lake City.[11] Back in Salt Lake City, McNiece thought otherwise, denouncing Middlemiss as "a scheming deadbeat" who reportedly walked into a real estate office waving a telegram from the General Assembly and shouting, "Here's a Presbyterian College and a million dollars for Middlemiss!"[12] McNiece sent telegrams to Portland advising General Assembly executives to abort the Middlemiss deal, an effort that proved partially successful. Commissioners at the closing session modified their previous action of outright acceptance of the gift by referring the matter to the Board of Aid for Colleges and Academies and empowering that board to make a final decision on locating the new college.[13]

In retaliation, Middlemiss charged McNiece with character assassination, triggering a public debate in local and denominational newspapers. Mormon writers tweaked the "sectarians" for their divisiveness and un-Christian displays of temper. In Presbyterian circles, potential benefactors were repelled by the acrimonious debate between Middlemiss and McNiece that suggested instability and confusion about the college's future.[14] Other Presbyterians left the Portland meeting thinking that the Utah college had received a generous land grant and thus were inclined to support other Presbyterian colleges in the West whom they deemed more needy.[15] As McNiece predicted, investigation exposed Middlemiss as a charlatan maneuvering to make large profits from marginal land. The College Board rejected the Middlemiss offer and advised college trustees to look elsewhere for suitable real estate.[16] Nevertheless, the episode had generated unfavorable publicity and cast doubts on the ability of college officials to control institutional affairs. As a result, trustees decided to replace the Westminster appellation with Salt Lake College, but they agreed to defer incorporation until the college was financially able to commence operations.[17]

Shortly after the Middlemiss affair, college trustees became embroiled in an interdenominational controversy with Congregationalists who also had plans to establish a college in Salt Lake City. Active in Utah educational missions through its network of day schools conducted through the New West Education Commission, the Congregational Church opened Salt Lake Academy in 1878, just three years after John Coyner commenced the Collegiate Institute, and Salt Lake Academy's history paralleled that of the Collegiate Institute. To the surprise of McNiece and his associates, academy trustees announced in 1894 that they had incorporated as Salt Lake College and planned to offer a wide range of degree programs. Classes began that same year with a faculty of six professors and approximately thirty-five students but ended abruptly two years later when financial difficulties proved insurmountable.[18] Cordial competition between Presbyterians and Congregationalists erupted into an energy-draining, acrimonious debate that extended for several years. The immediate question concerned use of the name "Salt Lake College." Because Presbyterian trustees had failed to incorporate in 1892, Congregationalists claimed prior rights and threatened litigation if Presbyterians continued to employ that name when referring to their institution. More important, however, was the struggle for territorial rights in a limited educational market. Both sides acknowledged the economic futility of promoting two Protestant colleges in Salt Lake City. Since neither group had sufficient endowment with which to sustain operations, a cooperative venture appeared to be the wisest and most "Christian" course of action.[19]

Congregational Church executives proposed a single Protestant college in Salt Lake City directed by a board of trustees equally represented by Presbyterians and Congregationalists. They also offered the use of Hammond Hall, the former academy building, as an interim campus while trustees organized a national endowment campaign. Initially prospects for rapprochement seemed favorable, but McNiece and Wishard denied Congregationalist claims of priority and argued that relationships between the two groups had so deteriorated that genuine cooperation was impossible.[20] Unable to resolve their differences locally, the disputants turned over negotiations to national mission board secretaries. Representatives from both denominations met in New York in 1895 to discuss ways of resolving the Salt Lake City conflict, with Duncan J. McMillan, now a secretary of the Presbyterian Board of Home Missions, participating. Influenced by McNiece and Wishard, McMillan came to the discussion convinced that a hybrid institution would never succeed in Utah and that Presbyterians were better prepared to undertake college work. Although the meeting disbanded inconclusively with both sides claiming priority for their respective institutions, McMillan boasted with typical dramatic flair that his arguments had "blown the Congregational craft into smithereens."[21]

Subsequent discussions also proved fruitless. Even though Congregationalists dropped their insistence for equal representation on the board of trustees, Presbyterians remained committed to an independent course of operations.[22] After extended correspondence between the executives of both denominations and public debate in denominational journals, the Presbyterian Boards of Home Missions and of College Aid finally rejected the proposal for a "Presbygational" College in Utah, arguing that their charters did not permit them to designate funds for union colleges. Utah Congregationalists retained legal rights to the name Salt Lake College and persisted for some time in their quest for a denominational college in the capital. They abandoned efforts when it became evident that the Presbyterians had secured the field.[23]

From the outset of his campaign to establish a college in Salt Lake City, McNiece maintained a steady flow of correspondence with Sheldon Jackson, who was then deeply involved in educational work in Alaska. Jackson retained a vital interest in Utah missions and encouraged McNiece to pursue the college project. Like McMillan, Jackson disapproved of cooperative ventures because he believed union colleges would not attract denominational funding. At McNiece's invitation, he agreed to stop in Salt Lake City en route to Alaska in the spring of 1894 to confer with church officials regarding strategies for promoting Presbyterian higher education in Utah.[24]

Before leaving New York, Jackson was a houseguest of Duncan McMillan for a week. According to McMillan, Jackson had inherited some cash and valuable land in Washington, D.C., assets which he wanted to invest in higher education. Jackson favored Santa Fe or Denver as sites for a college, but McMillan argued convincingly for Salt Lake City, pointing out its potential economic growth, the network of Presbyterian preparatory schools in Utah, and the absence of rival colleges within a five-hundred-mile radius. Jackson ultimately agreed that Salt Lake City was the prime location for a Presbyterian college in the intermountain west.[25] During his visit to Salt Lake City, McNiece and his fellow trustees impressed Jackson, who promised to promote the venture among denominational executives and to contact prospective benefactors among his friends and acquaintances. Jackson also urged college officials to begin an endowment campaign in Utah and indicated his intention to invest a considerable sum of his own money if they were successful. With such an endorsement from one of the best-known and highly respected Protestant home mission figures, McNiece believed the college could begin operations within a calendar year.[26]

College trustees made little progress in securing cash or pledges from the Salt Lake City community. Their feud with the Congregationalists caused local philanthropists to be hesitant about investing in either college venture. The only major contribution, a check for $1,000, came from Colonel Elliott F. Shephard of New York City.[27] Sensing a deterioration of morale among trustees and presbytery officials, McNiece implored Sheldon Jackson to intervene, and Jackson responded with a dramatic offer in the spring of 1895 that gave new life, new hope, and a new name to the Presbyterian college in Salt Lake City.[28] Jackson arrived in Salt Lake City early in May 1895 bearing a letter to the Presbytery of Utah in which he pledged a $50,000 endowment to be derived from the sale of real estate in Washington, D.C., contingent on acceptance of certain stipulations: that local citizens provide no fewer than fifty acres of land for a suitable campus; that college trustees make the Bible a regular textbook in the curriculum; that the college adhere to the "work and doctrines" of the Presbyterian Church in the United States of America; that the institution be known as Sheldon Jackson College, and that if any material changes in this agreement occurred, college property would revert to the denomination. Jackson also promised to underwrite the college president's salary (not to exceed $1,500) so that the executive could be free to concentrate on raising endowment funds.[29]

The original articles of incorporation of Sheldon Jackson College, dated November 14, 1895, codified the requirements of Sheldon Jackson regarding denominational affiliation and use of the Bible as a classroom text. Eighteen trustees, all Presbyterians, were to be elected by ordained clergy at meetings of the Presbytery of Utah. In addition, the articles defined Sheldon Jackson College as an "institution of learning for the education of youths without distinction of race, sex or religious belief" modeled after existing American seminaries, colleges, and universities. Courses of instruction were to include "scientific, technical, divinity, law, medical, normal and other classes of any and every kind."[30]

In crafting an official seal, the founders of Sheldon Jackson College selected a motto that they felt expressed the college's institutional mission,

Pro Christo et Libertati (For Christ and Liberty). The college was to be unequivocally rooted in Protestant Christianity and nurtured by an ethical system that stressed personal integrity and social responsibility. Moreover, its curriculum would emphasize biblical and religious studies taught by a faculty of dedicated Christians. At the same time it was to espouse devotion to country, adherence to participatory democracy, and acceptance of a capitalistic economy. The founders of Sheldon Jackson College viewed both Christ and liberty in juxtaposition to Mormonism, which they believed to be a threat to American values and principles.[31]

Following endorsement by the Presbytery of Utah and completion of incorporation procedures, college trustees met on January 20, 1896, to formally accept Sheldon Jackson's offer. At the same meeting, they also considered a proposal by a mining syndicate headed by trustee Gill S. Peyton and his partner E. H. Aires. The syndicate offered fifty acres of the three-hundred-acre Crissman farm, located four and one-half miles south of the city, and an additional thirty acres known as the Price Place, on the condition that Sheldon Jackson College be located on that site. Unlike the previous Middlemiss scheme, this offer had considerable merit both in location and respectability. The trustees unanimously accepted the proposal.[32]

Jackson played a decisive role in recommending the first president of Sheldon Jackson College, whom he determined should be a nationally known educator with proven ability as a money raiser. College trustees selected sixty-seven-year-old General John Eaton, Ph.D., former United States commissioner of education and past president of Marietta College in Ohio, to become the first in a series of nonresidential presidents. Eaton promised to bring experience and maturity to the challenge of establishing a college in Utah.[33] Keenly aware of the power of the press, he journeyed to Utah in 1895 to publicize Sheldon Jackson College. It would be the only time during his presidency, however, that he visited Utah. The *Salt Lake Daily Herald* carried an exclusive interview with Eaton and McNiece and editorialized that the two men were collaborating "on the most important educational theme ever suggested west of Chicago." Equating the proposed college with Princeton, the *Herald* announced that groundbreaking ceremonies would begin shortly after Eaton finalized arrangements with denominational officials in Chicago and New York.[34] Editorial comment in the *Deseret Evening News* was less enthusiastic. While acknowledging that the proposed project would benefit the local economy, an editorial questioned Jackson's integrity because of statements he had made regarding the increase of polygamy in Utah.[35]

After a tour of several Presbyterian mission points and an address to the Synod of Utah meeting in Ogden, Eaton returned to Washington,

D.C., armed with a strategy to differentiate Sheldon Jackson College from similar institutions clamoring for endowment funds. He would employ the issue of anti-Mormonism as its unique institutional mission. He told donors that what separated Sheldon Jackson College from any other Presbyterian college was "the cause of Christianity against Mormonism at the very headquarters of this delusion."[36] Eaton initiated his 1896 national fund-raising campaign with a series of anti-Mormon articles in the inter-denominational *Christian Herald*, citing alleged polygamous abuses, Mormon atrocities, and efforts by Latter-day Saints to curtail traditional American political freedoms. Eaton warned, "Their missionaries are propagating at our very doors. Shall we wait until Mormons have placed the statue of Brigham Young beside that of Washington and Lincoln in the old hall of the House of Representatives before we realize that Mormonism touches all parts of the country and imperils every interest?"[37] With polygamy officially abandoned and Utah statehood obtained, however, Eaton discovered that eastern newspaper editors and Presbyterian benefactors seemed disinterested in the topic.[38]

Sheldon Jackson also continued to emphasize the college's role as an antidote to Mormon evangelism. In his letter of condolence when Marie Louisa Kissam Vanderbilt died in 1896, Jackson suggested that each of her five surviving children give $10,000 for the construction of a women's dormitory in memory of their mother and in opposition to Mormonism "that dethrones the God-head, ruins the home and debases woman to the level of brute beast."[39] Jackson asked one daughter who had been making annual contributions to missions in Sitka, Alaska, to transfer her donations to Sheldon Jackson College, arguing that he could always get money for work among Indians and Eskimos from other sources.[40] Capitalizing on friendships cultivated over many years of missionary service, Jackson secured the first major gift to the college building fund in 1896. Mary J. Gunton Temple of Washington, D.C., one of Jackson's longtime acquaintances, left a bequest of approximately $40,000 to the Board of Home Missions to build a chapel memorializing her father, William Gunton. Jackson persuaded board officials to assign this legacy to Sheldon Jackson College. Although the money was not immediately available due to probate complications, trustees accepted the gift, hoping that it would stimulate other contributions.[41]

While Eaton and Jackson promoted Sheldon Jackson College in the East, McNiece and his fellow trustees coped with problems in Salt Lake City. The land syndicate, having invested $150,000, wanted a building on site to inspire public confidence and stimulate commercial sales. Peyton and Aires threatened to withdraw their offer unless some construction activity commenced soon. McNiece feared that the whole enterprise would be jeopardized unless Eaton and Jackson could raise a minimum of $10,000 to lay a foundation for the initial building by June 1, 1896.[42] That date passed with no funds and no construction, and a year later the news was equally discouraging. Referring to college officials as "paper trustees," one wealthy Presbyterian suggested that they abandon their project before precious financial and human resources were wasted.[43] Always optimistic, Sheldon Jackson assured college trustees that an endowment for the college would be secured.[44] He urged McNiece to commence offering classes, reasoning that donors would be more likely to give to a functioning institution. He suggested that McNiece recruit a few part-time faculty from local ministers, lawyers, and physicians, arguing that "the advertising and prominence it gives them will be compensation for their time."[45]

Lacking a campus, the college needed rooms in which to hold classes, and several were available at the Collegiate Institute. The trustees secured permission from the Board of Home Missions to rent space in the old adobe institute building that was only partially utilized for dormitory purposes. Failing to attract any adjunct professors, they agreed to begin with one faculty member, McNiece, who had recently resigned his charge as pastor of First Presbyterian Church and was teaching part time at the institute. Designated professor and dean, McNiece would teach Latin, Greek, and English literature while trustees searched for an additional instructor to cover the sciences. They subsequently selected George B. Sweazey to fill the second teaching slot, who, as noted in the previous chapter, would later become principal of the Collegiate Institute and academic dean of Westminster College.[46]

Classes commenced on September, 7, 1897, with seven men and women, two of whom were part-time students. Because the college had little to offer in the way of faculty and facilities, trustees waived tuition.[47] The entering students had the option of two curricular tracks on their way to a four-year baccalaureate degree. The traditional classical course emphasized English, Latin, Greek, and history with courses in mathematics including algebra and trigonometry. During their junior and senior years, students were required to take either French or German. The Latin-scientific curriculum featured courses in physics, chemistry, biology, and geology. Both curricula included courses in biblical studies during each of the four years, and each senior was required to take a capstone philosophy of life course as prerequisite to graduation.[48]

Along with the opening of classes, Sheldon Jackson College trustees noted several other encouraging signs. Although no major endowment gifts had materialized, a number of smaller contributions ranging from

$500 to $2,000 provided enough income to cover operating expenses. Wealthy Presbyterians such as Nettie McCormick, John Wannamaker, and John Converse had expressed interest in the college and were being cultivated by Eaton and Jackson.[49] In 1897 commissioners elected Sheldon Jackson moderator of the General Assembly of the Presbyterian Church U.S.A. This position made him highly visible as he traveled nationally and internationally to visit mission stations. It also afforded Jackson opportunities to promote Sheldon Jackson College as part of the denomination's missionary program. Ecstatic about Jackson's election and his selection of John Wannamaker as vice moderator, Eaton urged Jackson to take full advantage of his moderatorial year.[50]

Eaton's anti-Mormon campaign also gained momentum in 1897. Aroused by documented cases of new polygamous relationships, Utah Protestants called for government intervention and renewed their attack that had been muted by statehood. Led by McNiece and ministerial colleagues, Utah Presbyterians established a nationally distributed anti-Mormon newspaper, the *Kinsman*. In the same year, the Presbytery of Utah issued a pamphlet, later endorsed by other Protestant denominations, entitled, "Ten Reasons Why We Cannot Fellowship With Mormons," the content of which was reproduced in many denominational magazines. The offensive against Mormon theology and lifestyle evoked a counterattack by the Latter-day Saints that carried over into the first decade of the twentieth century.[51] The local controversy acquired national proportions in 1898 when Utah elected Brigham H. Roberts, a member of the First Council of the Seventy of the Mormon Church, to serve in the U.S. House of Representatives. Previously convicted for cohabitation under the Edmunds-Tucker Act, Roberts allegedly had entered a new polygamous relationship even after President Woodruff had issued his Manifesto counseling Mormons not to practice plural marriage. Active as a Mormon apologist and prominent in the political arena, Roberts offered a target that galvanized anti-Mormonists into a nationwide crusade that eventually would bar him from taking his congressional seat.[52]

Eaton sought to channel public sentiment against Roberts into support for Sheldon Jackson College by mailing out hundreds of form letters in which he described Roberts as "an avowed polygamist" and stressed the importance of Sheldon Jackson College as an antidote to Mormonism.[53] The *Presbyterian Banner* carried an advertisement for Sheldon Jackson College charging that "all the colleges within a radius of 500 miles are presided over by Mormons and teaching polygamy is just as much a part of the curriculum as are Latin and Greek and other classical subjects."[54] An article by Eaton in the *Home Mission Monthly* reminded readers that the mechanism for preventing Mormon control was a Christian college in Utah "to lead [young people] out of Mormonism into Christianity."[55] Even though the Roberts case heightened tensions between Mormons and Presbyterians in Utah, it failed to attract a single major benefactor for Sheldon Jackson College. Eaton wrote to Jackson, "I am utterly amazed that nothing has come in for the College, that not a hand has been lifted for it and that your steady and long time supporters are failing you. Can the Lord purpose that the enterprise is to be given up?"[56]

While Jackson refused to abandon hope, he admitted that prospects for the college in Salt Lake City appeared tenuous.[57] To complicate matters, Eaton accepted a federal appointment in 1898 in order to supervise the organization of public schools in Puerto Rico and left Washington without informing college trustees in Utah of his departure. McNiece subsequently wrote Eaton a plaintive letter indicating his concern about the future of Sheldon Jackson College. "If you are going to be fastened down there in Porto [sic] Rico and our College enterprise is thereby going to be weakened, I should hesitate about continuing in the work, for a College without a President cannot expect to succeed."[58] Although Eaton returned to Washington within a year, declining health limited his ability to handle presidential responsibilities.[59]

Intertwined with financial insolvency was the long-standing problem of relationships between the Collegiate Institute and Sheldon Jackson College. The college needed what the institute had to offer—a temporary home, a steady supply of students, and an affiliation with a respected educational institution. So long as the Collegiate Institute operated independently, however, the college could not fully develop its own institutional identity. Potential donors often made sharp distinctions between academy and collegiate work and were perplexed by the apparent overlap of high school and college curricula in Salt Lake City. In order to reduce confusion, college trustees referred to the institute parenthetically as "the preparatory department of Sheldon Jackson College" and inflated their enrollment by including high school students in attendance statistics. Eaton once told McNiece how he avoided the embarrassment of reporting that Sheldon Jackson College had only seven students. "I find as I talk about the way you are doing the work in interchange with teachers in the Institute that people like to say, 'Then there are sixty-five or seventy students in all.'"[60]

When plans for a new campus failed to materialize, college officials sought to attain ownership of the Collegiate Institute, drop its name, and transform it into a subsidiary of Sheldon Jackson College. Aware of these efforts, Principal Caskey corresponded with denominational officials in

New York regarding "the college people" and the threat they constituted to the financial solvency and academic integrity of the Collegiate Institute. He charged that college trustees were delinquent in rental payments and that McNiece was duplicating classes already offered in the institute curriculum. In addition, he complained that college students were negligent in attending daily chapel, setting a bad example for institute students whose attendance was required, and that McNiece had done nothing to alleviate the problem. More important, Caskey questioned the ability of college authorities to assume financial support of the institute. He told Sheldon Jackson, "The thing which I am now fearing is that before the College gets onto its own feet it may drag the Collegiate Institute to its death."[61]

The Woman's Board of Home Missions, which owned and operated the institute, sided with Caskey in supporting the school's administrative autonomy. The women had never supported traditional college work and saw no reason to reverse that policy. Moreover, with the financial exigencies facing Sheldon Jackson College, they did not consider it prudent to merge the two institutions. Unless officials could demonstrate the college's ability to pay the bills and guarantee quality education for preparatory students, the women were unwilling to relinquish administrative oversight of the Collegiate Institute.[62] Undeterred, Jackson continued to press for college control of the institute. According to one witness, Jackson told women leaders that he would rather close up missions in Alaska than see the work in Utah collapse.[63] Appearing before the Woman's Board in 1899, Jackson promised that by September 1, 1901, the college would have ample funds to assure the continued operation of the institute. If that goal were met, he requested that Sheldon Jackson College be awarded total responsibility for the high school and college departments.[64] After extended discussion, the Woman's Board granted Jackson's request with the provision that college trustees present proof by that date that they had adequate endowment funds to warrant such a transfer. They also granted trustees the right to sell the institute property and relocate on the condition that they agree to maintain the preparatory department.[65]

Despite their previous lack of success, Eaton and Jackson were confident that they could meet the September 1, 1901, deadline. In letters to McNiece they spoke enthusiastically of "prospects" and "un-named sources" who were on the verge of giving substantial sums to the college. McNiece expressed concern, however, about financial shortfall and long-range planning. "We need some definite and clear cut plan outlined for the support of the Institute, in order that we may act intelligently." He reported low morale among the trustees, with some beginning to concede defeat.[66] In order to facilitate the sale of Jackson's property, college trustees hired Thomas Gordon, president of the Kenilworth Building and Loan Association of Washington, D.C., as financial agent and granted him power of attorney to act on their behalf. Jackson and Eaton questioned giving Gordon such far-ranging authority but acquiesced in the board's decision. Gordon borrowed money, dispensed funds, sold and mortgaged college property without consultation, and failed to make monthly reports. When he spent $23,000 to construct eleven rental houses that remained unfinished and unoccupied, McNiece went to Washington to investigate. He concluded that Gordon had expended approximately $34,000 of college funds with nothing to show for it and recommended that his services be terminated.[67] Although McNiece contemplated bringing charges against Gordon, Jackson and Eaton advised against prosecution, fearing adverse publicity. Trustees complied, but the college suffered a financial blow from which it never fully recovered.[68]

Another money-raising scheme went awry. College trustees commissioned architectural drawings for an initial building to be called Eaton Hall in honor of their first president and proposed a real estate scheme to generate capital. They prepared an advertisement that described the educational mission of Sheldon Jackson College and contained a diagram of the undeveloped college campus in Salt Lake City. Surrounding the campus were hundreds of residential lots laid out in anticipation of suburban growth. Donors who gave between $125 and $400 to Sheldon Jackson College would be entitled to a free lot. Although the advertisement was widely distributed in denominational publications, it failed to generate much response. Various constituents criticized such a bait-offer promotion, and the Board of Home Missions advised Jackson to withdraw the offer immediately.[69] Other problems hampered the faltering financial campaign. Jackson experienced personal financial problems and requested permission to withdraw his original pledge of $50,000 cash.[70] The land deal in Salt Lake City that had been pending for several years suddenly collapsed. Peyton and Aires modified the conditions of their gift in 1899 to specify that $50,000 worth of buildings had to be erected on college property within three years or the offer would be withdrawn.[71] Two years later, Aires repudiated the transaction by refusing to accept anything less than $110,000 cash for the entire eighty-acre plot. College trustees had no choice but to withdraw from negotiations and begin a new search for a suitable campus site.[72]

Early in 1901 Jackson acknowledged that the September 1 deadline could not be met. He blamed a combination of factors: poor economic conditions, mismanagement of his Washington property, and the opposition of

Caskey, which he claimed had resulted in the loss of several large dona-tions.[73] McNiece conveyed the news to the Woman's Board of Home Missions but asssured the women that the college would become finan-cially solvent in the near future.[74] Although the women continued to own and operate the institute, they permitted college officials to refer to the institute in their annual catalogs as the college preparatory department and waived the rental fees for institute classrooms. Much to Caskey's relief, the name Salt Lake Collegiate Institute did not disappear, and the school continued to issue its own annual course bulletin and announcements.[75]

In the midst of these developments, Sheldon Jackson College held its first and only commencement exercises on June 4, 1901, in the sanctuary of First Presbyterian Church to honor a sole graduate, Theodore Manoff Keusseff. A native of Bulgaria who joined the army as a youth to fight the Ottoman Turks, Keusseff emigrated to the United States in 1886 and even-tually reached the west coast where he resided briefly in San Francisco. Attracted to a Methodist revival by some friends, Keusseff resolved to devote the rest of his life to Christian service. Even though he could speak only a few words of English, Keusseff enrolled at the Moody Bible Institute in Chicago to become an evangelist. By the time he reached Salt Lake City, however, his meager funds were exhausted, and he found refuge in a nondenominational rescue mission a few blocks from the Collegiate Institute. Through the influence of McNiece, Keusseff enrolled at the insti-tute to attain educational credentials to become a Presbyterian minister.[76] When Sheldon Jackson College opened in 1897, Keusseff was among the handful of students. He worked his way through college by doing construc-tion work and by giving lectures, dressed in native attire, to religious and civic organizations throughout the state on conditions in Bulgaria. At the commencement service, Keusseff delivered the graduation oration, entitled "Sabbath Observance in Relation to National Prosperity." McNiece praised Keusseff for diligence and perseverance in learning a new language and funding his high school and college education.[77]

In October 1901, President Eaton, in poor health and no longer an active participant in college activities, accepted emeritus status. After sev-eral unsuccessful efforts to enlist Sheldon Jackson as president, trustees turned to George Bailey, pastor of the Westminster Presbyterian Church in Salt Lake City, who assumed the presidency the same year. Although promised a salary of $2,500, Bailey agreed to serve without compensation until the cash flow improved. Like his predecessor, Bailey resided in Washington, D.C., and his primary function was fund raising.[78]

With the transition of leadership came a change in institutional name. Trustees had relied on the national fame of Sheldon Jackson to attract endowment capital, but the value of the name recognition had lessened with the unsuccessful attempts to secure funds and with public criticism of Jackson's educational activities in Alaska. Now that he had found it necessary to withdraw his promise of cash support for the college, Jackson also felt personal embarrassment about having his name associated with the institution.[79] In addition, Jackson's reputation as an anti-Mormon activist did little to rally local support in Utah. Latter-day Saints regarded him as an enemy, and gentile businessmen hesitated to associate themselves with such a controversial figure.[80] At first trustees reconsidered the name Salt Lake College, but lawyers reported that Congregationalists retained legal rights to that title. McNiece suggested that, to succeed in Utah, the college needed to project an image that transcended specific geographical or denominational associations, one that generated a more generic Protestant and Christian affiliation. He advocated going back to the original name of Westminster because it would be recognized as belonging to a Protestant tradition that included Presbyterians, Baptists, and Congregationalists. Although two other Presbyterian colleges in Pennsylvania and Missouri already bore the name, McNiece observed that "it seems to us no more objection than that so many towns and counties in different states are called *Washington*."[81] On February 6, 1902, trustees approved the new name and directed the treasurer to file the appropriate legal papers.

When Westminster College began the 1902–3 academic year, students, faculty, and staff experienced little change in day-to-day operations. The Collegiate Institute, still referred to parenthetically as the preparatory department, constituted virtually the entire student body. The only novelty was a new letterhead on college stationery which contained the notation "formerly Sheldon Jackson College." McNiece, continuing as dean and professor and attending to a small group of students in the shabby institute annex, remained optimistic about the future of Westminster College. Writing to a colleague, McNiece claimed, "I've never worked against greater difficulties in my life than during the past 5 years, but I begin to see light and victory now."[82] In 1902, he was probably the only person in Salt Lake City who could make that statement and actually believe it.

NOTES

1. Banker, *Presbyterian Missions and Cultural Interaction*, 142–49. See also Robert G. McNiece to Mrs. William Thaw, 8 January 1901, WC Archives.

2. For biographical information on McNiece, see Nyman, "A Short History of Westminster College," Appendix J.

3. Minutes of the Presbytery of Utah, 28 March 1892, PHS Archives. For background on the college resolution, refer to the meeting of August 29, 1891, when commissioners approved expansion of educational missions in Utah.

4. Robert G. McNiece to Board of Home Missions, 8 March 1892, RG 32-26-6, PHS Archives. See also "Sheldon Jackson College, Report on the Need for a Protestant College in Utah," 1895, WC Archives.

5. Minutes of the Presbytery of Utah, 28 March 1892, PHS Archives.

6. "On the Way to Portland," *Home Mission Monthly* (July 1892): 194–95; and "The Presbyterian Party," *Deseret Weekly News*, 14 May 1892.

7. The text of Penrose's address is in the *Deseret Weekly News*, 14 May 1892. See also Henry A. Nelson, "Across the Continent," *The Church at Home and Abroad* (July 1892): 3–8; and "Salt Lake City Meetings," *Presbyterian Journal* (4 May 1892): 240.

8. "Presbyterianism Rampant," *Salt Lake Tribune*, 16 May 1892; and "Our Presbyterian Visitors," *Deseret Weekly News*, 20 May 1892.

9. "Card from Dr. McNiece," *Deseret Evening News*, 20 May 1892. See also "Concerning Utah and the 'Mormons,'" *Deseret Evening News*, 7 July 1892.

10. "The Presbyterian Excursionists," *Salt Lake Tribune*, 17 May 1892; and "The Presbyterians," *Salt Lake Herald*, 15 May 1892.

11. "The Middlemiss Gift," *New York Evangelist* (14 July 1892): 4; and *GAMPCUSA*, 1892, 19–20. Although early trustee minutes simply refer to "the college," the name Westminster College of Salt Lake City was being used at the General Assembly and in newspaper accounts from May to July 1892. See "The Presbyterian School," *Salt Lake Tribune*, 21 May 1892; and "The Westminster, A Few Facts about the Proposed College," *Salt Lake Herald*, 17 July 1892.

12. Robert G. McNiece to E. C. Ray, 2 June 1892, RG 32-32-5, PHS Archives.

13. *GAMPCUSA*, 1892, 174. Writing shortly thereafter to the College Board, McNiece castigated the land deal as "a bogus thing all through—a windy real estate scheme without any foundation." He advised Ray to have nothing to do with Middlemiss. Robert G. McNiece to E. R. Ray, 2 and 15 June 1892, RG 32-32-5, PHS Archives.

14. "The Westminster," *Salt Lake Herald*, 30 July 1892.

15. John R. Middlemiss to E. R. Ray, 7 and 13 June and 16 July 1892, RG 32-3-5, Other correspondence supported McNiece. See Robert J. Caskey to E. R. Ray, 21 June 1892; and Samuel E. Wishard to E. R. Ray, 21 July 1892, RG 32-32-5, PHS Archives.

16. Robert G. McNiece to E. R. Ray, 16 July 1892, RG 32-3-5, PHS Archives.

17. WC Trustee Minutes, 30 August 1892.

18. "Salt Lake College," *Church Review* (29 December 1895): 59–60; and Robert G. McNiece to E. R. Ray, 16 July 1892, RG 32-3-5, PHS Archives.

19. Presbyterians considered an offer to locate in Ogden but rejected it because Utah Presbytery had specified Salt Lake City as the approved site. WC Trustee Minutes, 3 May 1893.

20. "Proposed Basis for the Consolidation of Salt Lake and Sheldon Jackson Colleges" (n.d., typescript), WC Archives; and Robert G. McNiece to Duncan J. McMillan, [1 May 1895?], Jackson Corres.

21. Sheldon Jackson to Duncan J. McMillan, 22 April and 29 August 1895; Robert G. McNiece to Duncan J. McMillan, 24 April 1895; and Duncan J. McMillan to Sheldon Jackson, 26 August 1895, Jackson Corres.

22. Robert G. McNiece to Sheldon Jackson, 26 April 1898, RG 239-6-14. Jackson told the Presbytery of Utah in 1898 that if they changed the college charter to accommodate

the Congregationalists, potential donations exceeding $100,000 would immediately be lost. Robert G. McNiece to E. C. Ray, 12 November 1898, RG 32-32-6, PHS Archives.

23. Robert G. McNiece to the editor of *Christian Education*, 14 May 1896; to John Eaton, 18 February 1899; and to Charles L. Thompson, 18 June 1901, WC Archives; and "Concerning Sheldon Jackson College," *Presbyterian Advance* (21 May 1896). Correspondence relating to the Congregationalist-Presbyterian efforts to develop a college can be found in RG 32-26-5, PHS Archives.

24. Robert G. McNiece to Sheldon Jackson, 22 January 1895, Jackson Corres. Although Jackson rejected union colleges, he advocated ecumenical cooperation in educational missions. Jackson envisaged an interdenominational educational consortium in Salt Lake City with Congregationalists, Presbyterians, and Methodists establishing colleges on adjoining tracts of land and sharing faculty and libraries. Sheldon Jackson to Duncan J. McMillan, 29 August 1895, Jackson Corres.

25. Duncan J. McMillan, "Early Education Days in Utah," *Utah Westminster*, anniversary edition (October 1922): 11.

26. Robert G. McNiece to E. C. Ray, 19 June 1895, RG 32-26-5, PHS Archives.

27. McNiece reported to trustees that because there was no likelihood that the $1,000 would be used immediately, he had loaned the money to First Presbyterian Church of Salt Lake City for one year at an interest rate of eight percent. Robert G. McNiece to Sheldon Jackson, n.d. See also WC Trustee Minutes, 3 August 1892 and 4 April 1893.

28. Robert G. McNiece to Sheldon Jackson, 22 January 1895 and 16 April 1895, Jackson Corres.

29. WC Trustee Minutes, 13 May 1895.

30. The original articles of incorporation of Sheldon Jackson College can be found in RG 11-4-1, PHS Archives and in WC Archives. Those filed following statehood in 1896 are located in the Commerce Office of the State of Utah in Salt Lake City.

31. WC Trustee Minutes, 17 May 1897; and Robert G. McNiece, "The Continued Encroachments of Mormonism," *Assembly Herald* (October 1900): 825–28.The wording of the original seal Pro Christo (ablative) et Libertati (dative) is more precisely translated, "In behalf of Christ and for the purpose of liberty." The dative of purpose requires no preposition. In recent years the college has modified the seal to read, "Pro Cristo et Libertate." This change links the two nouns together (both are in the ablative case) and employs an antiquated spelling "Cristo" that was used in Middle English. This information is derived from members of the Department of Classical Studies at Trinity University and from independent Latin scholars Mary Barrett and Mary Ann Rossi.

32. WC Trustee Minutes, 20 January 1896, "Sheldon Jackson College," *Salt Lake Tribune*, 10 January 1896; and "Big Real Estate Deal," *Salt Lake Tribune*, 18 February 1896. Trustees actually had reached an agreement several months earlier but kept negotiations secret in order to forestall any sudden jump in property values before final closure. See John Eaton to Sheldon Jackson, 2 November 1895, Jackson Corres.

33. Sheldon Jackson to Duncan J. McMillan, 29 August 1895; and Robert G. McNiece to Sheldon Jackson, 10 September 1895, Jackson Corres. See also WC Trustee Minutes, 26 August 1895; and "Sheldon Jackson College, Salt Lake City, Utah," pamphlet [c.1898], 2–3, WC Archives. A graduate of Dartmouth University and Andover Theological Seminary, Eaton had served during the Civil War as commanding officer of the Sixty-third Regiment of Colored Infantry and following hostilities as assistant commissioner of the Freedmen's Bureau. In 1870 he became United States commissioner of

education, serving until 1886 when failing health prompted his resignation. Subsequently he was elected president of Marietta College in Ohio, relinquishing that post in 1891, again due to poor health.

34. "A New University," *Salt Lake Daily Herald*, 10 November 1895; and "Presbyterian College," 10 January 1896. See also "Sheldon Jackson College," *Salt Lake Tribune*, 10 January 1896.

35. "For a Utah 'Christian College,'" *Deseret Evening News*, 30 November 1895.

36. Robert G. McNiece to Sheldon Jackson, 21 October 1895; John Eaton to Sheldon Jackson, 23 October 1895, Jackson Corres. See also John Eaton to Robert G. McNiece, 21 September 1898 and 21 March 1901, WC Archives.

37. John Eaton to Sheldon Jackson, Sheldon Jackson Scrapbook, II:71, PHS Archives. The articles were subsequently reprinted and circulated in pamphlet form in 1897 and 1898. For a typical article in a Presbyterian magazine, see John Eaton, "Presbyterian Missions among Mormons," *Assembly Herald* (February 1899): 69–72.

38. "There was not only indifference," he lamented, "but a strong disinclination to consider the facts both on part of the press and the pulpit. Americans seemed ashamed to take up anew the struggle with Mormonism." John Eaton to E. C. Ray, 6 August 1898, RG 32-32-6, PHS Archives.

39. Sheldon Jackson to Mrs. Elliot F. Shepherd, 9 November 1896, Jackson Corres.

40. "There is no section of the Globe—there is no people—there is no heathenism existing where God is so dishonored as in Utah by Mormonism." Sheldon Jackson to Mrs. Elliot F. Shepherd, 1 January 1897, Jackson Corres. Despite his pleas for funds, the family declined, suggesting that "the great cities in the West are the ones who should be called upon to support such a College." Mrs. Elliott Shepherd to Sheldon Jackson, 11 November 1896, Jackson Corres.

41. WC Trustee Minutes, 1 June 1896. Money from the Gunton estate did not become available until 1899. See Thomas Gordon to Sheldon Jackson, 9 September 1899, Jackson Corres.; and "Gunton Chapel Is Dedicated," *Salt Lake Tribune*, 20 March 1905.

42. Robert G. McNiece to Sheldon Jackson, 28 March 1896, Jackson Corres.

43. Mrs. William Thaw to E. C. Ray, 11 October 1899, RG 32-32-6, PHS Archives.

44. "I have no doubt, but that there is $50,000 for the college somewhere in the country, the point is to find it, and God will reveal it in answer to united prayer." Sheldon Jackson to Robert McNiece, 22 November 1895, Jackson Corres.

45. Sheldon Jackson to Robert G. McNiece, 10 December 1896 and 14 April 1897, Sheldon Jackson Corres.

46. "Sheldon Jackson College," pamphlet [1898], 2–4. Other early faculty members included John W. Cathcart (from 1900 to 1901), J. C. Lincoln (from 1904 to 1906), Margaret King Moore (from 1905 to 1907), and Grace Zorbaugh (from 1907 to 1909).

47. WC Trustee Minutes, 2 July 1897; and Robert G. McNiece to Sheldon Jackson, 14 April 1897, RG 239-6-10, PHS Archives. Of the initial seven students, only one returned the following year; two went off to the Spanish-American War, three transferred to other colleges, and one dropped out due to illness.

48. *Sheldon Jackson College Catalog*, 1900–1901, 16–18, WC Archives.

49. John Eaton to E. C. Ray, 6 August 1898, RG 32-32-6, PHS Archives; and John Eaton to Robert G. McNiece, 11 January and 6 August 1898, WC Archives.

50. John Eaton to Sheldon Jackson, 22 September 1897, Jackson Corres.; and Stewart, *Sheldon Jackson*, 423–37.

51. Copies of the *Kinsman* and various newspaper clippings relating to the anti-Mormon crusade are in the William Peden Papers, WC Archives. For Mormon response, see "J. B. Eaton and the Mormons," *Deseret Evening News*, 6 February 1897.

52. Davis Bitton, "The B. H. Roberts Case of 1898–1900," *Utah Historical Quarterly* 25 (Winter 1957): 27–46.

53. Form letter from John Eaton, 1 December 1898, WC Archives.

54. *Herald and Presbyter*, 27 September 1899. Other clippings are in Sheldon Jackson Scrapbook, III:35ff.

55. "The evil is not to be cured by merely lopping off the branches. It must be uprooted." Even if Roberts were unseated, Eaton pointed out, he likely would be replaced by someone who was sympathetic to the practice of polygamy. "A Christian College in Utah," *Home Mission Monthly* (January 1900): 65. See also "A Christian College Needed," *Kinsman* (July 1900): 282.

56. John Eaton to Sheldon Jackson, 28 March 1899, Jackson Corres.

57. Sheldon Jackson to John Eaton, 4 April 1895, Jackson Corres.

58. Robert G. McNiece to John Eaton, 18 February 1899, Jackson Corres.

59. McNiece remained committed to sustaining the college. He told the ailing president, "It requires more faith and courage to carry on this work here than anything else that I have ever tried. But I'm willing to hold on, small and disheartening as the work is, if that is the Lord's will." Robert G. McNiece to John Eaton, 24 February 1899, Jackson Corres.

60. John Eaton to Robert G. McNiece, 11 January 1898, WC Archives.

61. Robert J. Caskey to Sheldon Jackson, 9 April 1900, Jackson Corres. See also Robert J. Caskey to George McAfee, 12 December 1899 and 12 December 1900, RG 111-4-11, PHS Archives.

62. From their perspective, the Collegiate Institute represented one of their long-time investments that required careful nurturing if it were to survive as a workable educational institution. John Eaton to Robert G. McNiece, 12 January 1897; and Emeline Pierson to Robert J. Caskey, 19 July 1898, WC Archives. See also Sheldon Jackson to George F. McAfee, 10 April and 4 May 1899, RG 111-4-11, PHS Archives; and Charles L. Thompson to Robert G. McNiece, 18 June 1901, WC Archives.

63. George W. McAfee to Sheldon Jackson, 29 November 1899, PHS Archives.

64. Sheldon Jackson to George F. McAfee, 1 December 1899, Jackson Corres.

65. Copy of the agreement is in RG 111-4-11 and was confirmed by minutes of the college trustees, 9 January 1900. Caskey was not informed of the agreement "lest [he] should be able to make some complications before the Board of Home Missions should act." Sheldon Jackson to John Eaton, 7 May 1901, RG 239-6-4. PHS Archives.

66. Robert G. McNiece to Sheldon Jackson, 19 December 1899, Jackson Corres.

67. WC Trustee Minutes, 26 June and 18 August 1899; and "Report by John Eaton and Robert G. McNiece on Dr. Gordon's actions as financial agent for the College," 6 August 1900, WC Archives.

68. John Eaton to Robert G. McNiece, 13 April 1901, WC Archives.

69. Sheldon Jackson Scrapbook, III:21–25, 35; and L. Thompson to Sheldon Jackson, 8 December 1899, WC Archives. Westminster trustees also tried unsuccessfully to appropriate money from the Gunton Chapel fund to use for institute expenses, but the Board of Home Missions vetoed the effort. See Charles Thompson to Josiah McClain, 17 May 1901; and Josiah McClain to Charles Thompson, 17 May 1901, RG 111-4-11, PHS Archives.

70. WC Trustee Minutes, 26 April 1900. In lieu of his cash pledge, the trustees accepted title to Jackson's Washington, D.C., real estate that eventually yielded approximately $60,000 for college use. See WC Trustee Minutes, 15 August 1958.

71. WC Trustee Minutes, 26 June 1899, 29 November 1901; and Robert G. McNiece to Sheldon Jackson, 26 April 1898, Jackson Corres.

72. WC Trustee Minutes, 26 November 1901; and Robert G. McNiece to Sheldon Jackson, 26 April 1898 and 22 January 1900, RG 239-6-25, PHS Archives.

73. Sheldon Jackson to Mrs. William Thaw, 12 January 1901; E. C. Ray to Robert J. Caskey, 9 April 1900, RG 32-32-6; Robert J. Caskey to Sheldon Jackson, 7 April 1900, Jackson Corres.; and Robert J. Caskey to E. C. Ray, 9 April 1900, RG 32-32-6. These records are all in PHS Archives.

74. Sheldon Jackson to Mrs. William Thaw, 12 January 1901; Robert G. McNiece to George W. McAfee, 29 March 1901, RG 111-4-11, PHS Archives.

75. Minutes of the Woman's Board of Home Missions, 5 December 1900, RG 32-32-5; Charles Thompson to Sheldon Jackson, 22 March 1901, Jackson Corres.; and Robert J. Caskey to George F. McAfee, 22 December 1899, RG 111-4-11. PHS Archives.

76. Keusseff later attended Western Theological Seminary in Pittsburgh and served for thirty-five years in Utah, first as a pastor in Panguitch and then as a synodical Sunday school missionary. For a more detailed account of Keusseff's ministry, see R. Douglas Brackenridge, "Theodore M. Keusseff," *Westminster Review* (winter 1966): 4–6.

77. "Sheldon Jackson Exercises: The First in Life of Young Institution," *Salt Lake Tribune*, 4 June 1901. See also "One Boy Graduated," *Deseret Evening News*, 4 June 1901. Other early graduates were E. J. Hanks (1903) and Roderick Thompson (1904). A list of students and graduates from Sheldon Jackson and Westminster Colleges can be found in a roll-grade book belonging to Robert G. McNiece, WC Archives.

78. WC Trustee Minutes, 24 December 1901; and "George Bailey," *Church Life* 34 (September 1926): 2–4. See also George Bailey, "Is Mormonism a Present-day Menace?" *Presbyterian Examiner* 28 (November 1912): 9–12. A native of England, Bailey had served as a missionary for the Presbyterian Board of Home Missions in Broken Bow, Nebraska, prior to accepting a pastorate in Salt Lake City. Westminster Presbyterian Church was organized by the Presbytery of Utah in 1889 and had no official relationship to the college. See "Westminster Presbyterian," *Church Review* (29 December 1895): 10.

79. For a description of the latter part of Jackson's career, see Stewart, *Sheldon Jackson*, 452–60.

80. Sheldon Jackson's contribution to Presbyterian higher education in Alaska has been acknowledged through the naming of a college in his honor. First referred to simply as Sitka Industrial School, the institution was long known as the Sheldon Jackson School and later as Sheldon Jackson Junior College. Today a four-year baccalaureate institution, Sheldon Jackson College continues to embody the missionary spirit of its founder.

81. WC Trustees, 15 July 1902; and Robert G. McNiece to E. C. Ray, 24 January and 31 March 1902, RG 32-32-6, PHS Archives. The two Westminster Colleges were located in New Wilmington, Pennsylvania, founded in 1852 by the United Presbyterian Church of North America, and in Fulton, Missouri, founded in 1851 by the Presbyterian Church in the United States. The Presbyterian Church in the United States of America organized Westminster University in Denver, Colorado, in 1905, but it closed in 1917.

82. Robert G. McNiece to E. C. Ray, 31 March 1902, RG 32-32-2, PHS Archives.

5

A Campus without Students

The difficulty of getting students has been so great that some of them were only gotten by offering them free tuition. Indeed, were it not for the danger of sacrificing our charter, I would almost be ready to take the ground that it is useless to have classes at all.
—President Robert M. Stevenson, 1907.

After a decade of high expectations and dashed hopes that included three different names, two failed land schemes, and several unsuccessful financial campaigns, the movement to establish a college in Salt Lake City appeared close to collapse. Westminster College was a feeble appendage to the Salt Lake Collegiate Institute, upon whom it depended for students and facilities. At the beginning of the 1902–3 academic year, only two full-time students registered for college classes, and five others, listed as special students, concurrently attended high school at the institute. The two faculty members, McNiece and Sweazey, offered a wide range of subjects in the humanities and sciences in order to implement the rigorous curriculum. Due to the college's limited financial resources, their salaries often were six to eight months in arrears, forcing them to rely on family and friends for short-term loans. Businessmen in Salt Lake City deemed the college a laughingstock, an ephemeral dream of a few Presbyterian clergymen whose ambitions exceeded their grasp.[1]

Despite this environment, college trustees appointed a committee of three, McNiece, George Bailey, and Josiah McLain, to locate acreage and seek financial backing for a campus. McNiece and his colleagues surveyed possible sites in the southeastern quadrant of Salt Lake City and selected a twenty-one acre plat of land located in Perkin's Grand View

Addition, an area just east of Eleventh East, cornering on Eleventh South (now Seventeenth South) and Thirteenth East, and extending south to Emigration Creek. Ideally located high above the city center with magnificent views of the Great Salt Lake and the Wasatch Mountains and easily accessible by two streetcar lines, the site could be converted into an attractive college campus with adequate room for expansion.[2] With a piece of property in mind, the committee turned for funding to a fellow trustee, Colonel William Montgomery Ferry of Park City. Ferry came from a Presbyterian family long associated with denominational home missions. His father, William Montague Ferry, had a distinguished reputation as a resourceful home missionary and an astute businessman in Michigan, where he spent most of his career. A Civil War veteran and graduate of the University of Michigan with a degree in civil engineering, Colonel Ferry came to Utah in 1879, locating in Park City, where he made a fortune in mining. His Presbyterian ties and high civic profile led to his selection as a charter member of the Sheldon Jackson College board of trustees when it organized in 1895.[3]

Ferry's spouse, Jeannette Hollister Ferry, also had long-standing links with Presbyterian home mission work in Michigan and Utah. As an officer in the women's synodical in Michigan, Jeannette Ferry corresponded with John Coyner regarding support for the Salt Lake Collegiate Institute. Through her initiative, Michigan women helped fund the construction of the first institute building in 1880. Ferry continued to participate in missionary activities upon moving to Utah, representing Presbyterian churchwomen at regional and national levels. An advocate for women's rights and a critic of polygamy, she was president of the Industrial Christian Home of Utah, a house of refuge for neglected or discontented Mormon plural wives.[4]

The committee arranged a meeting with the Ferrys at the home of their daughter and her husband, George Hancock, on Seventh East Street. Acting as chief spokesman, McNiece listed reasons for establishing a Presbyterian college in Salt Lake City. By providing land for a college, McNiece concluded, the Ferrys would be underwriting an institution that would bring honor to the Presbyterian Church and to the family name. Without hesitating, Colonel Ferry responded, "Gentlemen, I cannot do anything for you. My own personal obligations must be met. I am sorry." Before McNiece could reply, however, Jeannette Ferry interjected a hopeful note into the conversation. "Well, Colonel, we know we have well in hand our personal obligations. I do not think that will be in the way." Taking courage from her comment, McNiece extended his emotional plea. "Colonel, we three men have given our lives to this work. That is all we have to give. The Lord has given you money. Cannot you take some of that money and put it into this work over against our lives?" Ferry appeared unmoved by McNiece's appeal, but he promised to consider the request and render a decision within a few days. As McNiece and friends walked out, Jeannette Ferry took them aside and whispered, "I think you will get what you are asking for."[5]

Three days later McNiece received a note from Ferry asking him to come to the Hancock residence to discuss college business. When McNiece arrived, Ferry announced that he had decided to purchase the land that McNiece had described and deed it to the college. He directed McNiece to secure clear title to every lot in the plat, sold or unsold.[6] Ferry placed stipulations on his beneficence: that the Bible be an integral part of the curriculum, that college faculty and teachings be in harmony with Presbyterian doctrine, and that the erection of a building worth not less than $25,000 be completed within five years. In addition, at the urging of Jeannette Ferry, he set apart a five-acre site for a woman's building and provided for a self-perpetuating board of five woman trustees to manage the internal affairs of the building such as furnishings, staff, care of grounds, and all repairs and improvements. He also required that all classes were to be open to female students and that they were to enjoy all educational advantages granted to their male counterparts.[7]

Reporting the news to Sheldon Jackson, an exultant McNiece concluded, "We have the deal now. The trustees hold the deal. Praise the Lord for that! Now the one important thing is a building. In fact, we have no College until we have a building of our own."[8] Trustees gave priority to the construction of a combination administrative and classroom building and dormitories for men and women so that the institute property could be sold and operations moved to the new campus. The only available source of income for construction, however, was the Temple estate, restricted to building and maintaining a chapel on college grounds. While some trustees thought the Temple money ought to be immediately utilized, others deemed it inappropriate to construct a chapel when the campus lacked classrooms and dormitories. McNiece took the latter position and used his considerable influence to veto the project.[9] The debate extended for several years, creating friction among trustees and causing denominational officials to reconsider their relationship with the institution. McNiece finally conceded that erecting a chapel constituted a step forward after more than a decade without any buildings, but he insisted that the chapel be situated where it could be put to immediate use, rather than sitting empty on an undeveloped campus. McNiece suggested that the chapel be built on the campus perimeter and made available to the nearby Third

Presbyterian Church, which had outgrown its present facilities. The trustees agreed and purchased two additional acres of land located at the present corner of Seventeenth South and Eleventh East, within two blocks of the Ferry Campus.[10]

McNiece presided at the dedication of Gunton Memorial Chapel on March 19, 1905, hailing the event as the first step in completing a master plan that would make Westminster College a permanent fixture in Salt Lake City. Erected at a cost of approximately $17,000, the attractive stone and brick chapel held special occasions such as baccalaureate, commencement, and religious emphasis week, but was utilized primarily by Third Presbyterian Church under special leasing arrangements with the college. Because the chapel was so closely identified with church worship and Sunday school activities, many townspeople were unaware that both building and property belonged to Westminster College rather than Third Presbyterian Church.[11]

Concurrent with the dedication of Gunton Memorial Chapel came the announcement that George Bailey had submitted his resignation as college president, a decision that had not been unexpected. He had assumed the presidency only after securing assurances from college trustees that they would acquire ownership of the Collegiate Institute and have a functioning campus within three years. Weary of unfulfilled promises and interminable delays, Bailey accepted a position as pastor of the Western Presbyterian Church in the nation's capital, where he had been residing for the past three years, managing the Jackson property and soliciting funds for Westminster.[12] In preparation for a presidential search, trustees drew up a position description listing experience as a fund raiser to be the number one prerequisite. Ministerial status, denominational recognition, and familiarity with Utah's unique religious environment were also important qualifications. Terms of employment included $2,000 salary, free use of a house on campus, and permission to establish a second residence in an eastern city as a base for development operations.

Their first choice, Samuel E. Wishard, fellow trustee and veteran missionary for the Synod of Utah, declined, citing age and health as primary factors in this decision. While the search continued, Wishard agreed to make an extended money-raising tour in the East, utilizing his many contacts with Presbyterian pastors and congregations.[13] After soliciting nominations from denominational officials, McNiece recommended Robert M. Stevenson, an ordained Presbyterian minister whom he had known since 1883 when they both served churches in the Synod of Colorado. Stevenson had held several pastorates and had served as vice president of Bellevue College near Omaha, Nebraska. A graduate of Wabash College and Princeton Theological Seminary, Stevenson was highly recommended as an effective speaker, a competent business executive, and a successful fund raiser. McNiece also praised Stevenson's wife, Emma, whom he described as "a captain for Christian work" and an able assistant in promoting the college program.[14]

The Stevensons came to Salt Lake City in August 1905 to meet with college trustees and the faculty and staff of the Collegiate Institute. Although they received a warm welcome and spent a week as houseguests of the McNieces, Stevenson hesitated about leaving a thriving congregation for the problems of a struggling institution like Westminster. Sensing his ambivalence, McNiece emphasized Westminster's potential to become the premier private college in the intermountain area, describing opportunities for leadership that the college provided. McNiece implored Stevenson to accept the challenge and promised him the unqualified support of faculty and trustees. Impressed by McNiece's sincerity and commitment, Stevenson agreed to assume the presidency by early November.[15]

In the meantime, Westminster's building program received an unexpected boost in the fall of 1905 from John Converse, a wealthy Presbyterian businessman in Philadelphia. An active churchman and philanthropist, Converse previously had given large sums to various Presbyterian educational institutions and missionary endeavors and to his alma mater, the University of Vermont. Although John Stuart Dickson, secretary of the College Board and confidant of Converse, actually finalized the gift, Wishard collected a check for $20,000.[16] Additional contributions from L. H. Severance and D. Stewart Dodge raised the amount to $27,480, a sufficient sum to engage a contractor and commence construction of a multipurpose administrative and classroom building.[17] Work on Converse Hall began in March, and college officials laid the cornerstone on August 23, 1906, in ceremonies led by Stevenson and McNiece.[18] The impressive modern Gothic administration-classroom edifice, constructed of pressed brick and gray stone, was completed in July 1907 but remained unoccupied because the campus lacked a heating plant and accommodations for boarding students. Despite security precautions, Converse Hall was repeatedly vandalized, resulting in broken transoms, smashed windows, and devastation to museum artifacts donated to the college by Sheldon Jackson.[19]

After a few months in office, Stevenson began to grasp the difficulties involved in developing the potential that had been so eloquently described by McNiece. For one thing, local support for the college was not nearly so solid as he had been led to believe. In his first annual report to the Board of College Aid, Stevenson commented, "So far as I can learn, no one in Salt Lake has given [money]. The College has been promised so often that as near as I can get at the public thought it has become a joke."[20] Given the small faculty, poor facilities, and inadequate funding, Stevenson marveled that any students were willing to matriculate at the college. Westminster's endowment was so poor that in response to a question, "By what committee are investments made?" he scribbled, "Have no need for such a committee."[21] Stevenson also learned that in order to qualify for annual grants from the Board of College Aid, Presbyterian colleges were required to meet certain educational and financial standards such as number of faculty, size of student body, and extent of endowment. Because Westminster had only two faculty members, fewer than a dozen students, and no endowment, the college was in noncompliance with minimal standards for receiving financial aid. The College Board informed Stevenson that until conditions at Westminster improved, no financial aid would be forthcoming.[22]

Stevenson operated the college as efficiently and economically as possible by reducing staff and eliminating unnecessary classes. With only six sophomores and four freshmen enrolled in 1906, he felt it impracticable to maintain a four-year degree program and insisted that trustees offer only first- and second-year classes until enrollment warranted resumption of work at the junior and senior level. Although McNiece opposed the decision as a hindrance to recruiting new students, the trustees sided with Stevenson and curtailed upper-division classes. Stevenson also economized by utilizing part-time and female instructors in cooperation with the Collegiate Institute. In a communication to the College Board, he noted, "In order to keep down expenses, we are employing a lady instead of a gentleman." Margaret King Moore was hired at a salary not to exceed $540, less than half what would have been paid to a man in the same position.[23]

In spite of financial limitations, Stevenson devised a series of goals designed to provide Westminster with the resources to become a fully accredited four-year college. Top priority was to develop a residential campus so that Westminster could rapidly expand its enrollment and generate tuition. For the long term, Stevenson wished to accumulate a substantial endowment to lessen dependence on tuition revenue and to permit expansion of faculty and staff. He also resolved to end the rivalry between the college and the Collegiate Institute by linking the two under one administrative unit on the new campus.[24] To accomplish these goals, Stevenson adopted the anti-Mormon strategies of his predecessors, especially when raising funds in the eastern states. When he assumed office in 1905, the country was experiencing a revival of anti-Mormon sentiment precipitated by efforts to deny Senator-elect Reed Smoot, a monogamist Mormon apostle, his seat in Congress. Charging that Mormons violated the separation of church and state by granting their religious leaders absolute authority, opponents of Smoot conducted hearings between 1903 and 1907 that featured a testimony of President Joseph F. Smith, who acknowledged that he continued to live with his plural wives in violation of cohabitation laws. Although Smoot eventually won his Senate seat and went on to a distinguished congressional career, the extended hearings riveted national attention once again on Mormonism as a major social issue. Popular magazines and newspapers featured stories of alleged polygamous practices and instances of Mormon control of public institutions in Utah.[25]

The first step toward a residential campus was taken by Jeannette Ferry shortly after Stevenson assumed office. Following the death of her husband in 1904, Ferry directed the family's philanthropy, supporting a variety of civic and religious causes. During her first conversation with Stevenson, she promised to contribute $15,000 toward the erection of a women's dormitory provided the college raise an additional $10,000 to complete the project. She also offered to enlist the support of church-women throughout the Synod of Utah.[26] At the national level, Emma Stevenson raised money for the dormitory by attending General Assembly and visiting various presbyterial and synodical meetings to present the claims of Westminster College. During her travels she secured substantial gifts from a number of prominent Presbyterian women including Mary E. James and Mary Jackson, wife of Sheldon Jackson.[27]

With approximately $25,000 in cash and pledges in hand, college trustees authorized contractors to break ground for the new dormitory. Jeannette Ferry turned the first soil at a dedication ceremony on October 10, 1907, at which time McNiece acknowledged the important role that she and her late husband had played in the development of Westminster College. Subsequently named Ferry Hall in honor of William and Jeannette Ferry, the building was located two hundred feet south of Converse Hall. Designed to house forty students and six teachers as well as provide instructional space for female music and art students, its colonial style of architecture with a large portico on the west front supported by eight large pillars offered an impressive background for the annual all-college photograph. Before workmen could complete the interior plastering and plumbing, however, funds were exhausted and work ceased. Two years would pass before the building was ready for occupancy.[28]

Raising money for Westminster as an absentee president proved to be a formidable task for Stevenson. He conducted college business primarily by letter and telegram, a process that frequently created confusion, misunderstanding, and occasionally gridlock. On one occasion, Stevenson received copies of the college catalog that had been printed and distributed in Salt Lake City without his prior approval. To his dismay, the catalog listed every college official except the president. In a sharply worded letter to trustee chair William Paden, Stevenson denounced the oversight and demanded that the catalog be reprinted with his name prominently displayed as president. Citing shortage of funds, Paden informed Stevenson that they would have imprints of his name pasted into undistributed copies and advised him to do the same. Similar conflicts and misunderstandings dominated his six-year presidency.[29]

Relationships with the Board of College Aid remained tenuous. In an era when scholastic achievement scores were unknown, church agencies ranked Presbyterian colleges not only by financial and enrollment statistics, but by the number of students who selected the gospel ministry as a vocation. According to statistics kept by the board, only two Westminster graduates had pursued a seminary career and entered the ministry. Board officials told Stevenson that unless the college could recruit more ministerial candidates to fill vacant pulpits in Presbyterian congregations, especially in the West where the need was acute, they could not justify the resumption of financial aid to Westminster.[30] Although women usually remained silent in matters of denominational policy, this criticism evoked a personal response from Emma Stevenson. She wrote board secretary Dickson that the college offered only freshman and sophomore classes and that most people usually chose the ministry during their junior and senior years. Stevenson also raised the question of sexism in denominational policies regarding ministerial ordination. "Why is it that so little is said and written about the great work Christian Colleges are doing for girls? I presume it is because girls cannot preach or become elders &c. So we have the frequent pitiful spectacle of seeing hundreds of bright cultivated consecrated women in our weak churches represented in our church courts by some stick of a man as elder."[31]

Despite efforts to recruit local students, college enrollment remained stagnant, largely due to lack of facilities and competition from the nearby University of Utah. McNiece reported that he regularly visited the graduating class of the city high school to interest them in Westminster, "but the University beats me every time." Even when trustees reinstituted their original policy of free tuition, the response was disappointing. In the fall of 1907, the entire student body consisted of four students, all of whom were freshmen. The following year the number rose to six, but by the end of the 1908–9 academic year only three students remained on the college roster. Even Westminster trustees elected to educate their children at institutions in the east, a practice that evoked criticism from McNiece, who accused his peers of institutional disloyalty.[32]

During the summer of 1909, the city building inspector declared the original institute building unsafe, thus closing the only classroom space available to Westminster students on the institute campus. Stevenson questioned the wisdom of relocating as well as maintaining a college with three students and two instructors.[33] In opposition to McNiece, who advocated continuing classes despite low enrollment, Stevenson confronted the trustees with an ultimatum: either suspend classes or he would offer his resignation and go public with his reasons. Rather than engage in open conflict with its president, the trustees agreed that until students could be housed and educated on the new campus, they would not attempt to resume college operations. In the meantime, high school classes at the Collegiate Institute constituted the sole academic program under college auspices.[34]

With classes suspended, the need to activate Converse and Ferry Halls and to acquire ownership of the Collegiate Institute became even more imperative. Stevenson launched a national financial campaign in 1909 following the death of Sheldon Jackson, whose commitment to the Utah college had been widely known. In a unanimous resolution, the General Assembly of the Presbyterian Church U.S.A. endorsed Westminster College and encouraged judicatories and congregations throughout the country to contribute to the college in memory of Jackson and his crusade against Mormonism. Stevenson placed advertisements in various Presbyterian publications to attract support for the college. A promotional article in the *Interior*, a highly regarded biweekly Presbyterian newspaper, emphasized Westminster's unique setting in Utah, surrounded by a dominant Mormon culture. Editor Nolan Best also praised Westminster as an outstanding liberal arts college and stressed its interdenominational appeal. Attractive photographs of campus buildings, student groups, and cameos of Jackson, McNiece, and Eaton accompanied the article. No mention was made, however, that college classes had been suspended and that the buildings were unoccupied.[35]

Although the campaign failed to generate an immediate influx of financial support, it did create an increased awareness of the college's precarious existence. Stevenson reported several significant new developments in 1910 that offered hope for the resumption of classes. Negotiations between the college and the Woman's Board of Home Missions regarding ownership of Salt Lake Collegiate Institute finally produced results. Although woman leaders continued to express a lack of confidence in the ability of Westminster College officials to sustain the institute financially, they agreed that "the destructive uncertainty" surrounding the two groups crippled both college and high school operations. In order to resolve the situation, the Woman's Board transferred ownership of the institute to Westminster College effective September 1, 1910, and authorized college officials to sell the institute property. Proceeds from the sale were designated for completing and furnishing Converse and Ferry Halls and constructing a campus heating plant. The Woman's Board also agreed to contribute $5,000 toward institute teachers' salaries during the 1910–11 academic year, reducing that amount by a thousand dollars each year until aid ceased entirely.[36]

During Christmas recess in December 1910, institute faculty, staff, and students participated in the move from downtown to the rustic Westminster campus. The winter term began on January 9, 1911, marking the first time since 1875 that institute classes had not been held on the so-called Presbyterian corner developed by John Coyner. Although officially the preparatory department of Westminster College, the Collegiate Institute retained its distinctive name, continued to issue an annual course catalog, and maintained separate athletic teams and school publications. Despite the absence of college students on the new campus, Stevenson issued a press release hailing the move as "the beginning of a new era for Westminster College."[37]

Other positive news in 1910 came from Mary E. James, an activist against polygamy, who had recently retired as president of the Woman's Board of Home Missions. Stevenson had asked James on several occasions to consider a contribution to Westminster in her extensive philanthropic activity, stressing the importance of having a Presbyterian college in Salt Lake City to combat Mormonism. Through her lawyer, James offered Westminster College $50,000 for its endowment and an additional $10,000 for operating expenses on two conditions: that the college secure an additional $190,000 in gifts and pledges to raise the total to $250,000 prior to December 31, 1911, and that the trustees amend the charter to make the college more interdenominational. This entailed removing or modifying a requirement that three-fourths of the Board of Trustees be Presbyterian.[38]

Confident that James's proposal if implemented would put Westminster on a sound financial foundation for the first time in its existence, Stevenson emphasized the importance of immediate support for the college. He told prospective donors that "the year 1911 is to be the crowning one, we trust, for the college. It's live or die, survive or perish by December 31, 1911."[39] Writing to college trustees from his Washington office, Stevenson called for immediate action on charter amendments, even proposing a few himself, but trustee chairman Paden, fearful of damaging relationships with the Presbyterian Church, advocated a slower, more cautious approach. Guided by legal counsel Henry Van Pelt, Paden crafted modifications that reduced Presbyterian representation on the board from three-fourths to two-thirds and made the board self-perpetuating subject only to ratification by the Synod of Utah. These changes satisfied Mary James and enabled the college to maintain its historic ties with the Presbyterian Church.[40]

During 1910–11 Stevenson worked at a furious pace to reach the $250,000 endowment goal and continued to invoke the threat of Mormonism as an incentive for supporting Westminster College. The excitement generated by the Smoot hearings had greatly diminished, however, and the Utah senator was proving to be an able legislator. Moreover, Mormon officials had disfellowshipped or excommunicated practicing polygamists, and American reformers of the progressive era had turned their attention to more pressing social problems such as assimilating immigrants from eastern Europe. Presbyterian Home Mission Board officials, weary of anti-Mormon controversies, were advocating a more positive, evangelical approach to relationships with Latter-day Saints.[41] Stevenson expressed disdain for his denomination's revised strategy, noting that it went counter to one of the principles on which Westminster was founded.[42] Although Paden sympathized, he reminded the president that Westminster's location in Salt Lake City necessitated good working relationships with the local citizenry, the majority of whom were Mormon. Nevertheless, Paden encouraged Stevenson to do what he thought necessary to promote Westminster among eastern benefactors.[43]

On several occasions Stevenson's strident anti-Mormonism generated unfavorable publicity for Westminster College in Salt Lake City. While residing in Washington, D.C., he wrote pejorative articles in eastern newspapers condemning Mormon missionary activities and alleged polygamous practices in Utah.[44] Copies of the articles were relayed to the *Deseret Evening News,* where they become the focus of editorial attention. One editorial charged Stevenson with being unscrupulous in misrepresenting educational affairs in Utah by claiming that the only way to get a "loyal American education" within six hundred miles of Salt Lake City was to attend Westminster College. According to the editorial, Stevenson had frequently related a story about a young Protestant woman who had met and married a Mormon while she was a student at the University of Utah and was now alienated from her family. Such propaganda, the editorial concluded, "will inhibit immigration into Utah and have serious negative economic implications for the intermountain region."[45]

Stevenson's uncompromising opinions caused some trustees to question his leadership, but he was determined to maintain his anti-Mormon stance even if it jeopardized his position. Writing to George Sweazey, he said, "I cannot work for the college and keep the Mormon question apart. I am at sea how to proceed. Possibly someone else can do the work to better advantage, and if so, I am ready to let such a one do it."[46] Stevenson also clashed with trustees regarding special treatment given to Robert McNiece, who had been in failing health for a number of years. He regarded McNiece as a liability rather than an asset and questioned offering him a faculty position if and when college classes resumed. Unemployed because of suspended classes, McNiece agreed in 1910 to serve as interim pastor of Third Presbyterian Church, which met in the Gunton Memorial Chapel. Unknown to Stevenson at the time, college trustees voted to augment McNiece's modest church stipend to the level of his former salary as dean. When he learned of the action, Stevenson accused both McNiece and the college treasurer of fiscally irresponsible and professionally inappropriate actions.[47]

Despite these tensions, Stevenson gathered approximately $86,000 in pledges and gifts by the beginning of 1911 and reported that several wealthy churchmen were seriously considering participating in the financial campaign. But large gifts never materialized, and the year ended with unrealized financial goals. Even though Mary James indicated a willingness to extend her deadline, Stevenson felt that a major opportunity to establish an endowment for Westminster College had vanished and could not be recaptured.[48] Physically and mentally exhausted, he wrote an open letter to college trustees in Salt Lake City chastising them for their apparent lack of support and ineffectiveness in raising money in the intermountain area. "From anything that has been written to me I would not even suppose that the people out there even knew that we were trying to secure endowment. Not even an allusion has been made to the fact, no letter has been received from any trustee or anyone else, even so much as asking how we were getting along." He further accused the trustees of drifting aimlessly while financial opportunities were passing them by. Concluding that he could do nothing more out east, Stevenson proposed to return to Salt Lake City. "I cannot conscientiously be a party to trying to get money for an enterprise when the people most concerned manifest no interest in it."[49]

Following his return to Salt Lake City in April 1912, Stevenson maintained an uneasy truce with McNiece and other members of the board of trustees. In order to raise money for college operating expenses, he canvassed Presbyterian churches in the Synod of Utah, beginning with First Presbyterian Church in Salt Lake City, one of the few self-supporting congregations in the state. Because they had recently pledged contributions to build a new sanctuary, members informed Stevenson that they were presently unable to support Westminster and would not be in a position to do so for some time to come. Moving south, Stevenson visited Benjamin, Payson, and Spanish Fork, where Presbyterians operated small mission churches. One congregation of seventeen members gave $5.00. At Spanish Fork an elderly woman pledged a turkey and a former pupil pledged two large chickens. Two others made pledges of $9.00 and $13.00. Payson congregants produced $2.00 in cash and $5.00 in pledges, making a total of $34.00 from the three congregations. When his tour of Utah churches was completed, Stevenson had netted a total of $400, mostly in pledges, from the entire trip.[50]

Stevenson received a similar response when he contacted members of the Salt Lake City gentile business community. While sympathetic to Westminster's financial plight, they cited poor economic conditions, other philanthropic projects, or very specific reasons for nonsupport. One industrialist claimed that efforts by Presbyterians to convert Mormons had a negative economic impact because once the converts became Presbyterians their former compatriots shunned them and denied them employment. Another wealthy executive who did business with Mormon merchants said that he really did not know much about Mormonism as a religion, but considered Mormons nice people with whom to do business. He was not inclined to support organizations like Westminster that were associated even indirectly with anti-Mormon activities. In relating this incident to a friend, Stevenson remarked, "Some evidently think that we who speak against Mormonism, not Mormons, are bigots."[51]

Although relieved to be free from his extensive eastern travels, Stevenson soon discovered that proximity to the Westminster campus failed to have any measurable impact on financial problems. His salary was several months in arrears, and bills for coal and other college supplies were unpaid in the treasurer's office. During the summer of 1912, the only contributions received were a small sum to purchase a cow and fifty dollars to support a vegetable garden. The 1912–13 academic year began with no college classes and only 42 high school students in attendance. Their tuition payments and $2,000 from the Woman's Board of Home Missions to assist with teachers' salaries constituted the only assured income for the academic year.[52] Beyond these problems was Stevenson's deteriorating relationship with McNiece and other members of the board of trustees. He felt isolated from key board members who rallied around

McNiece and maintained only perfunctory contact with the president's office. As a member of the board, Stevenson was subject to the process of nomination and election like any other trustee. At a meeting on October 8 when nominations for trustees were presented, Stevenson received only three votes out of eleven cast. He immediately offered his resignation as president, effective November 1. After postponing action for one week, the board accepted the resignation by a vote of ten to two.[53]

The internal dispute became public record the following week at the annual meeting of the Synod of Utah in Ogden. When board chairman William Paden read the slate of trustees for approval, the synod clerk noted that due to confusion in record keeping, the trustee class being presented had been elected the previous year. Consequently Stevenson had two more years to serve on a three-year term as trustee. Paden acknowledged that he did not have the original trustee minute in hand and could not verify the accuracy of his list. During the heated debate on procedure that ensued, Stevenson made a speech that quickly turned into a personal attack on specific trustees, including McNiece, who was seated in the audience. The moderator intervened, stopped Stevenson's address on a point of order, and appointed a special committee to investigate the dispute and report back to the synod the following day. After hearing conflicting testimonies from McNiece and Stevenson, the committee recommended that the Westminster board of trustees reorganize under the supervision of the Presbyterian College Board. Approving that recommendation, the synod also deferred endorsing the college's request for financial aid until Westminster's governing board had implemented the synodical directive.[54]

Initially Westminster trustees vacillated on responding to the synod's action, claiming that neither the principles nor the method of reorganization had been clearly articulated in the motion approved by that body. They requested a called meeting of the synod to discuss the issue of reorganization in more detail.[55] With fifteen commissioners including Stevenson present, the synod convened on January 14, 1913, and immediately became embroiled in procedural logistics. According to an eyewitness, "the air was electrified" when one member recommended that the synod appoint an investigating committee to visit Westminster and ascertain the situation. Wanting to avoid further public controversy, a majority of commissioners voted to rescind the action taken in October and approved a motion requesting only that the Presbyterian College Board send a representative to Salt Lake City to confer with Westminster trustees regarding the future of the college.[56] College trustees agreed to cooperate with this decision, but they maintained that everyone was working harmoniously except

Stevenson, who from their perspective had been stirring up trouble since his resignation.[57] The synod invited James A. Clarke, associate secretary of the College Board, to visit, ascertain facts, and make recommendations.

In a matter of weeks, Clarke arrived. He refused to confer privately with participants but instead convened the trustees as a group. Emphasizing the need for unity of purpose, Clarke urged board members to submit their resignations and petition the Synod of Utah to reconstitute an enlarged, ecumenically inclusive college board. Without a single dissenting vote (Stevenson was not present), the trustees concurred with Clarke's recommendation and passed a resolution of thanks for his fair-handed services.[58] This expanded board gave Westminster College an interdenominational dimension that it previously lacked. While conserving ties to the Presbyterian Church in the United States of America, the college could now enlist the support of intermountain Protestants affiliated with such denominations as Methodist, Congregational, and Baptist. The first two woman trustees, Kate Harwood Hancock (Presbyterian) and Clara Bowdle (Methodist), were elected at this time, both of whom also served on the Woman's Board of Ferry Hall. Bowdle ended her service in 1919 but Hancock, the daughter of William and Jeannette Ferry, was routinely reelected until her death in 1940.[59]

With the process of reorganization completed and relationships with the Synod of Utah solidified, Westminster trustees initiated a presidential search. Assuming that the tradition of ministerial leadership would continue, they again looked to denominational officials in New York and Chicago for assistance. Charles E. Bradt, a field secretary for the Board of Home Missions, recommended Herbert Ware Reherd, pastor of the First Presbyterian Church of Waterloo, Iowa.[60] Bradt and Reherd had participated in a world tour of foreign mission stations during the previous year, and Bradt rated Reherd as an accomplished preacher, a zealous advocate of mission enterprises, and a proven fund raiser. A graduate of Parsons College and McCormick Theological Seminary with additional studies at Princeton Theological Seminary, the Illinois native at age forty-two possessed the necessary intellectual acumen, physical vitality, and spiritual depth to undertake the presidency of a financially troubled and dissent-ridden educational institution.[61]

. Reherd came to Salt Lake City to interview on October 2, 1913, meeting with trustees, faculty, and townspeople. His experience and energy impressed the Salt Lake community. The trustees invited Reherd to become the fourth president of Westminster College at an annual salary of $3,500 and traveling expenses. Reherd accepted the offer with the contingency that he would stay five years, at the end of which time a decision would be made in consultation with the trustees whether to continue or to close the school. After a congregational farewell in Iowa, the Reherd family arrived in Salt Lake City on November 26, 1913, the day before Thanksgiving. The first bona fide residential president of Westminster College, Reherd would devote the remainder of his life to the educational enterprise in Salt Lake City.[62] During his initial visit to Salt Lake City, Reherd made a courtesy call on Robert McNiece, who was near death. For several hours the two men talked about the future of Westminster College. McNiece reaffirmed his confidence in the institution that he had nurtured for more than twenty years. He urged Reherd to accept the challenge of rebuilding confidence in Westminster College. The following day McNiece died at the age of seventy-four after a thirty-six year career in Utah.[63] His passing signified the end of an era during which the college had survived only by faith, determination, and fortuitous generosity. Reherd would renew Westminster's quest for academic respectability and financial stability.

NOTES

1. Robert G. McNiece to Sheldon Jackson, 15 July 1907, Jackson Corres. McNiece taught as many as eight different subjects during an academic year.

2. "Donation to College," *Salt Lake Tribune*, 31 March 1902; and Robert G. McNiece to E. C. Ray, 27 March 1902, RG 32-32-6. McNiece stated that twenty acres of land would be sufficient for the next two hundred years. See Robert G. McNiece to Sheldon Jackson, 30 December 1901, Jackson Corres, PHS Archives.

3. "The Woman's Building," *Utah Westminster* 2 (1 January 1908).

4. "The Homecoming of Mrs. Ferry," *Utah Westminster* 4 (December 1917): 1. Also see Mrs. William M. Ferry, *Our Schools in Utah: An Address to the Woman's Synodical Committee of the Board of Home Missions for Michigan* (n.p., 1883); and *Industrial Christian Home of Utah* (Salt Lake City, 1893). Jeannette Ferry, a college graduate and a linguist, taught French and German and read the New Testament in the original Greek.

5. Josiah McClain, "Early Days of the College," *Utah Westminster*, anniv. ed. (October 1922): 13–14.

6. Ibid., 14. See also William M. Ferry to Westminster College Board of Trustees Minutes, 13 February 1903, WC Archives (hereafter the minutes will be referred to without the archival designation). Although the land was unoccupied, it had nine owners in five different states, creating a formidable task for McNiece and his associates. Nevertheless, they were overjoyed. "We now had a resting place for our weary feet," said trustee Josiah McClain.

7. WC Trustee Minutes, 17 February 1902.

8. Robert G. McNiece to Sheldon Jackson, 1 May 1902, RG 239-7-3, PHS Archives.

9. Robert G. McNiece to George Bailey, 24 October 1902, WC Archives.

10. "Erection of the College Chapel," *Westminster Herald* (October 1903): 3. Also see WC Trustee Minutes, 3 February 1903.

11. "Gunton Chapel Is Dedicated," *Salt Lake Tribune*, 20 March 1905; and WC Trustee Minutes, 29 August 1905. The chapel remained the home of Third Presbyterian

Church until 1948 when it merged with the Westminster Presbyterian Church to form the Wasatch Presbyterian Church at the corner of Seventeenth South and Seventeenth East.

12. WC Trustee Minutes, 28 February 1905; and Sheldon Jackson to John Eaton, 7 May 1901, RG 239-6-4, PHS Archives.

13. WC Trustee Minutes, 16 March 1905; and Samuel E. Wishard to Sheldon Jackson, 26 April 1905, Jackson. Corres.

14. WC Trustee Minutes, 29 August 1905; and Robert G. McNiece to E. C. Ray, 7 March and 1 September 1905, RG 32-32-6, PHS Archives.

15. WC Trustee Minutes, 16 March and 29 August 1905. See also "A New President for Westminster College," *Salt Lake Tribune*, 30 August 1905.

16. John Stuart Dickson to Robert M. Stevenson, 10 December 1908, RG 32-32-7, PHS Archives. See also WC Trustee Minutes, 1 February and 2 March 1906.

17. "New College for Salt Lake City," *Salt Lake Herald*, 11 February 1906. See also "John Heman Converse," *Dictionary of American Biography* (New York, 1930), 360–61; Philip E. Howard, *Their Call to Service* (Philadelphia, 1917), 63–75; and R. Douglas Brackenridge, "John Converse: The Man behind the Building," *Westminster Review* (summer 1996): 12–14. Raised in a Presbyterian manse, Converse respected institutional religion and embraced an evangelical piety that shaped his personal life and public career.

18. "Corner-stone Laid by Presbyterians," *Salt Lake Tribune*, 24 August 1906.

19. Robert Stevenson to the Executive Committee of the College Board, 28 November 1910, WC Archives; and Robert G. McNiece to Sheldon Jackson, 15 July 1907, Jackson Corres.

20. Robert M. Stevenson to E. C. Ray, 7 December 1906, WC Archives.

21. Board of College Aid Information Form, 1906, RG 32-32-7, PHS Archives. Stevenson was so busy raising money for the building fund in the eastern United States that the current expense account went down to zero. Robert M. Stevenson to Sheldon Jackson, 15 July 1907, WC Archives.

22. E. C. Ray to Robert M. Stevenson, 6 August 1906, and Robert G. McNiece to E. C. Ray, 31 October 1903, RG 32-32-6, PHS Archives.

23. WC Trustee Minutes, 29 August 1905. On another occasion, when considering a talented female candidate for an administrative position, the principal of the Collegiate Institute commented, "If she were only a man, now, she would be the one for the position." George B. Sweazey to George B. McAfee, 13 March 1905, WC Archives.

24. Robert M. Stevenson to J. Stuart Dickson, 18 September 1905, RG 32-32-6, PHS Archives.

25. Stevenson told potential donors that Mormons controlled all private and public education in Utah and that Westminster was the only "Christian" alternative available to non-Mormon residents. W. Robson Kothman to J. Stuart Dickson, 21 December 1905, RG 32-32-6, PHS Archives. See also Alexander and Allen, *Mormons and Gentiles: A History of Salt Lake City*, 140–41.

26. Robert M. Stevenson to J. Stuart Dickson, 14 September 1905, RG 32-32-6; and Stevenson to Sheldon Jackson, 22 August 1907, Jackson Corres, PHS Archives.

27. "The Woman's Building," *Utah Westminster* 1 (October 1907): 2; Robert M. Stevenson to J. Stuart Dickson, 14 September 1905, RG 32-32-6; and Robert M. Stevenson to Sheldon Jackson, 15 February 1907, Jackson Corres, PHS Archives.

28. WC Trustee Minutes, 12 December 1910; *Westminster Catalog*, 1909–10, 13; Robert G. McNiece to Sheldon Jackson, 15 July 1907; and Kate Hancock to Sheldon Jackson, 23 November 1907, Jackson Corres.

29. Robert M Stevenson to William M. Paden, 7 September 1908; and William M. Paden to Robert M. Stevenson, 20 September 1908, WC Archives. The process for receiving funds from the Board of College Aid required application forms to be filled out by the college trustees, endorsed by the Synod of Utah, and signed by Stevenson. For two consecutive years, the trustees failed to complete the forms accurately and in a timely fashion, causing delays in distribution of funds. When Stevenson requested trustees to explain the reason for the delays, he received no response. Robert M. Stevenson to William M. Paden, 11 December 1911, WC Archives.

30. "Reports of Visits to Westminster College and Salt Lake Collegiate Institute," 17–18 February and 16–18 April 1904, RG 32-32-6; and J. S. Dickson to Robert M. Stevenson, 21 December 1906, RG 32-32-7; PHS Archives.

31. Emma L. Stevenson to J. S. Dickson, 21 December 1906, RG 32-32-7, PHS Archives.

32. "Westminster College Board of College Aid Form," 1909, 10, RG 32-32-7; Robert G. McNiece to J. Stuart Dickson, 14 January 1905; and Robert M. Stevenson to J. Stuart Dickson, 21 December 1906, RG 32-32-6, PHS Archives.

33. Robert Stevenson to E. C. Ray, 12 February 1909, RG 32-32-8, PHS Archives.

34. WC Trustee Minutes, 26 April 1909 and 27 June 1910; Robert M. Stevenson to Westminster Trustees (n.d., typescript); and Robert M. Stevenson to William M. Paden, 18 June 1910, WC Archives. Despite this decision, college trustees announced on several occasions their intention to resume classes. See WC Trustee Minutes, 27 March and 18 April 1911.

35. Nolan R. Best, "The College Situation in Utah," *Interior* (9 September 1909): 1232–36. Although not indicated anywhere in the article, the Westminster trustees paid $400 for its publication, an unusual practice at that time. WC Trustee Minutes, 16 March 1909.

36. Robert M. Stevenson to William Paden, 8 June 1910, WC Archives. Initially the Board of Home Missions proposed to purchase property from the college and erect a separate building for the Collegiate Institute. These plans were abandoned, however, because of the precarious financial condition of the college and accessibility problems. See George B. Sweazey to George F. McAfee, 6 July 1905, RG 111-4-11, PHS Archives; and WC Trustees Minutes, 14 January 1904.

37. *Salt Lake Collegiate Institute Annual Catalog, 1913–14*, 7; and Robert M. Stevenson, "A Happy Day" (n.d., typescript), RG 32-32-8, PHS Archives.

38. William Barman to Robert Stevenson, 7 May 1910, RG 32-32-8, PHS Archives; and WC Trustee Minutes, 19 May 1910. Like many of her contemporaries, Mary James believed that the future belonged to broadly supported Christian colleges rather than to narrowly focused denominational institutions.

39. Stevenson, "A Happy Day."

40. William Paden to Robert M. Stevenson, 31 March and 11 April 1910, WC Archives; and WC Trustee Minutes, 5 April 1910.

41. Correspondence between Utah missionaries and the Home Missions officials indicates that the board was moving away from the anti-Mormonism that had dominated its policies in the nineteenth century. See George F. McAfee to Robert G. McNiece, 7 October 1899, WC Archives. The history of these changing attitudes is described in Richard H. Morton, "'Means of Grace': Directions in Presbyterian Home Mission Work, 1870–1885," *American Presbyterians* 72 (summer 1994): 123–34.

42. Writing to Paden, he commented, "Under the new plan there is no Mormon Problem and there must be no mention of Joseph Smith, nor of Mormonism. I can think of

no plan that will cause more rejoicing among the Mormon leaders for all they wish is to be let alone. I suppose the next step will be to recognize Joseph F. Smith as a prophet of the Lord and the Mormon church as evangelical." Robert Stevenson to William Paden, 3 May and 9 November 1911, WC Archives.

43. William M. Paden to Robert M. Stevenson, 15 December 1911, WC Archives.

44. Robert M. Stevenson to William Paden, 5 July 1910, WC Archives.

45. "Education in Utah," *Deseret Evening News*, 9 June 1906; and *Journal History* (10 July 1907): 7. Stevenson claimed that Mormons put economic pressure on potential Westminster donors, threatening them with loss of business if they supported the school. See Robert M. Stevenson to Robert MacKenzie, 31 December 1910, RG 32-32-8.

46. Robert Stevenson to George Sweazey, 9 November 1911, WC Archives.

47. Robert M. Stevenson to Robert MacKenzie, 7 March 1911 and 12 and 16 October 1912, RG 32-32-8; and George Goodwin, Robert McNiece, and Henry Van Pelt to Robert Mackenzie, 25 March 1913, RG 32-32-9, PHS Archives. See also WC Trustee Minutes, 27 June 1910.

48. Robert M. Stevenson to Executive Committee of the College Board, 23 January 1912, WC Archives.

49. Robert M. Stevenson to Westminster College Trustees, 16 January 1912, WC Archives. See also Robert M. Stevenson, "A Statement Relative to Westminster College" (n.p., n.d [c.1912]), RG 32-32-9, PHS Archives.

50. Robert M. Stevenson to Robert MacKenzie, 10 September 1912, RG 32-32-9, PHS Archives.

51. Robert M. Stevenson to William E. Paden, 3 May 1911, WC Archives.

52. Robert M. Stevenson to George W. Sweazey, 23 February 1912, WC Archives.

53. WC Trustee Minutes, 8 and 15 October 1912; and George Goodwin, Robert McNiece, and Henry Van Pelt to Robert Mackenzie, 25 March 1913, RG 32-32-9, PHS Archives.

54. Minutes of Synod of Utah, 12 October 1912; and Wildman Murphy to Robert Mackenzie, 25 January 1913, RG 32-32-9. For Stevenson's version of events, see Robert M. Stevenson, "A Statement Relative to Westminster College" (n.p., n.d. [c.1912]), RG 32-32-9, PHS Archives.

55. WC Trustee Minutes, 3 and 17 December 1912.

56. Minutes of the Synod of Utah, 14 January 1913; and George W. Martin to William M. Paden, 18 January 1913, RG 32-32-9, PHS Archives.

57. WC Trustee Minutes, 15 January 1913; and George Goodwin, Robert McNiece, and Henry Van Pelt, to Robert Mackenzie, 25 March 1913, RG 32-32-9, PHS Archives.

58. WC Trustee Minutes, 4 and 13 April 1913; and James E. Clarke to Robert Mackenzie, 15 April 1913, RG 32-32-9, PHS Archives. See also Minutes of the Synod of Utah, 13 October 1913, 15–18.

59. WC Trustee Minutes, 16 September and 23 October 1913. See also R. D. Brackenridge, "Westminster's Founding Mothers," *Westminster Review* (fall 1995): 6–7.

60. WC Trustee Minutes, 6 March and 24 July 1913. The trustees had previously offered the position to Bradt but he declined.

61. "New President for Westminster College," *Continent* (12 November 1913): 4.

62. WC Trustee Minutes, 2 October 1913.

63. Minutes of the Synod of Utah, 8–11 October 1913; and Emil Nyman, "A Short History of Westminster College," 10.

6

A Unique Missionary College

As a minister I am in Christian college work on a mission field simply because I reckon it to be my place of greatest influence for God. If we cannot do with the Christian college something more religiously vital than is done by the tax-supported institutions, we had better close our doors and turn the whole educational task over to the state.
—Herbert W. Reherd, 1924.

Herbert Ware Reherd inherited an educational institution in 1913 that had been without a president for over a year. It had not offered college classes for eight consecutive semesters, and the Presbyterian College Board no longer included Westminster on its list of approved denominational colleges and universities, relegating it instead to a category of academies and secondary schools. Morale among trustees, faculty, staff, and students was at low ebb, and rumors circulated that the college was on the verge of closure.

The campus consisted of twenty acres of mostly unimproved rough terrain. One visitor observed that "it looked like a ranch" with its alfalfa fields and a few fruit trees. The bordering street, Thirteenth East, was a narrow dirt road with an open irrigation ditch and willows fifteen feet high. Campus mail was delivered via a horse-drawn carriage. The president's office in Converse Hall had no furniture, decorations, financial records, or correspondence files. Reherd remarked that he had come to an office "which had largely been a man's vest pocket and the man had gone off with the vest." With his limited funds, Reherd purchased two desks, two chairs, and a letter file and began constructing lists of students, alumni, and potential donors.[1]

Reherd's first administrative actions were staff appointments and the selection of an academic dean. Almira Dodge, who became secretary to the president and assistant to the treasurer, proved to be invaluable to Westminster as recordkeeper, editor of college publications, morale-booster, and counselor. Throughout her tenure of thirty-five years, she resided in Ferry Hall and was on duty virtually twenty-four hours a day.[2] Later he selected Parke M. Pontz, a Salt Lake City accountant, to serve as business manager. Referred to by students as "Pay-me-Pontz," for forty years he supervised buildings and grounds, collected fees, and paid the bills.[3] Reherd also promoted George Sweazey from principal of the preparatory department to dean of the college, a position that oversaw high school and college curricula as well as student activities. Because of Sweazey's scholarly reputation, his long association with the college and the Collegiate Institute, and his ability to cultivate interpersonal relationships, the college community applauded this selection.[4]

With a functional office and a competent staff, Reherd concentrated on fiscal problems. Westminster's 1914 operating budget was $9,230, two-thirds of which paid seven faculty salaries including the principal, who also taught classes. The college carried a debt on which only interest payments were being made. Support from the Woman's Board of Home Missions directed to the preparatory department, diminishing by $1,000 each year, was scheduled to terminate in two years. Although Westminster listed no endowment funds, a review of bank records revealed that the college actually had $1,250 earmarked for that purpose.[5] Needs were so basic that Reherd included on a campus want-list "the gift of six or seven dozen soup spoons" because students were eating soup with teaspoons.[6]

Following an inaugural ceremony in Gunton Memorial Chapel, Reherd introduced himself to Salt Lake City community leaders and traversed the backroads of Utah contacting scattered institute alumni, recruiting new students, and seeking donations.[7] In a battered Model-T Ford, he traveled over sandy roads and mountain trails that were engulfed in clouds of dust or pitted with deep ruts filled with water. To save money, Reherd frequently camped out at night in a small tent and on several occasions was wakened by the sound of bears rummaging for food outside the tent. Learning of the president's adventures through a mutual friend, a mission board executive remarked, "Mr. Reherd, I think you are tempting providence."[8] He also traveled to the eastern states, and during his first trip he met people whose personal fortunes could easily have accommodated the school's modest needs. Although he found these potential donors to be genuinely interested in Utah missions, Reherd also observed that they were besieged with requests for money from many worthy organizations and causes. Accordingly, they listened patiently and promised to "give the matter consideration" or proffered only a token donation. Preparing to return to Salt Lake City, Reherd had raised about $1,500 during a month of solicitation in New York, an amount a Board secretary thought "more than you had any right to expect on your first trip here."[9]

Reherd had an ambitious agenda that included enrolling a first-year class in the fall of 1914, landscaping the central campus, erecting a men's dormitory, exploring opportunities for interdenominational cooperation, and organizing committees to canvass Salt Lake community leaders for much-needed revenue. Reherd proposed using his personal contacts with Presbyterian administrators in New York and Chicago to promote Westminster among prospective donors. He also recommended that Westminster be renamed Salt Lake College in order to facilitate public relations in the places where it was frequently confused with similarly named institutions in Missouri and Pennsylvania.[10] Reherd affirmed Westminster's historic relationship with the Presbyterian Church, U.S.A., the college's primary benefactor, but he advocated ecumenism in Utah, where Protestants were minorities. Aware that Westminster's future depended on broad-based support, Reherd persuaded college trustees that the college would operate equally in the interest of all evangelical denominations. Reherd received pledges from Baptists and Episcopalians to contribute $2,000 annually toward the support of a Westminster faculty member and secured promises from several other denominations to consider future participation.[11]

Reherd demonstrated Westminster's new ecumenical interests in 1915 by hosting the first annual Intermountain Bible Institute, sponsored by the interdenominational Utah Home Missions Workers Council.[12] Designed to encourage cooperation among missionaries and teachers in the field, the week-long institute featured morning Bible study groups followed by afternoon plenary sessions and evening musical and preaching assemblies. At subsequent meetings, participants also discussed current theological issues and occasionally invited Mormon scholars such as Professor M. Wilford Poulson of Brigham Young University to comment on theological developments within the Latter-day Saint community.[13]

Reherd also reconfigured Westminster's anti-Mormon image that had featured so prominently in the college's early history. Although he acknowledged fundamental theological differences between Mormons and traditional Christians, Reherd repudiated the polemics that had characterized nineteenth-century Utah. When asked by audiences outside Utah to speak on Protestant-Mormon relationships, Reherd used what he termed "a descriptive approach" to Utah's dominant religion. "We are careful to tell a true story—a story which any Mormon could hear and not denounce, and yet a story which tells of the peculiar need of Christian Education in Utah."[14] Reherd nevertheless experienced difficulties in explaining his centrist position both to Mormons and Presbyterians.

On one occasion, an advertisement for Westminster written by Reherd and published in Presbyterian magazines stated that the Utah college did not combat Mormonism but rather attempted to build Christian character. Editor David Reed Miller of the *United Presbyterian* asked how one could build Christian character without combating Mormonism and suggested that Westminster administrators apparently wanted to keep on friendly terms with the devil to reduce interference with their Christian program. The editorial admonished potential benefactors to think carefully before investing personal or congregational funds in the Utah college.[15] In response, Reherd compared Westminster's attitude toward Mormonism to that of a foreign mission board toward false religions. Citing his year-long tour of Presbyterian mission colleges abroad, Reherd observed, "I have failed to visit a successful one which is not operating along the line of a helpful, constructive policy. We criticize by creation. Our best criticism of Mormonism in Utah is the building of strong men and women by Protestant Christian education."[16] With a touch of sarcasm, Miller accepted Reherd's explanation but insisted that Westminster's advertisement should be rewritten in order to eliminate any confusion about institutional goals.[17]

Reherd also evoked negative reactions from Latter-day Saint authorities in Salt Lake City when excerpts from his out-of-state sermons and addresses reached their desks.[18] On one occasion, a California newspaper quoted Reherd as calling Mormonism "a real danger in American life today" because it supported a gigantic business enterprise that threatened political freedom in the state and nation. The *Deseret News* condemned Reherd for these remarks and demanded a public apology. Reherd denied using any pejorative language and said that his remarks were apparently taken out of context. His explanation failed to mollify Mormon officials in Salt Lake City who complained that Reherd repeatedly made unfair and inaccurate assessments of Mormon community life on his fund-raising tours for Westminster College.[19]

Although Reherd spent many days on the road representing Westminster, he also had administrative responsibilities in Salt Lake City. College classes resumed in the fall of 1914 after a five-year hiatus with ten first-year and sixty-three preparatory students. The following year there were fourteen first-year and seven sophomore students enrolled with ninety-two preparatory students. Student recruitment and retention became problematic when the United States entered World War I. Enrollment in college classes dropped to three sophomores and eleven freshmen. College trustees switched to a combined high school and two-year college until enrollment conditions improved. Credit hour requirements for a two-year college diploma included English (twelve), foreign language (six), mathematics (eight), science (eight), history (six), Bible (four), and twenty elective hours for a total of sixty-four hours. Students could select courses from eleven areas—Bible, biology, chemistry, education, English, French, Greek, history, Latin, mathematics, and Spanish.[20]

The preparatory department continued to provide the bulk of enrollment and revenue for everyday operations, and high school students dominated extracurricular activities. In fact, the Student Association consisted entirely of high school students until 1915 when its constitution was amended to permit college students to participate as voting members.[21] The curriculum featured three major divisions: classical, emphasizing English and classical languages with additional courses in mathematics, history, and sciences; Latin-scientific, identical with the classical program except that German was substituted for Greek; and commercial, providing practical training in bookkeeping, stenography, and commercial law. All preparatory students were required to enroll in a literary society and participate in declamation, debating, and essay writing throughout their high school careers.[22]

Even with the geographical isolation of the school and its inadequate compensation, Westminster attracted experienced teachers with degrees from reputable liberal arts institutions. Although no information on their instructional methodology remains, their credentials appeared to be excellent. Early faculty members, such as Lou Rachel Paden, Rosa Bird Marimon, Louise Bowman Engle, and Elizabeth Hayes Simpson, came from such institutions as Pomona College, Coe College, Northwestern University, the University of Missouri, University of Chicago, Knox College, Western Reserve University, Colorado College, Wooster College, Colgate University, and Lawrence University. Most contacts with prospective faculty came through church channels, and applicants understood their position at Westminster to be Christian service as well as academic employment.[23]

Westminster's graduates performed successfully in universities such as Princeton, Harvard, Michigan, Pennsylvania, Stanford, and California, and colleges such as Occidental, Knox, Wabash, and Wooster. For example, John A. V. Davies, valedictorian of the junior college class of 1916, won a Rhodes Scholarship in competition with students from the University of Utah and other state and private colleges. He would become a professor on the Harvard University medical staff. Two years later his brother, Paul E. Davies, was first alternate as a Utah Rhodes candidate. Paul attended seminary and received a doctorate from the University of Edinburgh. Another graduate from this period, Reva Beck Bosone, did graduate work at the University of California at Berkeley prior to enrolling in the University of Utah law school. She was elected to the Utah House of Representatives, became Salt Lake City's first female judge, and was the first woman in Utah to be elected to Congress.[24]

In the fall of 1918 a flu epidemic caused Salt Lake City officials to close churches, schools, theaters, and other public venues. Because most Westminster students lived on campus, dormitory residents could continue classes while nonresidential students received assignments by telephone. Within weeks, though, a quarantine of the residence halls and suspension of classes was necessary. School officials transformed the second story of Ferry Hall into a temporary hospital with an attending physician and nurse. Although twenty-two students and two faculty members required hospitalization, all recovered. During the enforced break, Dean McKirahan set up a carpentry shop in Converse Hall where he constructed a chemistry lecture desk, a large bulletin board, and a bobsled for college faculty, the latter "designed to furnish healthy recreation for the tedious days of enforced absence from school work."[25] When rumors of a pending armistice circulated in Salt Lake City, students defied the quarantine to hold a premature mock funeral for the kaiser and buried him with appropriate ceremonies. When the armistice became official, students exhumed the coffin and dragged it around the campus attached by chain to the rear of a farm wagon. Accompanied with popular songs and college cheers, they symbolically cremated the ex-ruler in a large bonfire constructed on the athletic field. Reherd observed the event with a mixture of happiness and solemnity, noting that the armistice was only a beginning step in the quest for authentic world peace.[26]

In the first decade of his administration, Reherd organized a series of fund-raising efforts to secure endowment and expand Westminster's modest physical plant. His initial campaign, undertaken shortly after he took office in 1913, had a goal of $1 million. He began with an attempt to raise $110,000 to erect a men's dormitory and a gymnasium and to secure endowment for a Bible chair. With war in Europe fueling economic expansion, Reherd hoped to attract substantial contributions. The local campaign realized only $25,000, however, though a gift of $30,000 from the Woman's Board of Home Missions enhanced the endowment.[27]

Reherd initiated a second financial campaign in 1919, hoping this time to raise $600,000 for buildings, faculty salaries, and endowment. He began the campaign on October 1, 1919, in Detroit, where he had once been a pastor, and then concentrated on cities in Pennsylvania, Ohio, New Jersey, and New York in which there were sizable Presbyterian constituencies. The Presbyterian General Board of Education (formerly the College Board) promised Westminster 12.5 percent of an estimated $2 million portion of a New Era Fund designated for church colleges. To qualify for the apportionment, Westminster had to raise a matching $250,000 before January 1, 1921. Reherd hired several field representatives to assist him in money raising efforts that eventually extended from coast to coast.[28] Given the time, money, and energy devoted to the two-year campaign, results were disappointing. Reherd had hoped to raise enough money in Utah to remove a $16,000 debt and provide $100,000 for the national campaign but netted only $5,000. Frustrated at the poor showing, the General Board of Education sent Louis Holden, a member of its financial department, to Salt Lake City. After talks with college trustees, whom he quickly determined were too impoverished and passive to be money raisers, Holden asked a prominent local businessman if there were not five men or women in Utah who could come up with $25,000. He replied, "No, not unless they had to put in soak all they had to get it!"[29]

Despite efforts to capitalize on Westminster's unique role as a promulgator of Christian education in the Mormon heartland, the financial campaign never fulfilled expectations at the national level. Although a few pledges and gifts in the range of $5,000 to $10,000 were forthcoming, most contacts elicited only token contributions. Reherd and an assistant spent three days canvassing Presbyterian congregations in Altoona, Pennsylvania, where they managed to raise only $5. Frank Riale, an experienced financial campaign manager, expressed frustration about his inability to generate sizable donations for Westminster and on several occasions offered to resign when monthly receipts failed to cover his own salary and expenses. Riale acknowledged that the college faced strong competition from nearby highly respected Presbyterian institutions and that most easterners regarded Mormonism a dead issue.[30]

In the meantime, Westminster faced a rapidly mounting operating deficit. Enrollment growth was slow (123 total with only 16 college students in 1919–20), and tuition costs ($250 including room, board, and fees) were kept artificially low to compete with nearby state institutions. Proposed annual budgets invariably contained the notation, "deficit to be secured from friends."[31] For a time Reherd contemplated leaving the campaign in order to raise money locally.[32] In Salt Lake City, Louis Holden wrote denominational officials that deteriorating financial conditions at Westminster called for an immediate response. "One wrong step now will mean Dr. Reherd's resignation and the resignation of his board. The tension is great as you can read between the lines."[33] Twice within sixty days during the 1919–20 academic year Reherd had to borrow money to meet the payroll. He recognized that the faculty and staff were overworked and underpaid, with most annual salaries less than one thousand dollars. Even though it would increase the operating debt, Reherd promised modest raises of $50 to $100 for the 1919–20 academic year, informed the General Board of Education of his intention, and requested additional funding. He received a reassuring response from secretary James A. Clarke, who promised $2,500 to help meet immediate expenses.[34]

When the January 1, 1921, deadline arrived, the ambitious fundraising drive had fallen far short of its $250,000 goal. After expenses, only $85,000 in cash and pledges had been raised. Reherd attributed the failure to a small, poor local constituency and an extended business depression.[35] While continuing to express confidence in Westminster's future, Reherd realized that without extended financial support from the Presbyterians, the Utah college had no chance of survival. He framed an argument to convince denominational officials that from the list of forty-two Presbyterian church-related colleges, Westminster deserved special treatment as a "unique missionary college." Invited to make a personal appeal to the General Board of Education in New York City on September 20, 1921, Reherd requested a unique policy for Westminster College. He asked that the board treat Westminster as "a special object" and allocate the college a disproportionate amount of money for operational expenses and endowment.[36]

Reherd supported his request with three points. First, Westminster differed radically from other Presbyterian colleges in its geographical setting, serving an area a thousand miles wide and a thousand miles long without a competitor, and occupying a unique mission field in the Mormon heartland isolated from the main body of Protestants. Second, Westminster was attached to a financially weak synod in the denomination with only three self-supporting Presbyterian churches and a membership of two thousand. Protestant membership in Utah hovered around eight thousand, displaying little sign of growth. Under these conditions, Reherd insisted, "the college presents today a pitiful picture of the Protestant attempt to change Mormonism by higher Christian education." Third, only a concentrated denominational effort would enable Westminster to surmount its weak financial base and "win her case with Mormonism." Without such a commitment, he argued, Westminster could not provide adequate facilities, faculty, and endowment to become a four-year college and compete for students in the intermountain area.[37]

Influenced by Secretary Clarke's enthusiastic endorsement, the General Board of Education designated Westminster College a "special object" of denominational benevolence. Extending its previous offer of $250,000 from the New Era Fund, the board provided $10,000 toward building a men's dormitory and $10,000 to permanently endow a Bible chair. The board also authorized a publicity campaign to raise public awareness of Westminster's unique mission and needs. Pledging to use its entire publicity budget ($4,000) for promoting Westminster, the board also promised field representatives to assist Reherd in organizing a national campaign to raise $750,000 over three years.[38]

To enlist interdenominational support for Westminster College, Presbyterian executives persuaded the Home Missions Council, the Council of Church Boards of Education, and the Council of Women for Home Missions to underwrite an on-site study of Westminster in 1922 to promote the upcoming financial campaign. Dr. Robert L. Kelly, executive secretary of the Council of Church Boards of Education, visited Salt Lake City, conducted extensive interviews, observed classes, and participated in various aspects of campus religious life. Kelly's report gave Westminster high marks for dedicated and effective faculty members, productive students, cooperative trustees, and high Christian standards in its operation. Noting Westminster's support in the wider Utah Protestant community, Kelly encouraged the college to maintain its Presbyterian connections and to develop new relationships with other Protestant evangelical denominations.[39]

Once the national campaign got underway, Westminster received more publicity in one year than it had during its twenty-five year history. Professionally written articles emphasized Westminster's unique educational mission in an area dominated by a powerful and aggressive Mormon establishment. A two-page advertisement with former General Assembly moderators touting Westminster as a worthy "special object" of denominational support appeared in numerous Presbyterian journals and was mailed to selected individuals and congregations. President of the United States Warren Harding was among the educators and churchmen endorsing Westminster as a worthwhile investment in Christian higher education.[40] Although Reherd's professional team never attained their target figures, they raised a total of $264,744.84 to match the Board of General Education's projected share of $250,000. The New Era Fund drive meanwhile fell far short of its mark, and the board received less than half of its anticipated funds earmarked for church colleges.[41] Because of the intensive publicity, however, Westminster secured a place in the benevolence budgets of congregations, judicatories, and nonprofit organizations and attracted the attention of men and women who included Westminster in their annual contributions.[42]

Amid his fund-raising campaigns in the 1920s, Reherd also worked to provide the campus with new buildings and necessary equipment. Reherd asked his trustees to raise $1,500 among themselves to erect a college barn for alfalfa and other farm crops and cover for a team of horses and three cows. Eight trustees contributed a total of $736, which led Reherd to say, "I am disappointed in the reluctance of the Trustees to shoulder this light responsibility. I could raise the whole amount myself in a few days but my hands are full."[43] Trustees raised the necessary balance. The *Utah Westminster* featured a photograph of Reherd in front of the new barn with his quotation, "The up-to-date barn will serve as an object lesson to students who do the barn work and will render a long time service to the institution."[44]

After a series of interim arrangements for housing male boarding students, in 1917 the Woman's Board of Home Missions granted $10,000 to allow trustees to break ground for the long-awaited men's dormitory and construct a partial basement to which workmen later attached a temporary frame structure referred to by students as "the cracker box." This makeshift arrangement constituted Westminster's male boarding facilities until the construction of Foster Hall in 1926. Underwritten by contributions from the Thomas D. Foster family of Ottumwa, Iowa, and dedicated to the memory of Robert Hubie Foster, a college classmate of Reherd's, the three-story Foster Hall housed one hundred students and had a reading room, parlor, and resident director's apartment. A fourth floor was left unfinished for expansion. Reherd exclaimed, "This news makes me want to sing the doxology. I believe it is the dawning of a new and brighter day for Westminster College."[45]

As work neared completion on Foster Hall, Westminster suffered a fire that gutted Converse Hall early on the morning of March 12, 1926. The two top stories of Converse collapsed, destroying a library of fourteen thousand volumes, many of them classics donated by former trustee and pastor of First Presbyterian Church William M. Paden.[46] The University of Utah and the Salt Lake public school system offered rooms and facilities free of charge, and local businessmen gave financial support. In the meantime, officials reconfigured Gunton Chapel, Ferry Hall, and Foster Hall to temporarily accommodate classes. Assisted by the Presbyterian Board of Christian Education (formerly Board of General Education), Reherd launched a campaign to raise $60,000 to rebuild and upgrade Converse Hall. The goal was readily attained, and a much improved Converse Hall opened for classes for the fall semester.[47]

One final link remained to complete Reherd's essential campus. With a growing interest in athletics among male and female students, Reherd wished to develop intramural and intercollegiate sports, including football, baseball, and tennis, by hiring full-time coaches and providing adequate outdoor facilities. Lacking indoor facilities, however, students had to travel several miles by streetcar to practice basketball and other sports.[48] Fearful that out-of-state donors might view a gymnasium as inappropriate or unnecessary, Reherd confined solicitations to Utah residents. With financial support from F. R. Payne, president of the board of trustees and manager of the local J C Penney Company, the college broke ground for a $55,000 gymnasium in July 1928. Dedicated on January 11, 1929, it was named Payne Gymnasium in honor of its primary donor. The new facility was widely used not only by Westminster students but by a variety of clubs and teams from the Sugar House area.[49]

When a thirteen-acre tract of land east of the campus above Thirteenth East Street became available, Reherd persuaded trustees to purchase the land to develop both an enlarged preparatory department and a four-year college. Since the land surrounded a small tract on which Reherd had built a new home (now 1733 South Thirteenth East), trustees purchased the tract and were reimbursed by one of Reherd's boyhood friends, L. A. Cushman, in whose honor the home was titled Cushman Cottage. Trustees unveiled a campus master plan in 1927, incorporating tracts on both sides of Thirteenth East, but the heralded project never materialized, falling victim to the Depression of the 1930s.[50]

Although such financial campaigns and building programs consumed administrative energies, campus life during the 1920s centered on classes, religion, and extracurricular activities. Applying for admission to Westminster College required little paperwork and no extended interview process. Potential students completed a one-page form that asked for name, address, date and place of birth, and names and address of parents or guardians and their occupations. Information requested about previous schooling included name and location of school, number of years attended, date of graduation or withdrawal, and the name of the principal of the last school attended. The form asked for church membership or church preference and had four blank lines for students to state their needs for self-support, including amount of money needed, type of work desired, and qualifications to perform the work. A final question asked, "When do you desire to enter Westminster?"[51] Despite low enrollments, Westminster raised its admission standards on par with other accredited junior colleges. Students with admission deficiencies had been permitted to take both high school and college classes simultaneously, but Westminster gradually increased its standards to require fifteen units of high school work before students could take college classes for credit. Other new rules specified that any student who fell below a D average would be immediately dismissed and listed penalties for excessive absences.[52] A committee composed of the dean and selected faculty adjudicated special cases in regard to all academic requirements.[53]

Westminster College's academic mission called for religious motivation. Although Reherd had a keen eye for degree, teaching skill, and experience in selecting faculty, a candidate with expertise in all three areas who lacked religious commitment invariably received no appointment. Reherd told a gathering of religious educators, "No professor who is not interested in the spiritual welfare of his students has any place on the faculty of a college which claims to be Christian."[54] Individual faculty members varied in commitment and competency to communicate Christian values, but collectively they constituted a community of scholars who shared common religious traditions and educational goals. Reherd once asked faculty members to write down why they came to Westminster and what they enjoyed about the teaching environment. Respondents mentioned Christian values and ideals and commented on the close bond between faculty and students. They noted that most students evaluated Westminster's educational opportunities highly and that parents supported teachers in their efforts to inculcate knowledge. Many confirmed that students had to earn their grades and that administrators never complained about high class standards.[55]

Mandatory daily chapel, compulsory church attendance, required Bible courses, and an annual spiritual renewal or religious emphasis week constituted Westminster's religious regimen. Usually held at 9 A.M. for approximately thirty minutes, daily chapel in tandem with evening prayers in dormitory units framed each school day in a religious context. Led by the president or other faculty members, the service featured singing, scripture readings, and a brief homily.[56] Early college catalogs required chapel attendance but made no mention of penalties for nonattendance. By the 1930s, however, chapel absences above four were subtracted from the number permitted in other classes, and unexcused absences often resulted in disciplinary action.[57] Every Sunday morning dormitory students attended church school and worship services at Gunton Memorial Chapel. On Sunday afternoons, woman residents observed an enforced quiet time from 3 to 5 P.M. while men were left to their own devices. Students active in other local Presbyterian or evangelical congregations resented their lack of choice regarding church attendance. Through the intervention of several trustees in 1921 Westminster reported to the General Board of Education that the president and dean now "exercise[d] liberty in allowing certain Christian students to attend regularly the church of their choice."[58]

Each February Westminster conducted a religious life week featuring morning addresses by a guest speaker, often a noted Presbyterian clergyman from an urban congregation, and evening meetings and individual conferences, usually held in dormitory lounges. Although conversions and decisions to become church members were sought and counted, emphasis in these sessions appears to have been more on evoking decisions for Christian service or resolutions to seek divine guidance in selecting a vocation.[59] Statistics released in 1935 revealed that during the previous decade Westminster had produced three clergymen, five seminarians who were finishing their studies, one person in "other religious work," and two about to embark on religious careers.[60] The Young Men's Christian Association (YMCA) and Young Women's Christian Association (YWCA) added an interdenominational dimension to campus religious activities beginning in 1915. The earliest groups were organized and sponsored by Ralph W. Lloyd, director of men's athletics, and Margaret Bell, dean of women. Some thirty percent of the male students and seventy-five percent of the female students maintained active membership in these organizations.[61]

Westminster required every full-time student to study the Bible in an academic setting by a credentialed Presbyterian clergyman. Reherd once noted that some entering freshmen believed that the first commandment was "God helps those who help themselves" and that the Philippians lived in the Philippine Islands. A selection of survey courses, such as The Pentateuch, The Prophets, Wisdom Literature, The Gospels, and Acts and the Life of Paul, introduced students to Old and New Testament scriptures and Jewish and Christian history.[62] Despite its pervasive religious ethos, Westminster instructors adopted a nonsectarian, historical-critical approach to biblical studies. Competent scholars, such as John McKay, Harrison Pillsbury, and R. Grady Snuggs, were among a number of faculty members who taught courses in religion and philosophy during the Reherd-Steele eras. Asked to describe his teaching method, Pillsbury said he taught solely from a historical perspective and students were graded on their factual knowledge rather than opinions. Pillsbury also rejected a dogmatic literal approach to the Bible.[63]

Biblical instruction at Westminster was by no means value free and posited a goal of developing moral character. In response to why Mormons, Roman Catholics, Jews, and families with no religious affiliation would enroll their children in a school where they lived under strict dormitory rules and studied the Bible under the tutelage of a Presbyterian minister, Reherd said, "Because parents value scholarship and character above adherence to a formal creed. A Mormon expressed it well when he said, 'I would rather have my daughter become a good Protestant than a wild Mormon.'"[64]

Westminster College administrators and faculty monitored campus social life to enforce their religious and moral standards. Students caught smoking tobacco or drinking alcohol on or off campus faced suspension or dismissal. Despite unannounced room checks by faculty and staff, many students circumvented the rules. They gathered by Emigration Creek at the south end of the campus to smoke. Because "nicotine gulch" received periodic inspections by college faculty, the students maintained a lookout system.[65] Forbidden to drink alcohol on campus, some town students brewed beer at home and invited friends to parties. Others frequented neighborhood speakeasies in Salt Lake City during prohibition. The back room of Rosie's Grill was a favorite watering hole for Westminster students even though they had to be alert for surprise visits from male faculty members in search of violators. One coed admitted, "I learned to smoke and drink at Westminster College."[66]

Faculty deemed other kinds of student behavior questionable also. A Ferry Hall resident was campused for one month because a matron, conducting a random search of rooms, discovered a pack of playing cards tucked away in a closet. One student who came to class with high-piled hair concealed under a large tam was sent to the dean, who denied her social privileges for a month for such a brazen décolleté. Another coed related how Dean Stevenson called her into his office because he had observed a young man touch her chin with his hand while she was walking down the hall. She escaped censure, however, by convincing the dean that the young man was only helping her to tie a large bow which had come loose.[67] Students periodically petitioned administrators to rescind the prohibition against dancing. In 1921 Reherd circulated questionnaires to trustees and area clergy asking their opinion, but since they indicated no strong sentiment to modify the current policies, the social ban remained in effect.[68] In defense of the policy on dancing, Reherd cited Westminster's unique social environment.[69]

Student pranks taxed administrative disciplinary casuistry. Once three junior students climbed to the top of Converse Hall, painted the class numerals on the campus clock, and posted a flag. At the chapel assembly the next morning, Dean McKirahan called the juniors aside and asked the guilty parties to come forward. No one volunteered, so McKirahan told town students to leave campus and confined dormitory students to quarters until those responsible removed the flag and erased the numbers. In the meantime, students would receive failing grades for every missed class. Making the most of their free time, the town students went to the city center, formed a conga line, and danced in and out of theaters and restaurants. Concerned parents intervened and persuaded Dean McKirahan to reinstate the junior class. Workers removed the flag and cleaned off the paint. The culprits, however, were never apprehended.[70]

During Reherd's tenure, Westminster developed customs and traditions that generations of students and faculty remembered. Although some were inherited from the Collegiate Institute, others originated within the new college community. An institute tradition, awarding a large wooden spoon to the most voracious eater, apparently was transmogrified into an award for "spooners," the most devoted couple on campus. How or when this change occurred has not been preserved. When Reherd received letters from parents who objected to offering a prize for something that had nothing to do with education, he replied that "it is impossible to keep such sentiment off the campus, and it is probably much better to be open and above board about spooning."[71]

Other annual events on the school calendar were popular with faculty and students. Founder's Day observances in April and Homecoming parades in October attracted people from nearby residential neighborhoods. For the May college picnic, students and faculty took a streetcar and then walked two miles up into Bountiful Canyon where they hiked and picked wildflowers along the stream.[72] During commencement week in 1918 after final examinations, students and faculty gathered on the steps of Ferry Hall for an informal College Sing consisting of songs and stunts by students directed at faculty members. Described as a new event for Westminster, observers predicted it would be increasingly popular in coming years.[73] Included among the lyrics was "Westminster Evening Song," which subsequently became the official college alma mater. Written by two Westminster students, Lawrence Eberly (Collegiate Institute, 1915) and Elizabeth Gillilan (Junior College, 1919), Westminster Evening Song made its debut in the First Methodist Church on Sunday March 10, 1918, sung by the combined glee clubs of Westminster College.[74] On Washington's birthday faculty entertained students in Ferry Hall with a four-course dinner served by waiters wearing colonial costumes and powdered wigs.[75]

Sometimes social events engineered by the Reherds and the McKirahans involved an element of surprise. On one occasion, faculty members received a formal notice from the dean that an emergency meeting had been scheduled for New Year's Eve at 6 P.M. Faculty members showed up for the meeting, voicing their displeasure about being required to attend on such short notice and at such an unreasonable time. A few started to leave but were called back by Dean McKirahan who announced that the meeting was only a ruse to mark the beginning of a progressive dinner, hosted by a grateful administration. Following a soup course in Converse Hall, salad with the dean, dinner at the president's home, and desserts at Ferry Hall, faculty members ushered in the new year with music, songs, prayers, and best wishes.[76]

Westminster athletics assumed increasing prominence following the First World War. Students adopted purple and gold as school colors and modernized team uniforms to include numbers for the first time in school history.[77] The origin of the nickname, Parsons, is unknown. An unsigned article in the *Utah Westminster* speculated that the sobriquet had been imposed by a local sports writer who mistakenly assumed that Westminster (frequently mispronounced and misspelled as Westminister) was primarily a school to prepare students for the ministry. "The name is unsatisfactory," the writer asserted, "and a search is on for a new and more appropriate name. Suggestions will be welcomed." Various student generations reactivated the search, but Parsons remains linked with Westminster athletics.[78] Like other faculty and staff, the college required athletic coaches to be evangelical Protestants and expected them to encourage the student athletes to be active in campus religious activities as well as to perform on the field. Administrators also encouraged academic priorities over winning seasons. Reherd in particular stressed the importance of athletics that produced character rather than touchdowns, remarking, "that is the real test of athletics—whether it helps a boy to be a better man, physically, mentally, and morally."[79] Westminster athletic teams competed against regional junior college opponents and occasionally won league championships, but Student Association Minutes record complaints about poor attendance and the lack of student interest at athletic contests.[80]

Women's athletics flourished briefly during the same time period. Westminster's college women first fielded a basketball team in 1918, although it is not clear how many off-campus contests, if any, they played. During their first season they challenged the preparatory department team and won by a score of 10-7. Volleyball, tennis, and gymnastics were also popular female sports, but they apparently were confined to intramural competition.[81] In 1923 Westminster women formed the Girls' Athletic Association complete with constitution and bylaws. The association established a point system for determining eligibility for varsity letters, the first of which were awarded in 1924. Interest in women's athletics apparently waned during the 1930s. Team photographs appear only infrequently in the college yearbook and the *Utah Westminster* contains few references to their activities.[82]

Photographs of the college debate squad and descriptions of its activities garnered as much attention as football contests and baseball games. The Student Association provided travel funds for debate and athletic teams from the same budget. When the student magazine faced a deficit, the Student Association transferred money from the athletic account "because the promoting of athletic activities in the school this year does not require the amount of money allotted to said activities."[83] Debate squads defeated teams from other intermountain colleges and received numerous prizes. Varied topics included such issues as "Resolved, the United States should join the League of Nations" and "Resolved, trial by jury should be abolished in the United States." Large audiences gathered in Gunton Memorial Chapel to hear students compete for the R. G. McNiece Memorial Prize featuring speeches on the Fundamentals of Christianity. Oration topics included "One Who Prays," "Evidence of God," "Eternal Life," "Biblical Authority," and presentations on biblical characters such as Esther, Ruth, and Paul.[84]

As the 1920s ended, Westminster had made measurable progress toward fiscal stability, even though carrying a heavy debt burden. With basic facilities in place, a committed faculty, a growing student body, and substantial denominational backing, Reherd had reason to believe that the institution's future was secure. At the end of the 1928–29 fiscal year, he reported an enrollment of 263, of whom 62 were college level, and total assets of more than a half-million dollars.[85] The Great Depression of the 1930s, however, would curtail expansion plans and bring Westminster once again to the brink of closure. As national unemployment rose to twenty-five percent of the work force during the winter of 1932–33, Utah's reached a level of thirty-five percent. In Salt Lake City, banks failed, businesses closed, retail sales plunged, and bread lines became commonplace. By January 1933 about twelve thousand families in Salt Lake County were on some form of relief; in 1934 about two hundred persons per thousand were on relief in Utah, the fourth highest rate in the United States. The federal government cut its WPA programs in 1936 because Salt Lake City officials were unable to generate sufficient revenue to pay their share of the costs. Although the city cooperated with various private organizations, especially the Mormon Church, unemployment and poverty continued to be serious problems in Utah until the beginning of the Second World War.[86]

Westminster's economic situation mirrored that of the wider Salt Lake community. In 1931 Reherd reported an operating deficit of

$12,734.09, the largest in Westminster's history. College officials halted an endowment campaign until business conditions improved and postponed indefinitely plans to expand to a four-year college. To reduce operating expenses, they dropped the first two years of high school from the preparatory department program. Consequently, for the first time in college history, college enrollment exceeded that of the preparatory department. During a two-year period (1932–33), faculty experienced salary reductions of forty-eight percent, and several staff members, including the registrar, voluntarily reduced their employment to September, January, and June, when their services were most needed. Because loans were not available from local banks, the college began issuing nonnegotiable notes at six percent interest in part payment for salaries in 1932, the total of which eventually reached approximately $40,000. They were systematically redeemed as the financial picture brightened.[87]

During the early 1930s, enrollment plummeted as students chose state universities or deferred their educational plans. Westminster students covered their expenses in many ways. One sold fruits and vegetables carted in weekly from his family farm. Another housed his jersey cow in the college barn and sold milk to neighboring residents to meet monthly installments on his college loan. A local dressmaker agreed to make clothes in exchange for her daughter's tuition. One young man brought twelve hundred pounds of honey on a horse-drawn wagon as payment for tuition, room, and board.[88] The college in fact encouraged frugality among students. They were charged ten cents for meals served in their rooms and faced an unspecified "extra charge" for electricity used for anything other than lighting. Course changes or extra examinations cost one dollar each.[89] Campus rules required that all resident students perform cleaning chores in dormitories or work in the college garden, orchard, or athletic fields in order to keep operating expenses at a minimum. Resident students received nutritious meals prepared from low-cost recipes. Much of the food was produced on college acreage that over the years had been developed into prosperous alfalfa and corn fields, fruit orchards, and vegetable gardens. Apples, plums, pears, peaches, nectarines, raspberries, currants, and gooseberries were preserved for use throughout the year, and cows supplied most of the college's milk needs.[90]

With an institutional debt now in excess of $75,000, in 1934 Reherd proposed a modest financial campaign to raise $150,000 over a period of three years to retire the debt and stimulate cash flow.[91] Just prior to this decision, however, Reherd had become ill traveling to raise money among alumni residing in southern California and had undergone emergency abdominal surgery in a Pasadena hospital. Recovery was slow and never complete, and although he continued as president for another five years, he needed an associate to share administrative duties to allow him more time to raise money. Trustees selected his son-in-law, Robert D. Steele, who came to Westminster on September 1, 1934, as vice president and professor of Bible. The following year Steele assumed the title of associate president with full authority to direct all aspects of Westminster's academic programs. A graduate of Princeton Seminary and an ordained Presbyterian minister, the thirty-one-year-old Steele projected an engaging personality and bounding enthusiasm. Committed to Reherd's concept of Westminster as a unique missionary college, Steele began to make his presence felt on campus and in the wider community.[92]

One of Steele's first administrative decisions was to transform Westminster into a four-year junior college, a move that did not materially alter the curriculum but reflected progressive educational theory. After two years, lower-division (high school) students entered college as juniors, not freshmen. The arrangement simplified administrative structures and enabled Westminster to maximize its limited course offerings and resources. Citing Pasadena Junior College in California as a precedent, Steele emphasized that the change, which became effective September 1, 1935, established Westminster as the only four-year junior college in the intermountain region.[93] Although the shift from a two-year to a four-year junior college involved minimal internal change in college operations, it marked the end of an era of Westminster's history. No longer would the name "Collegiate Institute" appear in conjunction with Westminster on catalog title pages, administrative stationery, or promotional materials. While technically still offering two years of high school, Westminster eliminated references to the preparatory department and featured college terminology. "Old Collegiate," would linger as a nostalgic institutional icon recalled only occasionally on Founder's Day and at alumni gatherings.[94]

Steele upgraded academic standards in various ways. New courses in college physics, surveying, mechanical drawing, and the reinstatement of accounting brought diversity to the liberal arts curriculum.[95] He secured accreditation from the Northwest Association of Secondary and Higher Schools, a move that enabled Westminster to train elementary schoolteachers for the Utah public school system and open a potential market for students.[96] He established criteria for faculty appointments that included a master's degree (minimal), experience in high school or college teaching, and a "positive Christian attitude" exemplified by high moral character and active membership in a Protestant church. Steele advocated seeking out-of-state faculty who represented a variety of educational institutions and evangelical denominations. Responding to requests from trustees for more involvement in employment decisions, Steele appointed a teacher's committee to work in association with the president on making new appointments.[97]

The new associate president softened the austerity of Westminster's religious ethos. While committed to existing religious programs, Steele used his preaching skills to make daily chapel more varied and interesting. He introduced resident students to a variety of theological traditions and worship experiences during the Sunday services, including bus trips to Methodist, Congregational, and Episcopalian churches and to the Salvation Army. The Bible professors then integrated these visits into classroom lectures and discussions.[98] Steele eased some social restrictions, quietly eliminating the long-standing ban on campus dances. Restrictions on card playing were modified to permit recreational card games at authorized campus events, but the injunction against card playing in dormitory rooms remained in force.[99]

Advertisements for Westminster acquired a bright, modern format projecting the image of a dynamic institution poised on the cutting edge of academic excellence rather than an impoverished church school reduced to accepting farm produce in place of tuition. An advertisement in the 1937 *Etosian* described Westminster first and foremost as "an educational opportunity," and emphasized accreditation, scholarship, and wholesome social activities. Religion appeared at the end of a list of programs that featured athletics, dramatics, forensics, and departmental clubs.[100] College catalogs continued to stress the religious dimensions of a liberal education, albeit in more general terms than in previous years. The Objectives of Westminster College (1937–38) referred to Westminster as a Christian institution where "an integrated and positive view of life is presented in harmony with religious faith and intended to impart a sense of the reality of God."[101]

With Steele in control of college operations, Reherd tendered his resignation as president of Westminster College to become effective August 31, 1939. In deference to requests from trustees, he agreed to function as a college fund raiser, financial advisor, and consultant in his role as honorary chairman of the board. The search for a new president extended no farther than the trustee's meeting room. Having previously examined Steele's credentials and having ascertained his availability, the presidential search committee recommended that Steele be appointed president at a salary of $3,000, with free housing, $25 monthly entertainment expense account, and participation in the Presbyterian ministers' pension plan.[102]

Reviewing his twenty-six years at Westminster's helm, Reherd cited some significant accomplishments: campus growth from twenty-two to forty acres; faculty from eight to twenty; students from 64 high school pupils to a student body of 227, most of whom were college grade; annual budget from $7,500 to $65,000; total assets from $227,000 to $667,000; and a building program that produced a renovated Converse Hall, Foster Hall, and Payne Gymnasium in a landscaped setting. Overall, Reherd had raised in excess of $1 million for Westminster programs, facilities, and endowment. Expressing confidence in his son-in-law as successor, Reherd looked forward to participating in the future growth and development of Westminster. "I am assured that some things I have seen in my imagination may be actual sights to my eyes."[103]

In reality, two members of the Reherd family were retiring. During Herbert Reherd's prolonged absences from Salt Lake City, Louise McClure Reherd functioned unofficially as acting president. She hosted dignitaries, provided accommodations and meals for needy students, taught Bible classes when emergencies arose, assisted presidential secretary Almira Dodge with office paperwork, and provided leadership for the Westminster's Woman's Board. Like most ministers' wives of her era, Reherd served as mother, soulmate, counselor, and unpaid college staff member. In addition, Louise Reherd sponsored youth groups and taught Sunday school at First Presbyterian Church. For years she served as president of women's presbyterial and synodical societies and participated in Red Cross and other civic organizations.[104]

A grateful denomination honored Herbert Ware Reherd with a distinguished service award at the 150th General Assembly of the Presbyterian Church in Philadelphia, citing his accomplishments as Christian educator and denominational leader. Regional historians and college supporters also informally recognized Reherd as "the father of Westminster," a title bestowed in acknowledgment of his contributions to Utah education. Although Reherd never fully realized his vision for Westminster, by his imagination, fortitude, and sheer hard work, he had revived a floundering institution and given it new life during a tumultuous quarter-century of American history.

NOTES

1. Herbert W. Reherd [compiled by Emil Nyman], "A History of Westminster College" (n.d., typescript), 34–35, WC Archives. Admissions documents transformed these liabilities into assets, boasting that Westminster was only a twenty-minute streetcar ride from town and fortuitously situated "away from the smoke, noise, and temptations of the city." See "Campus Notes," *Utah Westminster* 1 (April 1915): 1.

2. Reherd, "A History of Westminster College," 3. When Dodge retired in 1949, she received the first staff pension from Westminster College: $30 per month.

3. Nyman, "Short History of Westminster College," 18.

4. For biographical sketches and photographs of the deans who served Westminster, please see Emil Nyman, "Westminster's Deans" (n.d., typescript), WC Archives. Family health problems forced Sweazey to resign in 1917 after thirty years of service in Salt Lake City. His successors, Walter W. McKirahan (from 1917 to 1927), Perry L. Stevenson (from 1927 to 1933), and Lincoln Barker (from 1934 to 1941), followed his tradition as responsible administrators, teachers, and counselors.

5. Reherd, "A History of Westminster College," 36–37. See also *College Board Application for Aid*, 1913–14, 2, RG 32-32-9, PHS Archives.

6. "College Notes," *Utah Westminster* 2 (January 1916): 3.

7. "Head of Westminster College Inaugurated," *Deseret Evening News*, 3 October 1914; and "H. W. Reherd Is Formally Installed," *Salt Lake Tribune*, 3 October 1914.

8. Reherd, "A History of Westminster College," 39.

9. Ibid., 38.

10. WC Trustee Minutes, 16 September, 2 October, and 9 December 1913. Although trustees did not change the institutional name due to legal technicalities (Congregationalists still owned legal title to "Salt Lake College"), every other aspect of Reherd's plan for Westminster eventually was realized.

11. "Its Interdenominational Work," *Utah Westminster* 1 (May 1915): 10; Reherd, "A History of Westminster College," 53; and WC Trustee Minutes, "President's Report," 15 December 1914, 3. Reherd later proposed a radical reorganization of Westminster to unite Utah Protestants in a major benevolence project. His plan called for each participating denomination to elect one trustee for each $100,000 capital investment in Westminster. In addition, each $5,000 contributed to current expenses merited an additional trustee, with individual denominations determining the appointee. The Depression ended any immediate hope of implementation. See WC Trustee Minutes, 18 March 1930; and Herbert W. Reherd to William L. Young, 7 February 1935, RG 32-32-15, PHS Archives.

12. Reherd, "A History of Westminster College," 27.

13. Ibid., 41–42. Later called Intermountain Christian Workers' Institutes, meetings were held annually on the Westminster campus until curtailed by the Depression in the 1930s. See "Intermountain Christian Workers' Institute," *Utah Westminster* 12 (July 1926): 2.

14. Herbert W. Reherd, "President's Report," WC Trustee Minutes, 9 January 1923, 1. Reherd wrote extensively in magazines and newspapers on Mormon theology and practice. For examples, see "Mormon Theology and Its Propagation," *Home Mission Monthly* 38 (December 1923): 25–26; and "The Mormon Centennial and the Protestant Program," *Missionary Review of the World* 53 (April 1930): 278–79. Reherd illustrated this strategy by relating an incident that occurred following a sermon that he delivered in San Francisco. As he was leaving the sanctuary, a visiting Mormon elder spoke approvingly of the sermon and engaged him in conversation about Latter-day Saint beliefs and practices. The two men walked to Reherd's hotel, where they continued their conversation for another hour. In parting the elder suggested that Reherd study Mormon theology and become a missionary. "If your church can give me the gospel as it is revealed in the New Testament," Reherd responded, "I will follow your belief." See "Mormon Attack," undated clipping [c.1922] from the *Salt Lake Tribune*, in Paden Papers, WC Archives.

15. "Shall We Combat or Condone Mormonism?" *United Presbyterian* 11 (December 1919): 4–5. "It is unthinkable," the editor wrote, "that a Presbyterian school should take the attitude of condoning, or apologizing for this iniquitous System."

16. Herbert W. Reherd, "Utah's Westminster College," *United Presbyterian* 12 (February 1920): 5.

17. "Mormonism and the Utah Westminster," *United Presbyterian* (January 1, 1920): 5.

18. A scrapbook collection of Westminster advertisements is in the WC Archives.

19. "College Head Gives Talk on 'Mormonism,'" *Deseret News*, 22 July 1921; and "President H. W. Reherd of Westminster College Submits Explanations," *Deseret News*, 4 August 1921.

20. Reherd, "History of Westminster College," 40; and "College," *Utah Westminster* 8 (May 1922): 32. Although junior colleges date back to the mid-nineteenth century, their major proponent was William Rainey Harper, president of the University of Chicago, whose support led to the establishment of the first public junior college at Joliet, Illinois, in 1902. By 1920, there were more than two hundred junior colleges in the U.S.

21. MSASLCI, 22 April 1915, WC Archives.

22. *Utah Westminster* 1 (April 1915): 2.

23. Faculty credentials were included in early college catalogs, and some of their letters of application can be found in Reherd's correspondence.

24. "Utah's Rhodes Scholar," *Utah Westminster* 4 (January 1918): 1. See also Reherd, "Protestant Aid to Utah Education" (n.d. [c.1952], typescript), 3, WC Archives; and Alexander and Allen, *Mormons and Gentiles: A History of Salt Lake City*, 215–16. She married Joseph Bosone, a fellow law student. As a legislator, Bosone pushed hard for legislation to provide greater protection for women and children in industry. Primarily through her efforts, the state legislature passed a minimum wage and hour law for women and children and created the Women's Division of the Utah State Industrial Commission. For a biography of Bosone, see Beverly B. Clopton, *Her Honor, The Judge: The Story of Reva Beck Bosone* (Ames, Iowa, 1980).

25. Reherd, "A History of Westminster College," 46; and "Influenza," *Utah Westminster* 5 (November 1918): 1–2.

26. Reherd, "A History of Westminster College," 47; and "Peace Celebration," *Utah Westminster* 5 (November 1918): 3.

27. Reherd, "A History of Westminster College," 43; and Alexander and Allen, *Mormons and Gentiles: A History of Salt Lake City*, 187–88.

28. Reherd, "A History of Westminster College," 49–50.

29. Louis E. Holden to James A. Clarke, 22 January 1919, WC Archives; and Frank Riale to Thomas Holden, 15 July 1919, RG 32-32-11, PHS Archives. Holden told denominational executives that while college trustees believed Reherd "to be the Moses that has led them thus far, they are not themselves leaders of men. He [Reherd] has the whole load in his wagon to draw as is usually the case in synodical colleges."

30. Frank Riale to Edgar P. Hill, 27 October 1919, RG 32-32-11, PHS Archives.

31. "Annual Report," *Utah Westminster* 3 (October 1916): 3. In 1921, room and board were listed at the rate of $320 per year, "a bargain compared to other schools." "The Call to Westminster," *Utah Westminster* 7 (August 1921): 2.

32. Herbert W. Reherd to Robert Mackenzie, 28 March 1931, RG 32-32-11, PHS Archives.

33. Louis Holden to Edgar P. Hill, 16 April 1919, RG 32-32-11, PHS Archives.

34. Herbert W. Reherd to James A. Clarke, 12 June 1919; and James A. Clarke to Herbert W. Reherd, 14 June 1919, RG 32-32-11, PHS Archives.

35. Herbert W. Reherd to Frederick E. Stockwell, 23 February 1921, RG 32-32-12, PHS Archives. Depressed markets for agricultural products and minerals between 1919 and 1922 had a negative impact on Utah's economy.

36. Herbert W. Reherd to Frederick E. Stockwell, 20 May 1921, RG 32-32-12, PHS Archives; and Reherd, "A History of Westminster College," 51–53.

37. Herbert W. Reherd, "Appeal Made to Presbyterian General Board of Education, September 20, 1921," WC Archives. Trustees had unanimously approved the appeal on September 13, 1921.

38. "Copy of Action Taken by the Board of General Education, September 1921," RG 32-32-13, PHS Archives; and Reherd, "A History of Westminster College," 53.

39. Robert L. Kelly, *Cooperation in Education in Utah, Report on Westminster College* (New York, 1922), 21–22. Kelly also recommended that Westminster drop its commercial and domestic science courses because he felt they detracted from the basic liberal arts curriculum.

40. For example, "Utah College Set ahead of All," *Continent* (23 November 1922): 4; and *Presbyterian Magazine* (May 1923): 270–71.

41. Frederick E. Stockwell to Herbert W. Reherd, 12 August 1921, RG 32-32-12, PHS Archives.

42. Reherd, "A History of Westminster College," 54–55.

43. WC Trustee Minutes, 29 August and 26 September 1922.

44. "College Notes," *Utah Westminster* 9 (December 1922): 4.

45. "Laying Foster Hall Cornerstone," *Utah Westminster* 11 (June 1925): 3–4; and "The New Year at Westminster" 11 (August 1925): 1.

46. "Westminster College Burns," *Deseret News*, 12 March 1926; and "Westminster's Loss," 13 March 1926. A passing milkman spotted smoke pouring out of the east door of Converse Hall at 5:30 A.M. and immediately turned in an alarm, but fire-fighters were unable contain the flames.

47. "The Fire," *Utah Westminster* 12 (April 1926): 1; and Reherd, "A History of Westminster College," 56–57.

48. "Athletic Activity," *Utah Westminster* 3 (December 1916): 3.

49. "Gymnasium Dedication," *Utah Westminster* 15 (January 1929): 1; and Reherd, "A History of Westminster College," 58.

50. Reherd, "A History of Westminster College," 49; and "The West Campus Plan," *Utah Westminster* 14 (November 1927): 1.

51. "Application for Admission," *Utah Westminster* 11 (May 1925): 63. If students required a dormitory room, they were instructed to include a $5 deposit with the application form.

52. "Westminster's Educational Standards," *Utah Westminster* 14 (September 1927): 3.

53. "Regulations," *Utah Westminster* 12 (June 1926): 31–32.

54. Herbert W. Reherd, "Educational Content of a Christian College," typescript, 5, WC Archives.

55. Westminster faculty to Herbert W. Reherd, January 1929, WC Archives.

56. Westminster College Annual Reports to Presbyterian College Board, 1914–20, RG 32-32-12, PHS Archives; and "Westminster's Educational Standards," *Utah Westminster* 14 (September 1927): 3. In interviews with the author, former students from this time period have described similar incidents.

57. "Chapel Attendance," *Utah Westminster* 17 (May 1931): 37; and Donald and Noreen Rouillard, interview by author, 1 June 1994, WC Archives. Chapel seating was

alphabetical to permit unobtrusive attendance checks. One coed related how she had agreed to change seats with a male student so that he could sit next to his girlfriend. A few weeks later the dean summoned her to his office and threatened her with expulsion because of excessive absences. Apparently the young man was skipping chapel, and her empty seat had not gone unnoticed.

58. Westminster College, Annual Report to the General Board of Christian Education, 1920–21, 5, RG 32-32-12, PHS Archives; and Robert Kelly, *Cooperation in Education in Utah: Report on Westminster College*, 3–5.

59. "Vocations Week," *Utah Westminster* 1 (February 1915): 3; and Herbert W. Reherd to Edgar P. Hill, 1 March 1922, RG 32-32-13, PHS Archives. Statistics on conversions and church membership were reported annually to the General Board of Education.

60. Herbert W. Reherd to Charles C. McCracken, 26 December 1935, RG 32-32-15, PHS Archives. Although unidentified, the latter three likely were women preparing for educational or missionary positions.

61. Reherd, "A History of Westminster College," 40; and "College Notes," *Utah Westminster* 5 (May 1919): 5. Periodically, the Wednesday chapel hour was devoted to "Y" meetings with other social and religious events held during the course of a month, including Bible study, discussion groups, and recreational outings. The YWCA, for example, sponsored a "Suffragette Convention" in Gunton Memorial Chapel to which the public was invited.

62. Reherd, "Educational Content of a Christian College," 5, WC Archives.

63. Harrison Pillsbury to Herbert W. Reherd, 10 January 1912, WC Archives.

64. Westminster College, Annual Report to the General Board of Christian Education, 1920–21, 5, RG 32-32-12, PHS Archives; Robert Kelly, *Cooperation in Education in Utah: Report on Westminster College*, 3–5; and "Westminster and the Bible," *Utah Westminster* 3 (March 1917): 2. Biblical study at Westminster, Reherd affirmed, "is not of the milk and water type so as not to offend the critical. On the contrary, it is frankly evangelical but does not insist dogmatically upon certain doctrines." See also "The College Department," *Utah Westminster* 5 (July 1919): 5.

65. Haydon Calvert, interview by author, 23 May 1994, WC Archives. The first endowed scholarship ($1,000) given to Westminster was from C. W. Black of Malvern, Iowa, who stipulated that income not be given to students who used tobacco in any form. See "First Endowed Scholarship," *Utah Westminster* 4 (January 1918): 3.

66. Lucille Bywater, interview by author, 31 May 1994, WC Archives.

67. Virginia Frobes-Wetzel, interview by author, 24 May 1994; and Lucille Bywater, interview by author, 31 May 1994, WC Archives.

68. "President's Report," WC Trustee Minutes, 15 November 1927; and Minutes of the Student Association of the Collegiate Institute, 12 March 1927, WC Archives.

69. Paul Patton Faris, "Protestantism's Oasis in the Desert of Mormonism," reprint from *Continent* (n.d. [1923], n.p.). All the town's social activities, Reherd claimed, were controlled by the Mormon church. Weekly dances under church auspices attracted Protestant young people into dance halls, where they were tempted to mix socially with Mormon youth. "To save their children from this Mormon dance, parents send their sons and daughters to us—and we try to be true to our trust," said Reherd. "We would not be so rigid if our school was in another environment."

70. "The Mystery of the On-Again Off-Again Chimes," *Newscope* (summer 1981): 3. On another occasion students disassembled a farm wagon and carried it piece by piece under cover of darkness to the platform surrounding the bell on top of Converse Hall.

They then reassembled the wagon and left it to be discovered the following morning. Again, no one confessed and no one was punished. Mansel Smith, interview by author, 7 August 1995, WC Archives.

71. Newspaper clipping, undated [c.1936], WC Archives.

72. "College Notes," *Utah Westminster* 5 (May 1919): 4.

73. "College Sing," *Utah Westminster* 4 (April 1919): 2; and "Commencement," *Utah Westminster* 9 (June 1923): 2. Caps and gowns were worn for the first time by faculty and junior college graduates in 1928. Students selected dark gray as the color of their robes. See "The 1928 Commencement," *Utah Westminster* 14 (June 1928): 2.

74. "College Music," *Utah Westminster* 4 (March 1918): 3–4. Eberly later became a member of Westminster's music faculty.

75. "Washington's Birthday Banquet," *Utah Westminster* 5 (February 1919): 3. The long tables were decorated with red tulips and red candles. Selected students dressed as Ben Franklin, Thomas Jefferson, Molly Pitcher, Patrick Henry, Betsy Ross, and George and Martha Washington. Each historical personage presented a toast based on some well-known saying associated with that individual. Following toasts, guests adjourned to the reception room where faculty presented two one-act plays.

76. "Recent Dinners and Banquets," *Utah Westminster* 7 (January 1921): 3.

77. MSASLCI, 10 March 1918, WC Archives.

78. "College Notes," *Utah Westminster* 18 (December 1931): 8. The name continued to be discussed. See "A New Name," *Utah Westminster* 20 (December 1933): 4; and "Origin of the Name 'Parsons,'" *Parson* (25 September 1953): 1.

79. "Autumn Sports," *Utah Westminster* 7 (November 1920): 4; and "Physical Education," *Utah Westminster* 11 (September 1924): 3.

80. MSASLCI, 20 October 1926, WC Archives.

81. *Etosian*, 1919, 84–85; and MSASLCI, 28 January 1919, WC Archives.

82. *Etosian*, 1924, 64 and 91, WC Archives.

83. MSASLCI, 10 March 1918, WC Archives.

84. "Commencement Announcements," *Utah Westminster* 5 (May 1919): 4; and "Recent College Events," *Utah Westminster* 17 (June 1931): 3–4.

85. WC Trustee Minutes, 2 October 1929.

86. Alexander and Allen, *Mormons and Gentiles: A History of Salt Lake City*, 197–204.

87. "The Story of 1932–33," *Utah Westminster* 20 (October 1933): 3; and WC Trustee Minutes, 1 March and 14 June 1932, 24 April 1933. As late as 1938, $10,000 in notes for past and current faculty members were still outstanding. See WC Trustee Minutes, 29 April 1938.

88. "The College Opening," *Utah Westminster* 20 (September 1933): 1–2. The honey-seller's photograph appeared in promotional brochures as an example of Westminster's innovative tuition policies. One Westminster advertisement listed tuition at $80 and room and board $260 with a note stating, "Farm Produce accepted on school bills," Scrapbook, WC Archives.

89. "Expenses," *Utah Westminster* 8 (May 1922): 46.

90. "The Coming Year," *Utah Westminster* 7 (June 1921): 4; and "A New Era For Westminster," *Utah Westminster* (September 1921): 8.

91. WC Trustee Minutes, 24 May 1934.

92. "Mr. Robert Steele, Vice President," *Utah Westminster* 24 (June 1934): 4; and WC Trustee Minutes, 1 October 1936. Steele met his future wife, Elizabeth Reherd, at Wooster College, where they both were undergraduates.

93. WC Trustee Minutes, 28 June 1935; "President's Report to Westminster Trustees," 28 June 1935; "College Opening," *Utah Westminster* 22 (September 1935): 1; and "Plan of Organization" (May 1936): 9. After completing the four-year curriculum, students received an associate in arts or an associate in science degree, which enabled them to continue their education at an accredited four-year institution.

94. In an effort to highlight college work, the high school and the college faculties had been formally separated and separate student organizations instituted as early as 1919. MSASLCI, 11 March 1919, WC Archives.

95. "Curriculum," *Utah Westminster* 23 (September 1936): 2.

96. "Westminster Accredited by Northwest Association," *Utah Westminster* 22 (April 1936): 1.

97. WC Trustee Minutes, 11 April and 13 September 1939.

98. "Church Attendance," *Utah Westminster* 24 (October 1937): 2.

99. "Clean Habits," *Utah Westminster* 25 (June 1939): 31; and "Religious and Moral Standards," *Utah Westminster* 25 (June 1939): 23. Steele contended that card games in the rooms were questionable and resulted in wasted time. To avoid suspicion, Steele advised students not to have playing cards in their rooms or about their persons.

100. *Etosian,* 1937, 107, WC Archives.

101. "Objectives of Westminster College," *Utah Westminster* 23 (March 1937): 3.

102. WC Trustees Minutes, 11 April 1939.

103. Herbert W. Reherd, "A Bird's Eye View of Twenty-Six Years at Westminster College," WC Trustee Minutes, 13 September 1939.

104. WC Trustee Minutes, 30 October 1945; and "In Memoriam," *Utah Westminster* 32 (October 1945): 4, WC Archives. She also published articles in denominational magazines. See, for example, Louise M. Reherd, "Mormon Temples, Tabernacles, and Meeting Houses," *Home Mission Monthly* 38 (December 1923): 28–29.

Part Three~

Four-Year College

*President Robert D. Steele and President Emeritus Herbert W. Reherd,
September 1, 1939.*

Previous page: O. C. Tanner Plaza and Fountain.

Presidents W. Fred Arbogast (1963–68) and Manford A. Shaw (1968–76).

Press conference, January 18, 1983, following college reorganization. Left to right, trustee Robert Weyher, President James E. Petersen, Vice President for Academic Affairs Douglas W. Steeples, and dean of admissions Craig A. Green.

Aerial view of campus, 1960s.

Malouf Hall dedication, 1974.

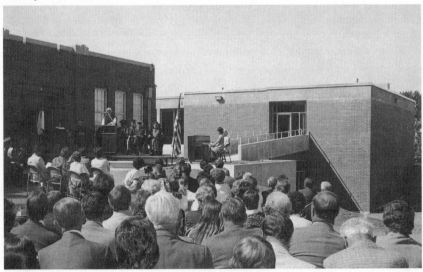

Viola Evans Chapman, professor of English (1948–72).

Jay W. Lees, professor of speech and drama (1946–1983).

Commencement, 1950. Left to right, Judge Tillman Johnson, Herbert W. Reherd, H. A. Hogle, J. S. Boughton, and Robert D. Steele.

President James E. Petersen (1982–85).

The Jewett Center for the Performing Arts.

President Charles H. Dick (1985–95).

The Bill and Vive Gore School of Business Building.
The Giovale Library.

President Peggy A. Stock (1995–).

7

Headed in the Right Direction

Westminster is on its way to securing a position of preeminence in Christian higher education in the Intermountain West. If we have some distance yet to go to realize our ambitions and make our dreams come true, we're on the road and headed in the right direction.
—Frank E. Duddy, Jr., 1959.

During the rapid expansion of American higher education following the end of World War II, Westminster College evolved from a combined high school and junior college with fewer than one hundred students into an accredited four-year institution with a college enrollment of five hundred. It also supplemented its Presbyterian relationship with regional ties to Methodist and Congregational (United Church of Christ) denominations. The three presidents who served during this time period mirrored Westminster's widening circle of church affiliations. Presbyterian Robert D. Steele (from 1939 to 1952), Methodist J. Richard Palmer (from 1952 to 1956), and Congregationalist Frank E. Duddy, Jr. (from 1956 to 1963) cultivated ecumenical relationships and enhanced Westminster's image as the only Protestant college in the intermountain region. Nevertheless, the college continued to suffer fiscal instability, surviving only by timely gifts, short-term loans, and use of undesignated endowment funds.[1]

On September 1, 1939, the day that Steele officially assumed the presidency of Westminster College, Adolph Hitler dispatched his war machine into Poland. Within a year of Hitler's invasion, the United States imposed the first peacetime draft in American history, and major industries began gearing up for wartime production. Westminster's enrollment plummeted with the military draft and war-related industry and service needs. In 1942 only twenty high school and fifty college students registered for classes and several key faculty members including the academic dean accepted more secure and higher paying positions at other educational institutions. The basketball coach reported for military service in mid-season and economics professor Brooks Anderson was drafted despite an appeal for exemption by college trustees. Even Steele seriously considered accepting an appointment as a military chaplain.[2] Hiring new faculty required patience and good fortune. Steele's first choice to fill a position in secretarial studies in 1941 agreed to a contract, then changed her mind. The second choice said he would come for a salary of $1,200 but sent a telegram on September 10 stating, "Am sorry to resign but received better job in college at home." A third candidate accepted the position on short notice but did not arrive until after the semester had begun. This was often repeated during the period 1942–45.[3]

Major policy changes by the Presbyterian Board of Christian Education adversely affected Westminster's finances. In 1942 the board informed Steele that it had recently approved operating procedures that removed colleges with mission status such as Westminster from receiving special financial consideration. Instead, funds for higher education would be divided equally among the forty-five Presbyterian church-related colleges regardless of need. This meant that Westminster could expect to receive only about half of its previous annual allotments, which had ranged between $8,000 and $10,000. Although the board subsequently awarded Westminster supplementary grants and other Presbyterian agencies contributed lump sums for special projects, the college became more dependent on local and regional resources for operating expenses and endowment.[4]

Steele nevertheless kept Westminster open with faculty, staff, and students helping. Every morning from 7:30 to 8:20, for lack of a housekeeping staff, dormitory students performed chores, an exercise Steele called "an extension of the educational process." The president and faculty members fired furnaces, mowed lawns, and handled other tasks as part of their portfolio.[5] Reliving the Depression period, faculty and staff received promissory notes in lieu of cash and accepted part-time appointments or reconfigured teaching assignments. Even with these measures, the drop in tuition revenue forced Steele to make periodic withdrawals from undesignated endowment funds. Each time they had to use these reserves, trustees pledged to restore the funds when financial conditions improved, promises they were unable to fulfill.[6] With a sharply curtailed curriculum, the intensely loyal faculty delivered courses. By 1944, however, Westminster had only forty-five students, most of whom were female, and the student-faculty ratio stood at an economically unfeasible six to one. Even the addition of civilian pilot trainees enrolled in a program at the University of Utah who occupied the lower floor of Foster Hall did little to increase cash flow. Steele acknowledged the grim situation, "Westminster is an idea, with a campus, buildings, some assets, and a governing Board. There is no faculty. There is no student body."[7]

Throughout this period, Steele prodded representatives of the Intermountain Conference of Evangelical Churches (ICEC), of which he was president, to endorse Westminster College as its denominational college. A survey conducted by the ICEC in 1941–42 concluded that Westminster could promote Protestant Christian education in the intermountain area but had little hope of surviving without an immediate and substantial infusion of cooperative financial support. The report also recommended that the national Home Missions Council call a meeting to study educational needs in Utah and to explore the role that Westminster College might play in meeting those needs.[8] Diverted by wartime problems, Home Missions Council executives failed to respond immediately to the ICEC recommendations. Several scheduled meetings were canceled due to inability to raise a quorum. A few denominational representatives finally met in December 1942 but failed to agree on any plan of action. Frustrated by ecclesiastical inertia, Steele told Westminster trustees that he did not expect much to happen in the near future. "Many difficult problems are settled by Interdenominational Committees by taking no action whatsoever. That is our case."[9]

Concerned about Westminster's future, Fay Campbell, secretary of the Presbyterian Board of Christian Education, visited Salt Lake City during the summer of 1943 to confer with representatives from various local churches regarding their interest in cooperative higher education in Utah. An enthusiastic local response led Campbell to arrange a meeting in New York of Presbyterian, Methodist, Baptist, and Episcopalian executives. When participants could not reach consensus on a plan of institutional support and control, Campbell proposed to conduct a more thorough survey of Westminster College, fully underwritten by the Presbyterian Church. Educational consultants Harry Morehouse Gage and George A. Works were selected to conduct the survey.[10]

Completed in 1944, the Gage-Works survey contained a mixture of discouraging statistics and hopeful projections about Westminster. Figures showed that enrollment had dropped sharply since 1938, especially at the high school level, that the maximum salary paid any full-time teacher was $1,600, and that the average remuneration was only $1,387. Even counting funds held by the Presbyterian Church in escrow, the college endowment amounted to less than $30,000, a figure the survey committee deemed negligible. Student fees accounted for only thirty percent of the college budget with the balance coming from annual gifts and bequests. The campus grounds showed deferred maintenance, and science and library facilities were deemed inadequate. Nevertheless, Gage and Works considered Westminster a worthwhile investment of denominational resources because of its unique location and potential influence on Utah society. Rather than abandoning the struggling institution, they concluded that Westminster should become a fully accredited senior college supported by all Protestant denominations in the intermountain area.[11]

With a report that urged continuation and expansion of academic programs in the face of financial deficits that threatened to close the college, Steele polled faculty and trustees. A two-thirds majority of faculty voted to maintain classes even if it meant further reduction or deferral of remuneration. Some volunteered to take unpaid leaves of absences in order to reduce expenses. One faculty member said, "Whatever you decide will be right for me. Merry Christmas. And I want to come back after the war." Basing their decision more on faith than facts, college trustees in 1944 voted unanimously to continue operations and to seek accreditation as a four-year college. Speaking for the group, trustee James A. Hogle said, "Salt Lake City needs a college of Christian Education. Salt Lake City can afford it. We need a school that gives the student something a state school cannot give."[12] With the end of World War II in sight, Steele believed that Utah would need additional educational accommodations for returning veterans. Moreover, because Salt Lake City had a rapidly growing non-Mormon population, Steele was confident that local philanthropy would maintain a church-related liberal arts college. In the meantime, he hoped that interdenominational support would enable the college to meet operating expenses and replenish its endowment. Steele acknowledged that working at Westminster always involved some ambivalence. "One is puzzled at times to know if one's attitude is faith or merely inertia, or just plain foolishness."[13]

Protestant denominations responded positively in principle to the Gage-Works proposal but offered little in firm financial commitments. Presbyterians agreed to budget $10,000 annually provided at least three additional denominations participated and a sum of $25,000 could be assured. Baptists offered $2,500 annually and indicated their desire to double that amount at war's end. Episcopalians, Congregationalists, Methodists, and Disciples of Christ, while declaring interest, declined to participate in the joint venture, citing internal financial problems. Steele expressed disappointment at the responses but continued to impress upon the various denominational executives the crucial role that their churches could play in assuring Westminster's future economic stability.[14]

Trustees revised the college charter in 1945 to make the board self-perpetuating, no longer subject to confirmation by the Presbyterian Synod of Utah. The new charter retained some denominational ties, however, by specifying that two members of each class be nominated by the Synod of Utah and that at least one member of each class be nominated by other participating Protestant denominations. In addition, the document affirmed that Westminster would operate in harmony with Protestant evangelical churches in so far as their doctrines and practices were not inconsistent with those of the Presbyterian Church in the United States of America.[15]

To alleviate the immediate cash flow problem, college trustees decided to sell property consisting of fourteen acres east of Thirteenth East Street which had been used primarily for recreational or agricultural purposes. Although long-range plans envisioned an expanded campus with new administrative, library, and class room facilities, trustees viewed the mortgage on the land as a liability. In need of immediate cash, they unanimously voted to ask $46,000, the amount which the college had invested in the acreage. The land sold quickly and was transformed into a subdivision to meet the growing housing needs of postwar Salt Lake City. The result, however, was that Westminster was landlocked into its original twenty-seven acre campus with no room for future expansion.[16]

Implementing their decision to transform Westminster into a four-year college, trustees in 1944 approved a plan to close down the high school department over a two-year period and to commence junior and senior level college classes. Although most of the forty-four college students who matriculated in 1944 chose the two-year associates degree, two women started on the four-year track. Commencement exercises in 1945 marked the end of an era that reached back to the founding of Salt Lake Collegiate Institute in 1875. Fifteen high school graduates received their diplomas, the last such group to do so at Westminster College. Trustee and then president of the board Edward Orson Howard and Herbert W. Reherd were the recipients of Westminster's first honorary degrees. The following year, Westminster awarded its first baccalaureate degree to Laurene Elizabeth Hodges, a music major from Salt Lake City.[17]

The new four-year curriculum included a bachelor of arts or bachelor of science degree with majors in secondary education, biology, chemistry, English, history, music, philosophy, and business education. Professional programs included a three-year premedical course leading to a bachelor of science degree upon completion of one year of medical school and two-year predental and secretarial science programs. Tuition was modest at $62.50 per semester with a matriculation fee of $5. Westminster College emphasized liberal arts education in its curriculum that required six hours of English, Bible, and history of civilization, five hours of physical education, and the second year of a foreign language. Beyond these basic courses, students took twelve hours in four divisions: language and literature, natural sciences and mathematics, social science, and philosophy, religion, and Bible. Each department administered a comprehensive examination for majors and offered a preparatory course for seniors during the second semester of their final year.[18] Music became increasingly important in Westminster's four-year curriculum. In 1945 the Department of Music organized into a conservatory offering a bachelor of music degree, at that time the only institution in Utah to provide such a program.[19] In the 1950s Westminster added a concert choir directed by William Bushnell and a community symphony orchestra conducted by Kenneth Kuchler. The Westminster Choir toured Utah, Nevada, and California, strengthening denominational relations and stimulating admissions. The orchestra presented an annual concert and offered student musicians an opportunity to work with professionals, including members of the Utah Symphony Orchestra.[20]

Over a period of time, Westminster expanded its offerings to include preprofessional and business courses designed to meet the needs of Salt Lake City residents. In 1949 Westminster formally affiliated with St. Mark's School of Nursing by providing academic courses such as English and biology for trainees enrolled at St. Mark's. By 1952, Westminster offered a bachelor of science in nursing education and an associate in science degree in affiliation with St. Mark's Hospital.[21] Engineering classes were first offered in 1954, and two years later a cooperative four-year tool engineering course administered in conjunction with Eastern Iron and Metal Company (Eimco) was established. In 1959, the college opened an Industrial Relations Center that was linked to a national program sponsored by the University of Chicago. The center offered twelve-week management training programs and conducted various workshops and seminars designed particularly to aid Utah industry.[22]

In framing their mission, Westminster administrators and faculty envisioned a maximum enrollment of five hundred in order to maintain a close-knit college community in which students received a personalized education. They wanted a selective admissions policy that would attract outstanding students who exhibited leadership qualities while also admitting students with potential ability. To enhance the image, Steele recommended that trustees invest $25,000 to erect a barrier wall, similar to one at Princeton University, made of stone, brick, or cement, that would provide the distinction and seclusion for the type of school he envisioned. Due to financial restrictions, however, neither the wall nor the selective admissions were ever implemented.[23]

Higher standards for faculty appointments and increased opportunities for their participation in curricular decisions marked Westminster's academic transformation in the post-World War II era. Trustees approved a faculty code in 1945 that established academic standards for the appointment and retention of professors. The code gave priority to teaching expertise, including classroom skills and interest in students, as well as ability to do scholarly work, institutional usefulness, and professional growth as requisite qualities for Westminster faculty. Faculty members were expected to serve on college committees, participate in professional organizations and community service, and demonstrate continuing scholarship and creative accomplishments in their respective fields. In addition to these criteria, faculty appointees were to be members in good standing of some evangelical church and committed to the principles of Christian education as articulated in the college catalog.[24]

A faculty profile derived from a self-study report in 1947 indicates that the twenty-one faculty members had an average teaching experience of 16.1 years, 4.4 of which had been at Westminster. Teaching loads averaged between fifteen and twenty hours per semester, but it was not uncommon for instructors in some departments to carry overloads of twenty-four to twenty-seven hours in order to accommodate student needs. Given the time devoted to classroom teaching and the limited opportunities for travel and enrichment, not surprisingly no faculty members had written any books or monographs and only a few had published in scholarly journals.[25] Faculty members did begin to take a more active role in academic policies and curricular development than when Westminster was a high school and junior college. Although formerly the president and dean played determinative roles in establishing academic policies, trustees now delegated to the faculty the responsibility to "select subjects and fix courses of study and regulate the admission, discipline and dismissal or graduation of all students." In the 1947 self-study report, the president and academic dean noted the growing authority of faculty in curricular decisions. "At Westminster the faculty seems pleased to accept the responsibility of forming academic policy, and the administration seems pleased to recognize the Faculty's authority to do so."[26]

At monthly meetings, the faculty discussed academic issues and introduced curricular changes and modifications of institutional policies that affected classroom operations. They also discussed the needs and problems of individual students. At every meeting, faculty members gave progress reports on probationary students and identified others whose work was marginal. By pooling information, instructors felt they could more effectively assist students whose performance fell below institutional expectations.[27] Because the faculty had no constitution or bylaws, eligibility to vote was established by custom rather than legislation. "If this seems careless or indifferent, let it be remembered that the ideal of the Westminster faculty is community—Christian community," wrote a self-study committee. "Rules are useful, and perhaps we should have some, but the prevailing Spirit is more important."[28]

The end of the war ushered in an enrollment boom fueled by the G.I. Bill that enabled the struggling college to survive despite inadequate interdenominational support. In the fall of 1946, the total enrollment at American colleges was fifty-seven percent higher than the figures for 1939, and Westminster shared in this sudden upswing. In September 1945 9 men and 39 women constituted the student body; the following year 176 students were enrolled, including the largest freshman class in history: 71 veterans and 18 married students. By 1949–50, enrollment had climbed to 355, surpassing the minimum enrollment of 250 recommended by the Gage-Works report as necessary to sustain college work.[29] Older, experienced, and diverse in religious and social backgrounds, this new wave of students challenged long-standing Westminster social regulations and traditions, including use of alcohol on and off campus. Students were not inclined to report their peers, and administrators elected to discipline offenders only when their drinking was excessive and occurred in public. Although discouraging the use of tobacco, in 1946 administrators permitted smoking at the south end of Payne Gymnasium and in private automobiles in designated parking areas. Shortly thereafter students gained the right to smoke in the campus lounge and in certain dormitory areas. In an editorial in the student paper, Dean Watkins lamented the campus smokers, complaining about bad breath and stained teeth. He wrote, "Nothing looks quite as awkward and ridiculous as a person, particularly a girl, learning to smoke."[30]

A comparison of house rules in Foster and Ferry Halls for 1951–52 reveals significantly different standards for men and women. Men could come and go as they pleased. Women who planned to be away overnight had to secure a leave slip endorsed by the housemother before leaving campus, with no leaves granted unless they had written permission from their parents on file with the college. Women were limited to one night out until 11:30 P.M. from Monday through Thursday and one weekend evening until midnight. On Sunday evening curfew was 10:30 P.M. Both sexes could entertain guests in public parlors or lounges, but male guests in Ferry Hall had to conform to specified closing hours. Women's regulations contained a prohibition that lacked a counterpart in men's rules: "When entertaining men in any parlor, lights must be on and the door to the room open."[31]

Westminster campus social life centered around the Do Flop Inn, a student-run lounge located initially in Converse Hall and later shifting to the basement of Payne Gymnasium where it was enlarged into a smoker and lunch room. Described as "a delightful meeting place where students can gather to smoke a cigarette and settle the problems of the world," the Do Flop Inn became popular with students and faculty.[32] Invariably shrouded in a haze of cigarette smoke and filled with the sound of popular songs blaring from a nickel-a-play jukebox, the Do Flop Inn provided an outlet for student enterprise and gave them a special space, separate from academic or religious settings. Alumni from the time period mentioned Do Flop among their favorite college memories.[33]

Campus newspapers and yearbooks suggest that Westminster students of the 1940s and 1950s were more interested in altering their marital status than they were in changing the world. Their social culture was organized around dances, parties, and sporting events, and their concerns appeared to be centered on dating. "Who spends their time in back of Foster Hall in a beautiful Buick?" and "What dorm boy and what town girl have been chasing each other?"[34] Events listed in student publications included a Mother and Daughter Tea, Halloween Party, Christmas Cantata and Christmas Dance, Cowboy and Lady Dance, St. Patrick's Day Dance, and the Spring Formal, a "girls" date dance where the May Queen was crowned and where "boys" were relieved of obligations to pay for the evening's entertainment. Betty Co-Ed Week featured a visit from professional grooming stylists who lectured to women on such topics as hair styles, posture, manners, and make-up.[35]

Other important events on the social calendar included Westminster Day (formerly Founder's Day) and Homecoming. Commemorating their origins back to 1875, students attended chapel, participated in campus clean-up activities, and had a picnic lunch followed by water fights and a tug-of-war between freshmen and sophomores. Owing to the demand for physical activity, students were permitted to wear jeans, shorts, and tee-shirts, items otherwise forbidden by campus dress codes.[36] The Homecoming parade, with decorated floats sponsored by each class and various campus organizations, originated in Sugar House and ended on the campus track. The parade, lunch, dormitory open houses, and coronation of the Homecoming Queen preceded an afternoon football contest.[37]

Reports of student apathy ranging from lack of interest in intercollegiate athletics to noninvolvement in contemporary social issues appeared in student publications. Although students wrote occasional editorials questioning the morality of atomic warfare or racial segregation, their attention appeared to be focused elsewhere. Trying to arouse discussion, a *Parson* editorial queried, "As students and citizens, are you concerned enough about our democracy to inform yourselves and seek a channel of action on [these issues]?" No replies were forthcoming.[38] Students were not isolated from national societal problems in Salt Lake City, in which laws, ordinances, and informal agreements restricted the access of minorities, especially African Americans, to public accommodations. Nationally known performers such as Marian Anderson, Harry Belafonte, and Ella Fitzgerald were denied entry to major hotels or permitted restricted access such as using rear entrances and freight elevators.[39] On campus, few minority students matriculated at Westminster. Those who did reported no incidents of campus discrimination, but ventures into the city center provided different experiences.[40] In the early 1950s, a group of Asian American students and a single African American student attempted to purchase tickets to a downtown movie house. Pointing to the African American student, the ticket seller said that if he accompanied the group they would all have to sit in the second balcony. The Asian Americans refused to enter the theater.[41] On another occasion, an African American student was denied admission to a Nat King Cole concert. His white friends returned their tickets and wrote letters to the theater owners, protesting the discriminatory practices.[42]

Anticommunism also triggered responses from the Westminster campus community. Some Westminster students editorialized on the values of democracy and the evils of communism. In a student editorial in the *Campus Crier*, Walter J. Miller challenged Westminster students to defend the American way of life. "Let us not be lulled to sleep by the suave propaganda of the Communists. The only hope for America is eternal vigilance. If we fail, all the world will fall under the domination of the menace from the East."[43] In 1949 a Westminster student and pastor of the African Methodist Church, Jerry Ford, invited African American vocalist and actor Paul Robeson to sing and speak on race relations and brotherhood. Ford, however, had not cleared the event through administrative channels. During his presentation, Robeson mentioned that he had sent his son to school in Russia in order to avoid the racial prejudice in American society. Responding to newspaper accounts of the event, college trustees queried President Steele as to why Robeson, "an avowed Communist," had been permitted to speak on Westminster's campus.

Noting that he had been out of town at the time of Robeson's appearance, Steele nevertheless defended Robeson's right to freedom of speech, but assured board members that his own convictions had no place for totalitarianism in any form.[44]

During the postwar period, Westminster faculty and administration underwent regional accreditation that validated transfer credit and degrees. Since the Presbyterian Church, still the college's largest financial backer, required that its church-related colleges be accredited before receiving any grants or loans, Westminster trustees apprehensively applied for accreditation to the Northwest Association of Secondary and Higher Schools. When a Northwestern Association visitation team arrived on campus in 1947, they found much to commend about the daily operations of Westminster College: dedicated faculty deeply committed to classroom teaching, a sizable, hardworking student body that displayed exceptional institutional loyalty, and a religious ethos that reflected institutional traditions and goals. At the same time, the team enumerated major obstacles impeding full accreditation, including low faculty salaries, inadequate facilities and equipment, and insufficient financial resources. Immediate needs were additional qualified scientists and laboratory facilities and instrumentation to conduct college-level experiments. Library holdings were deemed inadequate for on-campus research. Until at least one of these deficiencies were remedied, the team recommended only provisional standing for a period of three years. At that time a decision would be made either to deny or affirm accreditation.[45]

No construction had been undertaken on campus during a twenty-year period between 1929 and 1949, and buildings already in place required painting, repairing, and upgrading of lighting, plumbing, and heating. With minimal funds available and high postwar construction costs, Westminster trustees decided to erect a modest science building that would temporarily sustain a credible science program. With support from the James A. Hogle family, the science building was completed and equipped for opening classes in September 1949.[46] Simultaneously trustees authorized the construction of Dane Hansen Stadium, a gift of the George Hansen family in memory of a son and brother, Lieutenant Dane Hansen, class of 1940, who had lost his life in World War II. The twelve-hundred-spectator stadium was dedicated at a special homecoming ceremony honoring Lieutenant Hansen's military career.[47] After a careful review of Westminster's progress, the Northwest Association granted Westminster full accreditation in 1950. Prior to that, the state superintendent of education, E. Allen Bateman, had approved Westminster to operate a certification program for secondary schoolteachers, followed by an elementary certification program, which became one of the most popular majors among Westminster students.[48]

Despite such external signs of progress, Westminster operated on a fragile financial base. Exacerbated by attrition due to the Korean War, the institutional deficit mounted. Neither Foster nor Ferry Halls were self-supporting. In 1952 16 women resided in Ferry Hall, which had a capacity of 60, and 32 men in Foster Hall, which had room for 120. Once again the college verged on closure. Steele explained to officials on the Presbyterian Board of Christian Education that "It is more than a financial crisis. It is one of morale and attitude. I won't know until the meeting Monday whether the trustees of Westminster think it is worth the struggle."[49] Westminster survived with assistance from the Presbyterian Church, but Steele decided that it was time for him to take another administrative assignment. Stating that a presidential change might stimulate growth, Steele submitted his resignation, effective June 30, 1952. He moved to become president of Carroll College, a Presbyterian Church-related institution in Waukesha, Wisconsin. Steele's departure and the death of his father-in-law, Herbert W. Reherd, the following month marked the end of a family association with Westminster that dated back to 1913. Trustee B. C. J. Wheatlake agreed to serve as interim president until a search committee could be organized and a new president located.[50]

During the interim presidency, a group of trustees led by Manford A. Shaw sought to enlist the expertise of world-famous architect Frank Lloyd Wright in designing a fine arts building for Westminster on the south bank of Emigration Creek. A delegation from Westminster visited Wright's architectural college in Arizona and persuaded Wright to undertake the fine arts center venture.[51] Amid widespread publicity, Wright arrived in Salt Lake City in April 1953 to survey the situation. Wright advised Westminster to sell its present campus and build a new one on the rolling hills near Big Cottonwood Canyon which would be entirely the product of his creative mind. College trustees approved in principle but would make no public announcement until money had been raised to build and endow the new campus. No funds materialized, and the project was quietly shelved.[52]

While negotiating with Wright, trustees were also searching for a new president. After consulting with Presbyterian and Methodist officials, the trustees appointed J. Richard Palmer in 1953 as Westminster's sixth president. In hiring Palmer, college trustees broke the precedent of having a Presbyterian minister in the presidential slot. Pastor of Emmanuel Methodist Church, a thousand-member congregation in Denver, Colorado, Palmer brought organizational experience and an ecumenical perspective to the position. Just prior to his appointment, the Rocky Mountain Methodist Conference announced its recognition and financial support of Westminster as its regional church-related college.[53] Palmer immediately launched a campaign fund for campus renovation, faculty salaries, and endowment. Campus improvements included refurbishing Foster Hall, rebuilding what students termed the Burma Road (a dirt road running through the campus), constructing a new student lounge, and general landscaping and painting. The financial campaign fell short of its $300,000 target leaving the college with an operating deficit of nearly $40,000. The Presbyterian and Methodist denominations contributed emergency funds to assist with the debt retirement, but even with their help, Westminster ended the fiscal year deep in red ink.[54]

In spite of the well-publicized financial campaigns and increased efforts to improve public relations and student recruitment, college officials faced mounting deficits. Comparisons with the other forty-five Presbyterian Church-related colleges indicate that Westminster ranked 44th in operating surplus, 45th in library budget (2.01 percent), 44th on dollars spent for maintenance and operation, 43rd in endowment income, 38th in salary at professorial rank, 30th at associate rank, and 34th at assistant rank.[55] When the Northwest Association team visited in 1957, it cited as major problems the turnover of faculty and administrators due primarily to deplorable salaries, a serious drop in enrollment, and poor library facilities. The committee recommended accreditation only for three years subject to a progress report at the end of two years.[56]

Under Palmer's leadership campus religious life flourished during the 1950s in the context of a national religious reawakening that swept the United States. Influenced by the "positive thinking" of Norman Vincent Peale and the revivalistic crusades of Billy Graham, Americans attended churches and synagogues in large numbers. Reflecting this, Westminster eliminated mandatory Sunday worship services for dormitory residents, encouraging students to attend the church of their choice.[57] Chapel remained an important feature of campus religious life, however; by 1948, students gathered twice a week for chapel with a third period on Friday set aside for what one student described as "hilarious" student convocations.[58] A decade later, religious services were confined to Wednesdays with Mondays and Fridays designated for athletic pep rallies, student forums, and lectures.[59] Absence from chapel services or convocations resulted in loss of academic credit or suspension from college. Student handbooks warned new arrivals that if they could not abide by Westminster's religious requirements, they had chosen the wrong college and were advised, "It is not too late to transfer."[60]

Volunteer religious activities were directed by the Student Christian Association (SCA), the largest, most popular campus religious organization. An outgrowth of the earlier YMCA and YWCA groups, the SCA sponsored Bible study and discussion groups and a variety of community actions. One of its most successful programs was the deputation teams which began with only a handful of participants and gradually attracted fifty to sixty students who had a wide range of academic interests and came from varied religious backgrounds. At the invitation of regional congregations, groups of Westminster students conducted Sunday morning worship services, leading prayers, providing special music, and giving sermons. Students not only voluntarily gave up their weekends but also paid their own travel expenses. "Our student service work permeates life, it doesn't avoid it," said religion professor Joseph Uemura. "Our religion is part and parcel of the warp and woof of that life."[61] Westminster students also participated in a service program supervised by faculty members and local pastors to promote congregational lay leadership. Students in the program attended a one-hour class on campus taught by a member of the religion department and assisted in Sunday school teaching and worship services at a local parish. According to Palmer, the service project attracted some of Westminster's best students and prepared them for responsible church membership.[62]

Westminster students encountered changes in the content and methodology of the academic study of religion. Protestant educators for a number of years advocated broadening so-called Bible classes into inclusive theological and philosophical examinations of religious issues and questions. Westminster reflected this trend as early as 1938 when the Presbyterian Board of Christian Education enlarged the scope of what church-related colleges could include in biblical curricula. At that time Robert Steele demonstrated at a special meeting of Westminster trustees the configuration of Bible study to include a range of topics.[63] As research universities dominated in the twentieth century, church-related colleges emulated their stress on professionalization and academic excellence. While not abandoning the concept of piety, Presbyterian educators emphasized the importance of developing academically sound religion departments. In 1953 President Palmer recommended the establishment of the Department of Bible, Philosophy, and Religion and reconfigured religion classes from one- to two-hour sessions in order to give them more academic status.[64]

Religion was not the only aspect of college life that underwent change during the 1950s. Bolstered by the rise of television, intercollegiate football developed a following on campuses throughout the country.

Westminster had resumed nonscholarship intercollegiate athletics in 1946 after a six-year wartime interim, fortified by an influx of talent from returning servicemen. Students and alumni confronted President Palmer, arguing that scholarship football and basketball offered sources of revenue and name recognition. They opposed Westminster remaining in the Intermountain Collegiate Athletic Conference, composed solely of junior colleges, because it caused people in the surrounding states to classify Westminster as a two-year institution. By scheduling four-year peer institutions and producing winning teams, Westminster could both recruit new students and attract contributions from alumni and friends.[65]

Initially Palmer resisted pressure to involve Westminster in competitive intercollegiate athletics. When several influential trustees indicated their willingness to support the movement, however, he acquiesced. At the end of the 1954 season, Palmer announced that Westminster would expand its athletic program and cease competition with junior colleges. Beginning in 1955, Westminster offered a grant-in-aid program for prospective athletes and hired Alvin W. Mercer, a highly successful coach from the Palo Alto, California, high school, to serve as head football coach and athletic director. During the next four years Mercer's football teams won twenty-nine games, lost five, and tied two. Basketball teams won three Colorado-Utah college championships and were NAIA regional champions in district seven.[66]

The athletic program was not accompanied by increased revenues, neither at the gate nor from private donors. Overshadowed by Brigham Young University and the University of Utah athletic programs, Westminster's accomplishments seemed insignificant. The total athletic budget prior to Mercer's arrival was only $9,000 with a deficit of approximately $7,000. In 1955 Mercer proposed a budget for the upcoming year of $42,354 with an anticipated income of about $4,500.[67] Given Westminster's financial situation, trustees would not approve Mercer's request. Instead, they voted to discontinue intercollegiate football for a minimum of three years and directed Palmer to inform students and faculty of their decision.[68] In a rare public display of opposition to administrative policy, Westminster students hung and burned President Palmer in effigy from a wrought iron gate. Following the conflagration, they went to the student lounge where a dummy football player lay in state beneath a large cross surrounded by flowers and students eulogized their departed facsimile athlete at a mock ceremony. The demonstration ended only when Dean Watkins arrived on the scene and ordered them to disperse.[69] In the midst of the acrimony over athletics, Palmer resigned, a reprieve for Mercer and his football advocates. Encouraged by a successful student money-raising campaign and by contributions from several trustees, Westminster reinstated the football program but reduced the amount of scholarship aid to athletes.[70]

Seeking strong leadership during a period of financial crisis and community unrest, trustees in 1956 selected as president Frank E. Duddy, Jr., Westminster's first nonministerial chief executive. A graduate of Harvard with a Ph.D. in modern European history, Duddy was a university professor with extensive teaching experience, including ten years at the U.S. Naval Academy. He had strong Christian ecumenical commitments emanating from his upbringing in a Congregational manse. Through his initiative, in 1958 the United Church of Christ established formal ties with Westminster, joining the Presbyterian and Methodist churches in a unique tripartite interdenominational support group.[71]

Picking up on the athletic situation, one of Duddy's first priorities was to reduce the cost of intercollegiate football, which consumed too high a percentage of college operating funds. Following the 1958 season, Duddy released Mercer as athletic director and football coach, an action that received considerable attention in the local press. While publicly praising Mercer for his accomplishments, Duddy informed Northwest Association of Secondary and Higher Schools officials that Mercer had "never really [been] a part of the College community or able to understand the proper place in it of the athletic program."[72] Even with this decision, competitive athletics proved to be too fiscally burdensome. Student athletes received nearly forty percent of Westminster's scholarships, which a visiting accrediting team termed out of proportion for a small liberal arts school like Westminster.[73] After prolonged discussions, college trustees in 1961 voted to eliminate intercollegiate football. In an all-college assembly, Duddy explained the decision as based on problems of finding a suitable conference in which to play and excessive costs. It was imperative, he said, "to get out of an activity which costs far more than is warranted by the returns, in finance, morale, publicity, and otherwise."[74] Although a large segment of the student population opposed the cutback, they made no formal complaint nor did they hold any public demonstrations.

Having resolved temporarily the conflict over intercollegiate athletics, Duddy embarked on a ten-year development campaign to create a campus adequate for about eight hundred full-time students and to make faculty salaries competitive with similar institutions. Loans from the Housing and Home Finance Administration totaling $1 million enabled Westminster to erect two badly needed dormitories, Hogle Hall (1959) and Carleson Hall (1962). The former building was named in recognition of the James A. Hogle family for their many years of support and service to the college, and the latter in honor of the Harry E. and Fred A. Carleson families, who provided furnishings for the building. Completion of the new dormitories opened space in Foster and Ferry Halls for classroom and office facilities.[75]

Duddy also tightened admission standards and provided special programs for exceptional students. Westminster had routinely admitted high school graduates who presented a C average in all their total course work. Effective January 1961, entering students had to demonstrate a C average in academic subjects in order to qualify for admission. Students unable to meet this standard were accepted on a probationary basis and assigned to upper-class tutors who helped them adjust to college-level work. Two years later, Westminster began requiring Scholastic Aptitude Test (SAT) scores from students entering directly from secondary schools. These scores were not employed to regulate admissions but to provide additional information about entering students.[76] An honors program initiated in 1959 placed superior first-year students in special sections of required history and religion. Taught by department chairs, the program included group discussions and individual special projects. A second phase of the program permitted selected upper-class students to participate in interdisciplinary honors seminars.[77] Even so, Duddy acknowledged that economic considerations forced Westminster into a de facto open door admissions policy. "Our students are not yet of the highest possible type either in ability or in dedication to the ideals of the institution. They are, however, a more able (and restless) lot than they used to be."[78] A Northwest Association accreditation team articulated the problem more directly by charging that the college had "distressingly low admission standards." The first-year class profile for the 1964 fall semester showed that nearly forty percent of the men and twenty-five percent of the women had SAT scores of below 400 out of a possible 800 points. About twenty-five percent of the men and women scored below 400 in mathematics. In the distribution of high school grade point averages, one-third of the men and ten percent of the females had averages below a 2.0. The accreditation team concluded that the open admissions policy was a contributing factor to poor retention of students.[79]

During a period when some universities instituted loyalty oaths and dismissed faculty whose political views ran counter to popular sentiment, Duddy advocated academic freedom. The Salt Lake community, however, occasionally censured speakers from the college. A Westminster economics professor, allegedly identifying himself as speaking for the entire college, objected to the handling of a witness at a rate hearing before the Utilities Commission. Another professor identified in the press as from

Westminster leveled charges of corruption against a number of local businesses. Responding to business leaders, Duddy affirmed the faculty's right to free speech and reminded complainants that Westminster's teachers could exercise their rights of citizenship so long as they did not speak officially for the college.[80]

Duddy also worked on enhancing relationships with the Church of Jesus Christ of Latter-day Saints. The LDS Church was assimilating into mainstream American culture at a national level and in Utah had greatly reduced long-standing tensions between Latter-day Saints and Protestant minorities. By the mid-1950s, under the leadership of David O. McKay, the Mormon Church was contributing to Westminster's stabilization fund. In some years, Mormons actually outnumbered Presbyterians in the student body.[81] When asked by out-of-state people how he related to Utah Mormons, President Duddy reported that his answer, "Just fine," invariably was a conversation stopper.[82]

Ultimately Duddy fell victim to mounting financial instability and declining institutional morale. Westminster continued to balance its budget with gifts from outside sources because tuition covered only fifty-two percent of operating expenses.[83] This meant that revenues from fundraising campaigns were utilized to offset operational deficits rather than to increase faculty salaries or maintain the physical plant. As a result, tensions between faculty and administrators over budgetary priorities and program development led to a number of faculty and staff resignations and dismissals in 1963. Students, still unhappy about Duddy's decision to drop intercollegiate athletics, questioned administrative policies and expressed concern about the flurry of faculty resignations. During these troubled months, Duddy received an offer from Marietta College to become president of that Ohio institution. Although reluctant to leave Salt Lake City, Duddy informed the college trustees in February of his intention to resign effective June 1, 1963.[84]

The evening before the public announcement of Duddy's resignation, nine Westminster students were arrested for underage drinking and destruction of property at a local tavern. This marked the beginning of an extended period of campus turmoil and unrest. A local municipal court placed the offenders on six-months' probation, and the dean of student life suspended them from classes. A group of upper-class male students objected and organized a walkout that, according to eyewitnesses, involved some three hundred students and local alumni.[85] Faculty also voiced displeasure. In a sermon in chapel, Chaplain McDowell, who subsequently resigned his position, said that unlike the goldfish swallowing students of the 1940s and the panty raids of the

1950s, "the student of today chooses involvement and demonstration as a responsible method of redress of wrong. The students of today are no longer content to be treated as immature children, or as objects of exploitation, but demand a fair hearing, response, and consultation from their elders."[86] The baby boomers were making an impact on Westminster's campus.

NOTES

1. In a study of church-sponsored institutions of higher education conducted by the Danforth Foundation in 1966, the authors singled out Westminster for its unique tripartite sponsorship "that deserves to be studied carefully by other institutions." Manning M. Patillo, Jr. and Donald M. Mackenzie, *Church-Sponsored Higher Education in the United States* (Washington, D.C., 1966), 206.

2. WC Trustee Minutes, 2 October and 14 November 1942. The WC Trustee Minutes are all located in the WC Archives. See also Nyman, "History of Westminster College," 27–29.

3. WC Trustee Minutes, 10 September 1941. A similar situation developed with an appointment in history. A New York City resident who agreed verbally to a contract finally secured sufficient gasoline coupons to embark on a hurried trip to Salt Lake City. Steele received an airmail letter from Ohio two weeks before opening classes in which the teacher stated that he had changed his mind and had accepted another position in the buckeye state. WC Trustee Minutes, 11 October 1944.

4. Westminster received special grants from the Presbyterian Restoration Fund inaugurated following World War II and from Presbyterian women's organizations as well as individual Presbyterian donors. Grants ranging from $10,000 to $50,000 helped the college to upgrade facilities and reduce operating debts. See WC Trustee Minutes, 2 August and 20 September 1960.

5. *Utah Westminster* 28 (September 1941): 1; and David Steele, interview by author, 15 June 1995.

6. WC Trustee Minutes, 2 October 1942.

7. WC Trustee Minutes, 21 June 1944.

8. "Origin of the Interdenominational Idea for Westminster College" (n.d. [c.1945], typescript), n.p., WC Archives.

9. WC Trustee Minutes, 29 December 1942.

10. "Origin of the Interdenominational Idea for Westminster College," n.p., WC Archives.

11. George A. Works and H. M. Gage, "Statement on Westminster College," 20 January 1944, 3, WC Archives.

12. WC Trustee Minutes, 30 June 1944.

13. WC Trustee Minutes, 29 December 1942.

14. WC Trustee Minutes, 24 March 1944.

15. WC Trustee Minutes, 13 April 1945; and Minutes of the Synod of Utah, 30 August 1945. Trustee minutes indicate considerable ambivalence regarding the college's relationship to the Presbyterian Church. On the one hand, the trustees did not want to cut ties with the national church and lose financial support. On the other hand, they did not want to be seen locally as sectarian. Their compromise was to maintain national

Presbyterian connections, but to emphasize interdenominational relationships regionally. See WC Trustee Minutes, 10 November 1944.

16. WC Trustee Minutes, 11 September 1945. The following year Westminster sold Gunton Chapel to a local businessman for $10,200, and the money was placed in a trust fund for the construction of a new chapel at some future date. A room in Converse Hall was set aside for chapel services and designated Gunton Memorial Chapel.

17. "Commencement Exercises," *Utah Westminster* 32 (July 1945): 2–3; and "Graduation" 32 (June 1946): 1. Hodges's photograph is in *Etosian*, 1946, 24. According to incomplete college records, the last baccalaureate degree awarded prior to 1945 went to Roderick Thompson in 1904.

18. "Fees and Expenses," *Utah Westminster* 31 (June 1945): 21; and "Course Requirements," *Utah Westminster* 32 (June 1946): 36–37.

19. "Seventy-first School Year," *Utah Westminster* 32 (October 1945): 1.

20. "President's Report," WC Trustee Minutes, 9 February 1955.

21. WC Trustee Minutes, 1 June 1949; and "Nursing Education," *Utah Westminster* 38 (May 1952): 97–98. The required academic courses were given on the Westminster campus and the professional courses were conducted by medical and nursing staff at St. Mark's Hospital.

22. "General Engineering," *Utah Westminster* 40 (May 1954): 51–55; "Westminster's Cooperative 4-Year Tool Engineering Course," *Utah Westminster* 42 (May 1956): 53–56; "Westminster Selects Woman Engineer," *Deseret News and Telegram*, 2 September 1954.

23. WC Trustee Minutes, 21 March 1946. Subsequently enrollment goals were expanded to include a student body in the eight hundred to one thousand range. "Westminster College Fact Sheet," 1956, WC Archives.

24. WC Trustee Minutes, 3 April 1947. Statistics on faculty religious preference after 1945 are not recorded in college publications as they had been during Reherd's presidency. At least one professor of Mormon background dates from this era (1946), and there may have been others. From interviews with former Westminster instructors, it appears that by the late 1950s the question of church membership was not a part of hiring procedures. As late as 1965–66, however, the *Faculty Handbook* specified that instructors were expected to be "Christian in professional functions and personal life." For a discussion of this topic, see Keith Wilson, "The Process of Secularization at Westminster College of Salt Lake City: A Case Study" (Ph.D. diss., Brigham Young University, 1995), 163–68.

25. "Statement of Criteria Prepared for the Commission on Higher Schools of the Northwest Association of Secondary and Higher Schools," October 1947, 61–62, WC Archives.

26. Ibid., 62–63. Westminster granted tenure after a three-year probationary period and provided optional participation in TIAA retirement program with the college and faculty member contributing five percent. In 1947 only six professors had availed themselves of this option. No sabbatical program was provided.

27. "Statement of Criteria Prepared for the Commission on Higher Schools of the Northwest Association of Secondary and Higher Schools," October 1947, 34–35, WC Archives; and WC Trustee Minutes, 3 October 1947.

28. "Westminster Self-Evaluation Report," August 1957, I-1-b, WC Archives.

29. "President's Report," WC Trustee Minutes, 28 October 1946 and 30 October 1952. See also "Progress Report Submitted to the Commission on Higher Schools of the Northwest Association of Secondary and Higher Schools," October 1959, 3, WC

Archives. Although enrollment declined during the Korean War, it gradually recovered, reaching 450 by the end of the decade.

30. "Campus News," *Campus Crier*, 18 October 1946, 2; "Ferry Hall," November 1947, 2; and "Editorial," *Parson*, 6 November 1953, 5.

31. "Ferry Hall—Rules for 1951–52" and "Foster Hall—Rules for 1951–52," WC Archives.

32. *Etosian*, 1947, 34; and 1949, 8.

33. Herb Dunn, "I Remember," *Newscope* (fall 1984): 10. The Do Flop Inn was started in 1946 by Virginia Moffat, Mary Kumereles, Fannie Zaharias, and Mrs. Baldwin. See *Etosian*, 1949, 8.

34. "Campus Chatter," *Campus Crier*, 18 October 1946. Such comments were typical during this time period.

35. *Westminster Student Handbook*, 1954–55, 20–24.

36. Levis, peddlepushers, and shorts were not permitted in Converse Hall or any classrooms. See *Westminster Student Handbook*, 1954–55, 18.

37. *Westminster College Student Handbook*, 1954–55, 16–24. Students found it necessary to confer with the college president to permit women to wear jeans on Westminster Day because many of them would not have time to go home and change clothes. See Student Council Minutes, 10 May 1949, WC Archives.

38. "Editorial," *Parson*, 1 November 1956, WC Archives.

39. Alexander and Allen, *Mormons and Gentiles: A History of Salt Lake City*, 262–63.

40. Westminster had only a few Black students at this time, and they were natives of Africa rather than American-born. A small group of Asian Americans of Japanese and Chinese descent became an integral part of Westminster's student body, many of whom were associated with Cameron House in San Francisco, a Presbyterian inner-city mission located in the heart of the tourist district known as Chinatown.

41. David Ng, interview by author, 4 September 1996, WC Archives.

42. "Reappraisal Study of Westminster College," June 1963, 9.

43. Walter J. Miller, "The Menace of Communism," WC Trustee Minutes, 5 May 1948, reproduced from *Campus Crier*, n.d.,

44. WC Trustee Minutes, 13 October 1949, WC Archives. See also "Paul Robeson Sings in Ogden," *Salt Lake Tribune*, 3 March 1947; "Robeson Spirituals Highlight Concert," *Salt Lake Tribune*, 6 March 1947; "Westminster Pupils Hear Paul Robeson," *Deseret News*, 6 March 1947.

45. "Westminster Self-Evaluation Report," August 1957, A-1-2, WC Archives.

46. WC Trustee Minutes, 2 October 1947. For background on the Hogle family, see "Salt Lake Engineer Wins Success," *Salt Lake Tribune*, 3 November 1946.

47. "Stadium Dedicated," *Salt Lake Tribune*, 2 October 1949. While constructing Hansen Stadium, an old campus landmark fell victim to earthmoving equipment. The Coyner Gate, located at the east end of Wilson Avenue about one block west of Converse Hall and consisting of two massive sandstone pillars, was demolished. Dedicated in 1915 by the Synod of Utah in memory of John M. Coyner, founder of the Salt Lake Collegiate Institute, the twin pillars and a double row of black locust trees extending up to the campus provided an artistic frame for early photographs of Converse Hall.

48. *Utah Westminster* 51 (January 1948): 1; and WC Trustee Minutes, 25 May 1950.

49. Robert Steele to Fay Campbell, 16 March 1951, WC Archives; and "President's Report," WC Trustee Minutes, 30 October 1952.

50. WC Trustee Minutes, Executive Committee Report, 9 May 1952; and "Dr. Reherd," *Utah Westminster* 38 (August 1952): 1–4.

51. WC Trustee Minutes, 30 October 1952.

52. WC Trustee Minutes, 8 May and 16 June 1953. See also "Almost Frank Lloyd Wright," *Parson*, 3 November 1978, 2.

53. "Introducing Our New President," *Utah Westminster* 38 (July 1952): 1–2; and WC Trustee Minutes, 7 July 1952.

54. WC Trustee Minutes, 25 February 1955; and J. Richard Palmer to Trustees, 11 January 1955, WC Archives.

55. "Memorandum to Board Members," WC Trustee Minutes, 6 June 1958 and 18 May 1963.

56. "Visiting Committee Report, Northwest Association of Secondary and Higher Schools," September 1957, 16, WC Archives.

57. "General Dormitory Regulations," *Utah Westminster* 35 (May 1949): 19; *Utah Westminster* 39 (May 1953): 16.

58. *Etosian*, 1948, 50.

59. "Westminster Report," 1952, 4, WC Archives.

60. *Westminster Student Handbook* 1954–55, 16, WC Archives. Periodic attempts to revamp and revitalize chapel programs in the 1950s met with mixed responses. Students deemed the coercive aspect of chapel more problematic than the content of its services. An editorial in the student papers concluded that Wednesday chapel "is about the most unanimous gripe on campus." "Editorial," *Parson*, 13 March 1959, 2.

61. "This College Has a New 'Team'—God's," *Parade Magazine* (12 September 1954); reprinted in *Utah Westminster* 40 (October 1954), supp: 5–7.

62. J. Richard Palmer to Fay Campbell, 23 February 1955, WC Archives. Westminster also instituted an undergraduate degree program for Christian educators in lieu of seminary training. The Presbyterian Church created the office of certified church educator and granted a certificate to men or women who had received a bachelor's degree from an accredited Presbyterian college which offered an approved program of preparation for service in Christian education. Adopted almost exclusively by women, the certified church educator program eventually was discontinued due to dissatisfaction with working conditions and pay scales. Westminster dropped its program in 1963. See Elizabeth Verdesi, *In but Still Out: Women in the Church* (Philadelphia, 1976), 130–31.

63. WC Trustee Minutes, 29 April and 15 September 1938.

64. Emphasizing that religion should be presented in a manner "INTELLECTUALLY RESPECTABLE" and by a "DESIRABLE PERSON," preferably with strong academic credentials, Palmer announced the appointment of Joseph Uemura, a Phi Beta Kappa graduate of the University of Denver and recipient of a Th.D. degree from the Iliff School of Theology. See WC Trustee Minutes, 16 June 1953. In an effort to involve townspeople and local clergy in academic theological dialogue, Westminster initiated an annual college theological conference in 1959. Highly publicized, the conference featured nationally known theologians such as Theodore A. Gill, president of San Francisco Theological Seminary, and Nels F. S. Ferre, professor at Andover Newton Theological Seminary. Due to high costs and poor attendance, however, the conference was discontinued in 1961. See WC Trustee Minutes, 24 February 1959; and "Reappraisal Study of Westminster College, Salt Lake City, Utah," June 1963, 9, WC Archives.

65. Subsequently a public relations survey conducted for Westminster by the Dudley Parsons Company recommended that "the trustees and administration ought to explore the

possibility of replacing at some future time the present athletic program, especially in football, with a strong intramural program." "A Report to President of Westminster College," 5 April 1956, conducted by the Dudley L. Parsons Company, New York, 3, WC Archives.

66. Howard D. Richardson to W. Fred Abrogast, 23 December 1963, WC Archives.

67. WC Trustee Minutes, 21 October 1954 and 28 March 1956. Mercer received an annual salary of $7,000, almost double that of most senior professors.

68. WC Trustee Minutes, 28 March 1956.

69. *Deseret News*, 3 April 1956.

70. The college continued to offer forty athletic scholarships but only at a maximum of eighty percent of tuition.

71. WC Trustee Minutes, 14 August 1956 and 13 May 1958. The United Church of Christ was formed in 1957 by a union of the Evangelical and Reformed Church and the Congregational Christian Churches. In affiliating with the United Church of Christ, the college noted that the new relationship "involves no denominational control or invasion of the autonomy of the college, and does not prevent further affiliation with other church bodies." WC Trustee Minutes, 16 June 1958.

72. "Progress Report Submitted to the Commission on Higher Schools of the Northwest Association of Secondary and Higher Schools," October 1959, 7, WC Archives.

73. "Visiting Committee Report [Northwest Association of Secondary and Higher Schools] Westminster College, September 1957," WC Trustee Minutes, 57.

74. "Trustees Vote to Drop Football," *Utah Westminster* 48 (December 1961): 2; and WC Trustee Minutes, 19 December 1961.

75. WC Trustee Minutes, 4 August 1959 and 18 September 1962. See also, "Hogle Hall Completed," *Utah Westminster* 46 (August 1960): 2; and "Residence Hall Open to Students," *Utah Westminster* 49 (September 1962): 1–2.

76. "Academic Policies," *Utah Westminster* 48 (April 1962): 34.

77. "Honors Program for Gifted Students," *Utah Westminster* 46 (October 1959): 1.

78. "Reappraisal Study of Westminster College," June 1963, 4–5, WC Archives.

79. "Report to the Higher Commission of the Northwest Association of Secondary and Higher Schools by Visitation Committee October 25–27, 1964," 6–7, WC Archives.

80. WC Trustee Minutes, 15 May 1962; and "Reappraisal Study of Westminster College," June 1963, 7–8, WC Archives.

81. The LDS Church gave $5,000 annually in unrestricted funds, and President Palmer reported that church officials "regarded Westminster highly." "President's Report," WC Trustee Minutes, 5 April 1956; J. Frank Robinson to I. George Nace, 19 July 1954; and Sterling McMurrin, interview by author, 1 June 1994.

82. Frank E. Duddy, Jr., "Westminster College and the Synod of California," 11 January 1960, WC Archives. Despite these changing attitudes, many Westminster officials continued to denigrate Mormon theology. "If there is a people anywhere needing enlightenment, sound Christian doctrine, a chance to escape the shame of a shoddy religious structure, and an opportunity to find intellectual respectability, more than the Mormon people, I have yet to hear about them." J. Richard Palmer to Fay Campbell, 23 February 1955, WC Archives. Occasionally articles about Westminster emanating from noncampus sources had an anti-Mormon slant. F. S. Dick Wichman, "Westminster College: In Heart of Mormon Empire," *Southern California Presbyterian* (July 1956): 10.

83. George W. Renneisen to Frank Duddy, 27 May 1957, WC Archives.

84. WC Trustee Minutes, 19 February 1963; and "College Chief Resigns at Westminster," *Salt Lake Tribune*, 20 February 1963.

85. WC Trustee Minutes, 19 February and 23 April 1963, "Walk-Out," *Parson*, 1 March 1963, 2; and "Student Dissensions," 19 April 1963, 1.

86. "Chaplain McDowell Resigns," *Parson*, 19 April 1963, 1. See also WC Trustee Minutes, 23 April 1963.

8

A College of Change

Westminster is a college of change. Through the years there has been an unfolding definition of its educational role and an ever-evolving development of its character, its values, its perspectives.
—"Change and Purpose: A Centennial Perspective of Westminster College," August 1975.

Adhering to its historic mandate, Westminster entered the 1960s as a small church-related liberal arts college with a mixture of residential and town students, most of whom were recent high school graduates. It emerged a decade later a different educational institution, altered not so much by philosophical choice as by pragmatic response to a changing educational environment. Westminster modified its liberal arts curriculum to accommodate a variety of professional and career-oriented courses and programs, some of which were offered off campus and in conjunction with other educational institutions. Enrollment patterns also shifted, with the eighteen- to twenty-one-year-old residential cohort joined by a contingent of commuters and second-career matriculants generally over twenty-five years of age. The college also ended legal ties with the national Presbyterian denomination for covenant relationships with regional synods, and it reduced commitments to the Methodist Church and the United Church of Christ regional organizations.

Nowhere was change more evident than in the selection of presidents. Instead of seeking candidates through denominational channels, Westminster turned elsewhere for institutional leadership. Following Frank Duddy's resignation in 1963, college trustees selected W. Fred Arbogast, a Westminster alumnus and former principal of East and

Highland High Schools in Salt Lake City. A recipient of graduate degrees from the University of Denver and the University of Utah, Arbogast served as president for five years. His successor, Manford A. Shaw (from 1968 to 1976), also a Westminster graduate, held degrees from Yale University and the University of Utah. Shaw was followed by Helmut Hofmann (from 1976 to 1979), a Ph.D. from Heidelberg University, whose previous employment included academic vice presidencies at Weber State College and Westminster College. These three men were neither ordained clergy nor active leaders in their respective denominations.[1]

The only constant in Westminster's changing educational environment was its ongoing struggle for financial stability that culminated in a declaration of financial exigency in 1979 and major cutbacks in programs and services. Even during good financial years, the college survived by previously used practices of taking out short-term bank loans, borrowing from endowment funds, deferring campus maintenance, and keeping faculty and staff salaries low. In spite of several successful financial campaigns, Westminster fell victim to a combination of uncontrolled expansion and loss of denominational funding that brought the college to the brink of closure. But such fiscal conditions failed to quench the determination that had characterized the college since its inception. Fred Arbogast, a popular choice among students and faculty, summoned optimism and stability on the troubled campus when he assumed the presidency in 1963.[2] A solid academician, Arbogast envisioned a period of steady growth based on attracting a larger percentage of local students by aggressive recruiting, varied course offerings, and flexible scheduling. Begun on a modest scale, Arbogast's curricular modifications resulted in enrollment growth that carried over into the next decade.

A new program initiated in 1966 in affiliation with the American International Academy of Salt Lake City enabled Westminster to grant first-year credit to approximately 270 of the 500 high school graduates who participated in a summer study tour of Europe. The tour featured visits to such cities as London, Paris, Geneva, and Rome with sidetrips to other archaeological and historical sites. Westminster faculty and administrators reviewed the program for academic standards and sent three of its faculty members as teachers and advisors. Student tuition covered the complete cost of the program including special office staffing on the college campus.[3] Westminster joined forces with Kelsey-Ellis Air service in 1967 to offer the first aviation course offered by a four-year college in the intermountain area.[4] During the same year, Arbogast initiated a new six-week summer school program that proved popular and profitable. Expanded to an eight-week session, the summer school program provided service to local students and utilized campus facilities.[5] Concurrently, Westminster offered graduate courses when trustees approved a new master of arts in teaching degree in elementary education designed primarily for in-service teachers who took part-time evening and summer courses to fulfill degree requirements.[6] Continuing education had its beginnings through a Management Center that provided courses for business supervisors in the Salt Lake City area. Using a quarter-system calendar, classes averaging about thirty-five to forty students met once a week and earned two credit hours. Another program conducted in cooperation with the Craft House, an adult continuing education institution, offered two or three undergraduate credit-hour art classes taught by qualified non-Westminster faculty. Courses not available in the regular college program, such as wood carving and basic design, were offered to small classes of seven to ten students.[7]

Applying for federal grants and loans that became available during the John Kennedy and Lyndon Johnson administrations, especially the Educational Facilities Act of 1963 and the Higher Education Act of 1965, Arbogast oversaw the planning and construction of much-needed campus buildings. When he assumed the presidency, trustees were considering plans to remodel Foster Hall to provide more facilities than those available in Converse Hall. Arbogast advocated a more extensive project that included a modern library, an administration building, a student union, and additions and renovations to existing structures. By demonstrating that the master plan could be financed through a combination of federal loans and local gifts, Arbogast received approval from the board of trustees to move forward with campus expansion.[8]

Completion of the Nightingale Memorial Library in 1964, named in honor of W. T. Nightingale, one of the primary benefactors and supporters of the project, marked the first time in Westminster's history that the college had a free-standing library with adequate shelf space for an expanding collection of books and periodicals. The new library contained open stacks for sixty thousand volumes, a conference room, an audio-visual center, and an archival area.[9] Other buildings in the master plan were Bamberger Hall (1967) for administrative offices, a student union building, additions to the gymnasium and science buildings, and the renovation of Converse Hall. Although no longer in office when all of the latter projects were completed, Arbogast arranged for government funding and initiated local financial campaigns.[10]

Arbogast inherited a new generation of students who questioned the values on which academic communities had operated since colonial times. Talented, idealistic, and assertive, they sought participatory rights in the educational process through demonstrations, sit-ins, and walk-outs patterned after the Berkeley student revolts of 1964–65. Westminster felt the impact of social change, debating issues such as civil rights, the war in Vietnam, and feminism, all of which impinged on pedagogy and administrative policies in ways that had not been anticipated a decade earlier.[11] The behavior of resident students also changed in the 1960s. In a letter to returning residents of Carleson Hall, the dean of students recited a litany of offenses that had occurred during the 1964–65 academic year, such as theft, water and shaving cream fights that resulted in building damage and destruction of property, and abuse of recreational equipment. Beer parties in rooms, loud noise and profanity, and sporadic raids on the women's dormitory added to the problems.[12]

Although Westminster students did not choose the route of extreme protests, they displayed an interest in self-determination. "We don't wear dirty sweatshirts or grow long Beatles hair-dos and we don't picket much," said junior Marilyn Pierson, "but this is not to say that we ridicule the right to do so, or that we don't rebel when we see the need. All in all we are a mild-mannered group, but we don't want to be pushed around either. Have you noticed?"[13] Another student, reflecting on reasons for the riots in Berkeley and Columbia Universities, thought that the fundamental problem was the lack of participation by students in college affairs, especially curriculum development, methods of instruction, class attendance, and faculty evaluation.[14] Westminster students also had been pressing for more participation in nonacademic disciplinary matters. An editorial in the *Parson* proposed a student court. "It is an attempt to bring to this community a freedom which it has long lacked," said the writer, who called for student support and administrative action.[15] After formal endorsement by the Westminster faculty, trustees in 1963 approved on an experimental basis a five-member student court elected by the students' peers. Protocol indicated that decisions by the student judiciary could be appealed to a review board consisting of three faculty and two students, subject to final review by the college president.[16] Although the court had its critics among both students and faculty, results demonstrated that students could act responsibly.[17]

Changing religious attitudes also impacted Westminster's campus life. Many students in the 1960s claimed only a nominal church affiliation and expressed little interest in campus religious activities. Faculty members in the Department of Philosophy and Religion observed that more than half of their students appeared indifferent or antagonistic to organized religion. A random survey conducted by an urban sociology class revealed that seventy-six percent of Westminster students considered themselves to be "inactive."[18] The revised constitution of the Student Government Association (SGA), approved in 1960, contained no references to Christian values or church relationships, and administrators noted that SGA leaders were not necessarily men and women of strong Christian commitment as had been true in previous student generations.[19]

In spring of 1965, student government leaders circulated a petition calling for the abolition of required weekly chapel. Citing "too much religious indoctrination," the students complained that college administrators had never provided a rationale for required chapel. "Yet we continue to be the victims of religious onslaught every Wednesday morning when one minister or another gives us the usual 'Sunday school' sermon."[20] To reinforce the claims of their petition, students organized a "walkout" of chapel that found wide support. Arbogast raised the possibility of ending required chapel at a meeting of trustees in December 1964, but when some board members expressed shock at the proposal, Arbogast moved on to another subject.[21] He raised the issue again in September 1965, this time asking trustees either to affirm or reject the policy of required chapel. After a lengthy discussion, Donald G. Christiansen, pastor of the Wasatch Presbyterian Church, moved that required chapel be ended and that efforts be undertaken to develop a sound religious life program on campus. His motion passed unanimously. In affirming the change, Arbogast assured trustees that it did not marginalize religious life at Westminster College and added, "We are determined to strengthen and emphasize it more than ever."[22]

Subsequent efforts to encourage religious activities included the addition of a college chaplain in 1966 as a part-time member of the Department of Religion. He coordinated religious activities and was available for religious and personal counseling. The college also replaced Religious Emphasis Week with Living Issues Week, which featured guest speakers on contemporary topics designed to stimulate critical thinking and discussion instead of issues of Christian commitment and vocational choices. Topics included "Involvement or Apathy," "Civil Disobedience," "The U.S. Role as Big Brother," and "Religion, Relevant or Irrelevant?" One session featured Alex Haley, biographer of Malcolm X; Lester Kirkendall, professor of family life at the University of Oregon, who spoke on the sexual revolution; Father John Leary of the University of Utah who discussed the meaning of the films *Easy Rider* and *Alice's Restaurant*; and John Fry, Presbyterian social activist, who talked about injustice, violence, and racism.[23]

Arbogast took another step in modifying religious practices by linking the college more closely with the Church of Jesus Christ of Latter-day

Saints. Through conversations with President N. Eldon Tanner, Arbogast was assured that the leadership of the Mormon Church endorsed the work being done by Westminster and would be supportive financially as conditions permitted. When Tanner suggested having a Mormon on the Westminster board of trustees in order to keep the church informed of institutional needs and concerns, Arbogast in 1966 recommended the appointment of Mormon businessman Frederick R. Hinckley to the board. Although some board members expressed concern that the appointment of a Mormon would conflict with the institution's historic denominational links, they unanimously endorsed the appointment following assurances from Arbogast that representatives from the Presbyterian, Methodist, and United Church of Christ denominations supported the proposal.[24]

After a four-year hiatus, Westminster's board of trustees reinstituted intercollegiate football in the fall of 1965. Although Arbogast had misgivings about the added burden to operating expenses, trustees assured him that additional funds would be forthcoming from interested alumni and friends of the college. Participating in the Rocky Mountain Athletic Conference, Westminster fielded competitive teams despite their limited scholarships and modest expense accounts. The Parsons' new coach, a young man named George Seifert who would later be well known as the NFL coach of the San Francisco 49er's, led the team to a 3-3 record but resigned after one year to become assistant coach under Ray Nagel at the University of Iowa.[25] Athletics became the target of negative editorials and letters to the editors in the *Parson*. Some complained that too much money was being diverted from curricular needs to support athletic scholarships and team expenses.[26] One student suggested that if the college could provide $40,000 for athletic scholarships, then it should do the same for student leaders. "Why not scholarships for editors and student government leaders?" queried *Etosian* editor E. T. Schomburg.[27] Others complained that athletes' behavior in the dorms and on campus impinged on the freedom and rights of their peers. *Parson* editor George Wood noted that Westminster football players were boisterous in dinner lines, rude to young women, and contemptuous of school policies. He described one situation when athletes returned from a road trip and initiated a food fight in the cafeteria.[28] While such incidents reflected negatively on Westminster's athletic program, most students endorsed the concept of intercollegiate athletics so long as they did not detract from the central educational goals of the college. In particular they appreciated the talents of Ken Hall, an outstanding basketball player for the Parsons who achieved national All-American honors in 1969, the first Parson ever to accomplish that feat.[29]

Students expressed their opinions on other topics including the widening and divisive war in Vietnam. In 1965 the SGA passed a resolution favoring the administration's policy in Vietnam and sent it to President Johnson. When two men appeared in the student lounge wearing "Peace in Vietnam" buttons, they were physically ejected and the air let out of their automobile tires. A student poll asking if students thought that the United States ought to withdraw from Vietnam received a ninety-five percent negative response. Asked also if they supported recent protest marches in support of peace, only six percent of Westminster students answered in the affirmative.[30] The college never encountered any campus violence that threatened orderly management of the educational enterprise. In fact, editorials in the *Parson* during the 1970s indicated apathy rather than activism was the biggest problem. One proclaimed that Westminster had no need for police or national guard to control student behavior. "The campus has one thing in its favor—apathy." Another identified the campus as being "liberally conservative," taking the middle road on most issues with little evidence of strong opinions. In the wake of the Kent State shootings, a student editor described the Westminster campus as "calm and serene" with the majority of Westminster students "totally unaware of what the six million other college students are thinking."[31]

Although Arbogast coped with changing student mores, he fell victim to the fiscal problems that had plagued his predecessors. In an effort to compete with the University of Utah and other state schools, the trustees insisted on keeping tuition unrealistically low, forcing Westminster to rely heavily on gifts from outside sources to maintain a balanced budget. With a growing faculty and expanding physical plant, operating costs escalated. Interfund borrowing became so extensive that the Presbyterian Board of Christian Education withheld payment of annual gifts until the situation was corrected. In response, Arbogast told Christian Education treasurer Renneisen, "This is only part of the 'mess' into which I unwittingly walked, when I assumed office. If all our donors were to adopt the same course of action, we would find it necessary to close our doors tomorrow."[32] Following a pessimistic fiscal projection report in 1967, trustees commissioned Arbogast to prepare recommendations on how Westminster could avoid closure and be placed on a self-supporting basis.[33] A few months later he submitted his resignation to a startled group of trustees who delayed making a public announcement until they could discuss procedures for seeking a replacement.[34]

After an abbreviated search, the trustees selected Manford A. Shaw, a trustee since 1941 and a classmate of Arbogast's at Westminster in the

1920s. A successful businessman and military veteran, Shaw was a well-known and highly respected figure in the Salt Lake community, and his long association with Westminster made him a popular choice with college faculty and students. During his eight-year administration Shaw accelerated the development of nontraditional professional courses and programs, presided over the severing of legal ties between the college and the United Presbyterian Church in the U.S.A., and completed the building program that had been initiated by his predecessor.[35]

Reflecting national trends in higher education, church-related colleges after mid-century adopted many of the values of the secular universities, such as academic specialization, professionalization, and research. University standards of academic excellence increasingly determined the policies and practices of colleges related to mainline denominations. A study of Presbyterian-related colleges in 1952 reported that "in practice, church-related institutions seem to follow largely the patterns and policies of other colleges and universities which make no claim to be Christian. They reflect to a large degree the secular influences of our society."[36] Some denominational theologians questioned the feasibility of Christian colleges and others argued that unless church-sponsored institutions hired faculty on the basis of academic qualifications rather than piety they did not merit collegiate status. When schools like Westminster continued to affirm Christian principles and denominational relationships, their statements often reflected the ideals of a past generation rather than the realities of the current operations.[37]

The United Presbyterian Church in the U.S.A. facilitated the trend toward secularization on college campuses. During the early 1960s, the denomination reexamined its historical relationship to Christian higher education. A study document entitled "The Church and Higher Education," approved by the General Assembly in 1961, concluded that modern church-related colleges should not be based on indoctrination or curtailment of academic freedom but on academic excellence undergirded by competent faculty and quality curricula. "If the education offered does not demand the highest standards of excellence, it had better not be offered in the name of the church and the Christian faith."[38] Responding to the study document, Presbyterian college presidents prepared a new set of criteria for church-related colleges "to assist these colleges to be free, responsible, and creative institutions of higher learning" without any demands for uniformity in academic policies and practices. Faculty were no longer required to be members of some evangelical Christian church but only to be committed to the declared institutional purpose. Instead of mandating a course in Bible, the new guidelines specified simply "a mature classroom encounter with the Judaic-Christian heritage." Accreditation by a regional association as an indication of academic quality completed the major criteria.[39]

Subsequent General Assembly reports informed the colleges that a decline in benevolent giving in the 1960s precluded new funds from the Board of Christian Education for the escalating needs of higher education. It followed that if the denomination could not produce financial support, then it should not insist on any form of legal control either through election of trustees or ownership of property. One Christian Education official said, "The relation can only be one that is open and free, clearly the will of both the church and the college."[40] Accordingly, Presbyterian colleges would no longer have legal ties to the national church but would be related to regional synods through mutual covenants under which each acknowledged the autonomy of church and college, but voluntarily agreed to cooperate and support one another to the best of their ability. In proposing these changes, the Board of Christian Education noted with irony that during years of expansion and change in higher education, United Presbyterians were pulling back from active participation.[41]

Westminster trustees implemented denominational policies while regretting that relationships that dated back to the college's beginnings were being altered. In 1970, with the consent of the Board of Christian Education, trustees deleted Article X of the college charter which specified forfeiture of college property to the Board of Christian Education if the college became "alienated from the work and doctrines of the Presbyterian Church."[42] Subsequently the college entered into a covenant relationship with the Synod of Colorado and Utah in 1970 and its successor, the regional Synod of Rocky Mountains in 1974, which encompassed Montana, Wyoming, Utah, and Colorado. The synod promised to support Westminster financially as resources permitted, to assist the college in recruiting students, and to supply a slate of three nominees for each class of college trustees. In turn, the college agreed to assume the primary role of promotional agent for the college within the bounds of synod, to provide facilities for synod, presbytery, and related groups as circumstances permitted, and to present the synod with an annual report of college activities.[43]

Although Westminster retained a nominal relationship with the Presbyterian, Methodist, and United Church of Christ denominations, the religious ethos that once dominated the campus was disappearing. Only nine percent of the student body were Presbyterians and almost forty percent listed no preference to religious affiliation. The 1971–73 college catalog featured a new seal that replaced "Pro Christo et Libertati," which symbolized Westminster's Christian roots, with the inscription "Advancing Independence and Diversity." At the same time, trustees also approved recommendations from the faculty to eliminate categories of creed and religion in the faculty hiring code and to omit the traditional practice of opening faculty meetings with prayer.[44] In 1975 trustees adopted a new mission statement formulated by a committee of faculty and administrators that emphasized Westminster's commitment to a four-year liberal arts and professional program in selected disciplines, but contained no mention of church relationships or religious values. Although subsequently modified to include a reference to Judeo-Christian values and traditions, the statement clearly reflected a major shift in college priorities. The adjectives Presbyterian and Christian had been replaced by private and independent.[45]

In keeping with new church relationships, college catalogs emphasized that the study of religion "is assumed to be an area of objective and scholarly investigation" rather than sectarian indoctrination. In addition to Bible offerings, students could take courses in American religions, religions of the world, sociology of religion, psychology of religion, and contemporary religious thought.[46] The philosophy of life course once required for graduation became optional in 1971. By 1974, the religion requirement, now listed under the title "Cultural Heritage," specified at least two classes from two of three areas that included philosophy, religion, or history. Students could avoid religion classes entirely and still graduate from Westminster College.[47]

Other changes in Westminster's academic programs occurred during Shaw's administration under academic vice presidents James Boyack and Helmut Hofmann. In 1968 the St. Mark's Hospital phased out its diploma nursing program and voted to cooperate with Westminster in establishing a baccalaureate degree nursing program. The program received temporary accreditation in 1969 and graduated its first class in May 1972.[48] An experimental miniterm between the first and second semesters of the 1969–70 school year became a fixture as a January term in a 4-1-4 curriculum. Initially courses were limited to seminars in traditional subjects in the humanities and the sciences and a few offerings in business, physical education, and aviation. As the program developed, however, offerings included such courses as "Human Sexuality: A Re-Evaluation of Identity and Sexuality," "The Occult and Parapsychology," and "The Meaning of Death in a World Perspective." Off campus, "Spaceship Earth and Population Control" was a course in which fifteen adults and fifteen children lived in a rustic cabin and explored the dynamics of group living and creating a learning experience out of nature; "The Way West" was a tour of pioneer trails and ghost towns in Utah, Idaho, and Wyoming.[49] Jazz was added to the music program in the early 1970s. Nationally known musicians such as Frank Zappa, George Duke, Chester Thompson, Ralph Humphries, Claire Fisher, and Don Menza performed on campus and interacted with students. During the January interim term, the Jazz Band toured southern California and performed at Dante's jazz club in Los Angeles.[50]

Course expansion accelerated after the appointment of a full-time director of continuing education in 1973. Between 1973 and 1976 the number of evening courses increased from nine to sixty with an enrollment of some eight hundred students. Summer school grew from 374 credit and zero non-credit students in 1971 to 600 credit and 150 non-credit students in 1976. Interim term increased from 311 in 1970–71 to 730 in 1976.[51] Other new programs in the early 1970s included interdisciplinary environmental science, early childhood education, computer science, a human relations interdepartmental major, and a real estate option in business administration. Many of these new programs were short lived because of their initial dependence on support from foundations. When grants were not renewed, the college could not keep them operating.[52]

By 1972 almost twenty percent of students on university and college campuses were twenty-five years or older and by the end of the decade the figure stood at thirty-three percent. Responding to changes in the college population, Westminster instituted an Alternative Entry Assessment (AEA) program in 1974 to encourage older students to submit verification of job-orientation training sessions, conferences, workshops, or correspondence courses as well as personnel and military records for evaluation. These experiences and accumulated knowledge were then translated into college credit and applied towards a baccalaureate degree. The AEA began with a group of thirty Federal Aviation employees, Veteran Administration employees, and peace officers, and rapidly expanded to include eighteen participating industries such as Mountain Bell, Western Electric, Mountain Fuel, and Kennecott Copper Corporation.[53]

Initiated during the same year, the Cooperative Education Program enabled some forty students to formally blend academic study with work experiences in business, industry, governmental agencies, social services, and private agencies. Instead of attending conventional classes, cooperative education students drew up a list of goals and learning objectives in consultation with employers and faculty advisors. During the semester, students attended periodic seminars and completed a study project assigned by their faculty advisors.[54]

Curricular changes were accompanied by an increase in student demands for wider participation in college governance and more freedom

of expression in personal life-styles. Anti-establishment sentiments sur-
faced in the form of underground student newspapers that critiqued college policies and practices. In March 1969 the *Newspaper*, edited by a
group of students including Jerry Rose, Amy Trimble, and Daryl Hunger,
promised to force the regular weekly (the *Parson*) to "seek accurate
news in a conscientious manner." During the same year, the first copy of
a mimeographed sheet entitled the *Torch* announced a forthcoming public debate on the war in Vietnam. A third underground paper called the
Westminster Wash presented an alternative voice to what it called "the
formal establishment." These papers articulated an undercurrent of dissent that characterized many Westminster students in the late 1960s and
early 1970s.[55]

Shaw's interpersonal skills enabled him to keep channels of communication open with the student dissenters. When he learned that some students
were calling for Westminster to participate in a national moratorium on the
Vietnam War by staging a campus walkout of classes, Shaw worked with
student government leaders to organize a public forum featuring speakers
on both sides of the Vietnam issue. Bruce Phillips, state leader of the Peace
and Freedom Party, spoke for the "doves," a number of military personnel
represented the "hawks," and several local clergymen discussed moral
issues. According to reports in the *Parson*, student-faculty participation was
high and debates were engaging and intense in contrast to the apathetic
responses to previous forums on other social issues.[56]

On another occasion, Shaw found himself engulfed in the issue of
college trustees selecting commencement speakers, as they traditionally
had done, without consultation with students. As a symbol of the changing relationship with Latter-day Saints, trustees had invited Harold B.
Lee, president of the Mormon Church, to address the graduating class of
1973. When the invitation became public, student leaders claimed that
they should have the right to determine who would address their class. At
an open meeting, Shaw defended the right of trustees to bestow the honor,
but offered to let the senior class select a second speaker to represent
them. The student protests generated so much unfavorable publicity, however, that Shaw was forced to withdraw the invitation.[57]

Students also called for an end to the *in loco parentis* tradition of
imposing restrictions on women who lived in campus residences. An editorial in the *Parson* complained that Westminster women had "the most
antiquated and archaic hours imaginable" and that they should be granted
the same rights afforded to men living on the same campus. "It's about
time we caught up with the rest of the world and remember that women
can vote, do wear pants, and have enough intelligence not to have to be

herded like sheep and tucked into bed by a nanny every night."[58] Expressing her frustration with the anachronistic rules in Hogle Hall, women's editor Mary Siciliano concluded, "Basically we are just damned tired of fighting with the hierarchy, and being turned out when we try to reason with their pattern of authority."[59] In the mid-1970s women were issued keys to the front door of Hogle Hall so they could access the building at all hours. By the end of the decade no adult supervisors lived in male or female dorms. Under the direction of student resident assistants, women developed their own rules and regulations for dormitory life and exercised discipline through their dorm councils.[60]

To monitor student concerns, Shaw held weekly meetings and annual retreats with campus leaders at which students set the agenda and voiced their opinions on a variety of topics. Student body president John S. Young, class of 1972, cited Shaw for his fairness, patience, and openness with students who did not always reciprocate. "President Shaw never generated any resistance, no matter how long-haired and weird some of us were," Young recalled.[61] When students raised student representation on the board of trustees, Shaw indicated that he would support a request to change the bylaws to permit such representation.[62] Student body president Edward Sweeney argued before the board of trustees for student participation in decisions affecting their college careers. With Shaw's encouragement, trustees voted in 1971 to grant two student representatives speaking and voting rights, making Westminster the first institution of higher education in the intermountain area to grant such privileges.[63] At the same time, students gained representation on some faculty committees, such as Admissions and Registration, Discipline, Honors Program, and Library and Student Life, and they secured the right to participate in formal class evaluations of faculty performance.[64]

The two student representatives to the board of trustees, Edward Sweeney and Lori D. Pinder, typified the diversity of Westminster students in the 1970s. As president of the student government, Sweeney urged his peers to become involved not just in social activities but in academic and curricular decisions that affected their college careers. In a feature story in the *Salt Lake Tribune*, Sweeney was quoted as saying, "Question everything and anything, you have the right. Paying your tuition gives you the right."[65] A dropout after the eighth grade, Lori Pinder took the GED at the urging of friends; results indicated that she had academic potential. Westminster admitted her on a probationary basis, limiting her to six hours for the first semester and summer school. After twelve hours of straight A work, her course load was gradually increased until she became a full-time student. She graduated in 1976.[66]

Following the lead of other undergraduate institutions, Westminster trustees approved the *Westminster Student Code* consisting of a series of statements regarding students' rights and responsibilities. Prepared jointly by the Student Life Committee and the Trustees' Committee on Student Affairs in 1972 and endorsed by the board of trustees in 1973, the document addressed issues of racial, ethnic, and gender discrimination, academic and religious freedom, confidentiality of student records, unreasonable searches and seizures, and due process. The *Westminster Student Code* marked the culmination of more than a decade of efforts by students to end what they considered arbitrary and improper control of their rights as students and citizens.[67]

Some traditions such as freshman initiation week and hazing died slowly even though periodically questioned by student leaders. Wearing yellow beanies, holding slave auctions, participating in scavenger hunts, and deferring to aggressive upper-class students remained part of the Westminster campus activities until the mid-1970s.[68] Occasionally some students rebelled and called attention to the nature of so-called initiation rites. Six first-year students, tired of being tortured with insane questions and insults, captured two seniors coming out of a bowling alley. They dressed their two captives in long underwear and bathing caps, applied a liberal quantity of grease, and handcuffed them to a flag pole in front of a local radio station. A plea from a radio announcer secured their release after several hours of public display. A few hours later, the culprits were seen rolling eggs down the steps of Converse Hall with their noses in retribution for their kidnapping.[69] About the time that beanies disappeared, streaking hit campus. During its short reign in the spring of 1974, Westminster had ten reports of student streaking. The first incidents occurred outside Hogle Hall where a group of students raised ten dollars for any male who would flash across the lawn three times after advance warning had been given to women residents so that they could view the spectacle. In the ensuing activity, one coed walked through a glass door and had to be taken to the hospital for treatment. Following the accident, streaking episodes dwindled, probably due as much to unseasonably cold weather as to concerns about student safety.[70]

Students modified other traditional activities during the 1970s. In 1971 student leaders canceled the annual Homecoming parade and dance and instituted a party on a restored passenger train, the Heber Creeper. In place of the May dance and crowning of a May Queen, students created Mayfest, featuring a variety of music ranging from country-blue grass and folk to jazz, boogie, funk, rock and roll, and big band orchestra. Four years later, the *Parson* wrote, "In 1971 Mayfest was a revolutionary idea, concept and production—in 1974, it's a tradition."[71] The institution's long-standing prohibition of alcoholic beverages on campus was also altered in the early 1970s. Editorials in the *Parson* and petitions from student organizations called for the end of what students termed "ridiculous rules and regulations."[72] While not endorsing the consumption of alcohol, college trustees adopted a policy that granted residents twenty-one and over the right to drink after 5 P.M. in dormitory rooms and in the Ghetto, a lounge in the basement of the student union. Advertisements in the *Parson* for dances and "bring your own beer" parties heralded the change in administrative policy.[73] Following two separate incidents of vandalism in 1978 which led to closing of the Ghetto, drinking privileges on campus were confined to residence rooms for students of legal drinking age. Undaunted, students held their parties off campus in private homes or at outdoor gatherings. Most popular was a Friday afternoon keg party in Mill Creek Canyon that dispersed in time for a steak and baked potato dinner in the campus dining room. Not all students approved of the unofficial parties that they claimed conflicted with organized social events and impacted negatively on school spirit. A contributor to the *Parson* charged the participants with engaging in "a drunken brawl" and then returning to campus "breaking windows, shouting obscenities, and throwing up all over the damn place."[74]

The drug culture also made its impact on campus life as Westminster students experimented with LSD, peyote, speed, and homemade highs such as dried banana peelings and perfume-soaked cigarettes. A poll of three hundred Westminster students conducted in 1970 revealed that thirty-seven percent had used marijuana at least once since their sixteenth birthday and almost a third used the drug on a regular basis. Twenty-four percent admitted to occasional use of LSD.[75] In 1974 narcotics agents arrested four first-year students in Carleson Hall for selling amphetamines.[76] In response, the board of trustees quickly approved a policy on drugs that forbade possession or consumption of drugs on campus. Students complained that this policy had been released to the local press before they had an opportunity to see it, noting that this demonstrated administrative insensitivity to participatory campus government.[77]

As Westminster entered its centennial year in 1975, the campus experienced a brief moratorium from financial, curricular, and social problems during extended celebrations of the college's one hundred years of higher education in Utah. Shaw used this event to promote a $2.5 million financial campaign and to garner area media coverage. Homecoming featured a 99-year-old queen, and the "Women of Westminster" sponsored a gala Centennial Ball. Pollster George Gallup, Jr., astronomer and physicist

Carl Sagan, and jazz musician George Shearing were among many individuals who appeared on campus during the year. Events culminated with a Centennial Dinner at the Hotel Utah on May 17 featuring a slide show depicting Westminster's history.[78]

At the conclusion of the centennial celebrations, Shaw announced his retirement as of July 1, 1976. In his annual report to the trustees he listed the accomplishments of his administration, which included curricular expansion, enrollment of more than one thousand, and a greatly improved physical plant anchored by the new student union building with its attractive O. C. Tanner Plaza and Fountain. Other improvements included the Eccles Art Center, Malouf Hall, and the Malmsten Amphitheater. Shaw also announced that through contacts established by trustee A. Walton Roth, Irene Nunemaker, a Presbyterian philanthropist from New York City, would underwrite building a sanctuary on campus near the amphitheater on Emigration Creek. Completed in 1977, Nunemaker Place functioned as a center for religious activities, an area for theatrical and musical performances, and a retreat center for students, faculty, and staff.

Shaw also reported that Westminster's financial condition had improved. The college ended the 1974–75 budget year with a surplus of more than $100,000. Although acknowledging that this was the result of gifts that would not likely be repeated, Shaw remained hopeful that "the specter of unpaid bills will not soon reappear on the Westminster scene."[79] C. T. Klein, board chair, praised Shaw for his leadership, affirming that the college had never been stronger in terms of fiscal and human resources and campus spirit. In recognition of his distinguished service, trustees named the student center in his honor and appointed him college chancellor, the first Westminster president to be so designated.[80]

Choosing not to institute a national search for Shaw's successor, trustees elected as president the academic vice president, Helmut Hofmann. Although some students and administrators questioned aborting the search process, Hofmann had support among various segments of the college community, including a majority of the faculty. Various student groups also expressed confidence in Hofmann as an academician and administrator. His confirmation as president was acclaimed by the local press as a wise choice.[81] Hofmann continued his interest in curricular expansion and enrollment growth.

Enrollment soared to fourteen hundred in 1977 and reached an all-time high of sixteen hundred the following year. New programs appeared as Westminster continued its shift from a liberal arts emphasis toward career preparation and adult education. In 1976 trustees approved a master's degree in education designed for employed teachers and tailored to their particular needs.[82] The Institute for Humanistic Studies, initiated with an $80,000 start-up grant in 1977, featured adult education courses for credit or noncredit, emphasizing classic works of philosophy, literature, history, sciences, art, and eastern and western anthropology. Also funded the following year was the Dayspring Ecumenical Project, based in Nunemaker Place, which focused on theological education for clergy and laypeople from all denominations. Directed by Horace McMullen, a United Church of Christ clergyman, Dayspring attempted to provide a "spiritual center" on campus to reflect Westminster's continuing interest in church relationships. Other Hofmann innovations included weekend and on-site (off-campus) adult courses and programs for troubled youth, geriatric care, and emergency medical technicians.[83]

Under Hofmann, Westminster made a number of changes in its academic structures and policies including a major reorganization that revamped the administration of academic departments from three division heads in charge of twenty departments to seven division heads responsible for only a few departments. The new configuration reportedly facilitated the supervision of Westminster's expanding curricular offerings. At the same time, tenure procedures were modified so as to insure that the entire faculty would not be tenured and to provide for periodic tenure reviews. For the first time in Westminster's history, a sabbatical leave program was in place with four faculty on leave and their courses covered with part-time replacements.[84] Officials also provided funds for a part-time director and space in the Shaw Center for a Women's Center, described by its founders as a "place to come with problems and leave with answers." During its brief existence, the center sponsored retreats, lectures, and discussions on a variety of women's issues, including rape, sexual discrimination, and marital relationships. Budgetary cuts in 1979 terminated the director's position, and the center closed shortly after.[85]

As the 1970s closed, despite construction of a modern campus, innovative programs, and increased enrollment, Westminster College administrators faced serious fiscal questions about the institution's future. Like many private colleges in the late 1970s, Westminster struggled for survival in an inhospitable environment of double-digit inflation that sent operating expenses skyrocketing and hampered the acquisition of endowment funds and nondesignated income. A larger percentage of students were enrolling in state universities, attracted by lower tuitions and diversified curricula. Coupled with reductions in federal support for higher education and a smaller pool of prospective students, 172 private colleges closed during the decade 1974–1984. Given its long history of marginal finances and recent loss of denominational support, Westminster was a prime candidate for closure. Operating expenses during the 1970s had outrun enrollment and inflation, rising 351 percent to $4.7 million before the end of the decade.[86]

When Helmut Hofmann assumed the presidency in 1976, he inherited two consecutive operating deficits totaling $405,000. The next two years produced deficits of $495,000 and $429,000, and in 1978–79, when student head count fell, the college was able to cover losses only by a $600,000 bank loan and interfund borrowing amounting to $650,000. The fiscal crisis was exacerbated by inadequate financial controls brought on in part by the hasty adoption of flawed computer accounting programs. Budget accounts frequently were in such disarray that it was impossible to determine where and by whom money had been spent for departmental and other operating expenses. When the student editor of the *Parson* asked for information about the paper's financial status, he discovered the account under the heading of "Picnics." No one in the office could explain why it was so listed.[87] Details on cash and bank transactions were so vague that it was not until 1981 that college officials ascertained that the 1975 centennial campaign believed to have raised $2.5 million actually only realized $1 million.[88]

With no clear linkage between student registrations and billings, some students actually completed degrees without paying any tuition. One student recounted his experiences in a letter to the editor of the school paper. When he went to the business office to pay his fees, he discovered that there was a check in his name for $888 because he had been "over awarded" in financial aid, even though he actually owed $200. Accepting the check, he took it to the financial aid office and signed it over to the college. The accounting department did not have him listed as a dormitory student but they posted his aid for being resident assistant. When he went to pay interim term tuition, the office had run out of receipts so they simply wrote "paid in full" on his registration form. Then the financial aid office informed him that he was due a refund of $34.35 for the second semester, but when he went to the business office they told him no refund was in order. Not satisfied with the answers he was receiving, the student brought someone from the financial aid office to confer with staff in the business office. His account card said that he owed $208.75, but they had not posted a government award of $888, which meant that Westminster owed him $600, which he did not believe was correct. Returning to the financial aid office, he was informed that he had not paid his fees for the interim term. After presenting his check stub and marked registration form, they apologized and gave him a check for the incorrect amount of $44.25.[89]

Hofmann attempted to halt Westminster's plunge into bankruptcy. During one four-month period, he held fourteen meetings with the college business staff, four sessions with the financial committee of the board of trustees, and hired an outside consulting firm to make recommendations regarding the improvement of fiscal policies.[90] Hofmann and key trustees sought funding from the state legislature for campus improvements and operating expenses, but the bill died on the senate floor.[91] Late in 1978 the college received a "qualified opinion" from an external audit conducted by the firm of Coopers & Lybrand who reported that the actual deficit was higher than previously stated and that there were substantial errors and assumptions in the budget that had been prepared in September. By the latter part of December, it was apparent that the college could not continue.[92] With an accumulated deficit of $1.3 million, and $573,000 more projected for the coming fiscal year, college trustees assembled on January 26, 1979, to take action amid charges that inadequate supervision had precipitated the latest financial crisis. Dean Dale Johnston called for a major retrenchment, including cuts in personnel and programs. The board declared a state of "bona fide financial exigency" and announced the resignation of Helmut Hofmann, which had not been requested. One trustee questioned accepting the resignation, stating that it looked like the board was seeking a scapegoat for the deficit which had grown over more than a decade. After extended discussion, the board accepted Hofmann's resignation but modified the press release to note that it had been received "with regrets."[93]

Despite the severity of its financial problems, the college was not without hope. It had survived similar crises, and loyal college supporters assumed that it would surmount the present predicament. Indeed, many faculty and staff pursued their campus duties with an attitude that softened the harsh reality of the situation. Administrators and trustees also continued to believe that the century-old institution had a future in Utah's configuration of higher education, and students remained committed to the school that had provided them a personalized education and opportunities for future employment. All these constituencies would play important roles in the days ahead.

NOTES

1. For biographical sketches of recent Westminster presidents, refer to Christopher Thomas, "The Legacies of Leadership," *Westminster Review* (summer 1995): 10–13.

2. "Unity A Must," *Parson*, 21 September 1964: 2. "Welcome to the NEW Westminster College," heralded the *Parson*. "Yes, Westminster College is growing up in every conceivable way."

3. "Westminster College Interim Report for Extension of Accreditation, March 1967," 7, WC Archives, hereafter cited as "Interim Report," with date.

4. "Students Enrolled in Westminster's Newest Course," *Parson*, 14 November 1967, 2; and "Jet Orientation Lab," *Westminster College Catalog 1969–70*, 4. Fourteen students enrolled in the program, which offered at completion a commercial pilot's certificate with an instrument rating as well as eighteen to twenty hours of college credit. Subsequently the college added a jet orientation lab utilizing a Lear Jet 24 to incorporate instructional business jet systems into the curriculum. The program was acclaimed in the local press and utilized by Westminster students from a variety of ages and backgrounds.

5. "Interim Report," 1967, 7. Initially eighty students enrolled in sixteen classes for an average of 4.52 credit hours each.

6. "Graduate Program," *Westminster College Catalog 1969–70*, 7. The program began in the summer session of 1967 and the first degree was conferred in 1968. See *Westminster Self-Study Report 1970*, 106–110, WC Archives.

7. *Westminster College Catalog 1969–70*, 7.

8. WC Trustee Minutes, 19 November 1963 and 21 January 1964.

9. "Library Set for Occupancy," *Utah Westminster* 50 (November 1964): 2.

10. For an overview of the building program, see WC Trustee Minutes, 16 May 1967.

11. For an overview of student life in the 1960s and 1970s, see Calvin T. B. Lee, *Campus Scene 1900–1970* (New York, 1970), 108–43.

12. Tom Fuhr, dean of students, to returning residents of Carleson Hall, June 1965, WC Archives.

13. "Rebels Loudly Seen but Not Heard," *Parson*, 29 October 1965, 3; and "Newer Breed of Students Occupy Today's Campus," 28 October 1970, 2.

14. "Editorial," *Parson*, 9 January 1969, 2; and "Editorial," *Parson*, 14 November 1967, 2.

15. "Student Court Proposed," *Parson*, 18 January 1963, 3.

16. *Etosian*, 1964, 85. Their first plea came in the form of an anonymous note, "Dear Sirs, Can't you do something about noise abatement in the student lounge? Signed, 'Frantic.'" After a decade of operation, the student court was transformed into a college disciplinary board composed of four students, two faculty, and one administrator. WC Trustee Minutes, 22 September 1976 and 11 May 1977.

17. "Westminster College Self-Study Report," 1964, 96.

18. "Student Survey," *Parson*, 14 May 1969, 4.

19. "Reappraisal Study of Westminster College Salt Lake City, Utah," June 1963, 8–9, WC Archives.

20. "Convocation—No Show, Must Go!," *Parson*, 23 April 1965, 2.

21. WC Trustee Minutes, 15 December 1964.

22. WC Trustee Minutes, 21 September 1965. For a time Westminster continued to require occasional convocations that featured presentations on a variety of educational topics and campus issues. These continued until the mid-1970s when through the leadership of student government president Edward Sweeney trustees voted to end mandatory attendance. See "Dean Stewart Clarifies Policy on Convocations," *Parson*, 3 November 1967, 1; and Nyman, "A Short History of Westminster College," 67.

23. "Interim Report," 1967, 2–3; and "Living Issues Week," *Parson*, 16 November 1967, 1 and 27 February 1970, 2.

24. WC Trustee Minutes, 21 March 1967.

25. WC Trustee Minutes, 16 December 1964 and 21 September 1965. See also Christopher Thomas, "From the 'Sugar Bowl' to the Super Bowl," *Forum*, 24 January 1994, 1.

26. "Editorial," *Parson*, 25 October 1968, 2. "We are becoming a gym with a school attached," lamented one editorial in the late 1960s.

27. "Letters to the Editor," *Parson*, 9 January 1969, 2.

28. "Editorial," *Parson*, 6 December 1968, 2. "In their wake they left broken furniture, floors filthy with food, and a sickening memory of people at their rudest."

29. "A Tribute to Kenny Hall," *Parson*, 14 May 1969, 6; and *Etosian*, 1969, 107, 117. Under the tutelage of coach Tom Steinke, Hall, a business major from New York State, led Westminster to a Rocky Mountain Athletic Conference championship with a 22-5 season record. A feature story in the *Parson*, lauded Hall "not only as a great basketball player, but a great person as well." Walt Love, drafted by the New York Giants in the tenth round, became the first Westminster athlete to reach the National Football League. *Etosian*, 1972–73, 50.

30. "Letter to the Editor," *Parson*, 1 December 1965, 2; "Muscle-Bound Reason Does It Again," 8 December 1965, 2; and "Student Opinion Poll," 15 December 1965, 1. Even a bearded professor was deemed a novelty on the Westminster campus. The *Parson* commented, "The bearded wonder will be a welcome change to many students and a wonder to most." "Two New Profs," *Parson*, 14 April 1969, 11.

31. "Colleges Prepare for Anything," *Parson*, 9 September 1970, 2; "Newer Breed of Students Occupy Today's Campus," 28 October 1970, 2; and "Colleges Air Tension," 4 November 1970, 2.

32. W. Fred Arbogast to George W. Renneisen, 17 February 1965, WC Archives.

33. WC Trustee Minutes, 22 August 1967.

34. WC Trustee Minutes, 19 December 1967; and W. Fred Arbogast to Harold H. Viehman, 8 January 1968, WC Archives. In a letter to a colleague, Arbogast explained the reasons for his decision. "My apparent inability to 'lick' the apathy and lethargy of most constituencies of the College, the meager resources, the almost nonexistent endowment, and the almost perpetual state of emergency with respect to finances, finally convinced me that for my own peace of mind and for the good of the College, I should resign."

35. Nyman, "A Short History of Westminster College," 62; and "New President," *Parson*, 12 January 1968, 1.

36. *GAMPCUSA*, "Blue Book," 1952, 166.

37. For a brief summary of changing church relationships, see Bradley J. Longfield and George M. Marsden, "Presbyterian Colleges in Twentieth-Century America," in Milton J Coalter, John M. Mulder, and Louis B. Weeks, *The Pluralistic Vision: Presbyterians and Mainstream Protestant Education and Leadership* (Louisville, 1992), 99–124.

38. "The Church and Higher Education," *General Assembly Minutes of the United Presbyterian Church in the U.S.A. (GAMUPCUSA)*, 1961, I:149–82.

39. "Administrative Guidelines for Colleges Related to the United Presbyterian Church in the United States of America," *GAMUPCUSA*, 1963, I:135–37; and *Sixth Annual Report of the Board of Christian Education of the United Presbyterian Church in the U.S.A.*, 1963, 31.

40. Harold H. Viehman, "The Church and the Church-Related College," a speech given to the annual meeting of the Presbyterian College Union, 15 January 1967, WC Archives.

41. "Recommendations Relating to Higher Education," *GAMUPCUSA*, 1965, I:131–37; and 1967, I:193–94. See also "Synod Relations to the Colleges," *GAMUP-CUSA*, 1968, I:163–64.

42. WC Trustee Minutes, 17 March and 15 July 1970.

43. WC Trustee Minutes, 19 February 1970 and 25 September 1974. Technically this agreement was voided in 1983 when the college reorganized and did not renew this relationship with the Synod of Rockies.

44. *Westminster Catalog 1971–73*, 1; and WC Trustee Minutes, 11 April 1972, 20 February 1973, and 25 September 1974. Earlier, President Shaw opened the college library on Sunday in response to student petitions. Traditionally the library had been closed on Sunday to accommodate Presbyterian Sabbatarian practices. "Library Hours," *Parson*, Homecoming Edition, 1968, 1.

45. WC Trustee Minutes, 15 October 1975 and 15 February 1978. For an analysis of these changes, see Keith Wilson, "The Process of Secularization at Westminster College of Salt Lake City: A Case Study," (diss., University of Utah, 1995), 79–85.

46. *Westminster College Catalog 1979–80*, 122–23.

47. *Westminster College Catalog 1974–75*, 54. An LDS Institute adjacent to campus began operations in 1973. See "LDS Institute Flourishes under Jenkins," *Forum* (25 October 1985): 7.

48. "Westminster College Self-Study Report," 1970, 29–30.

49. WC Trustee Minutes, 22 August 1967; and *Westminster College Summer Session Catalog*, 1975, 5–8. A black studies course was offered for the first time as an evening course in 1969. See "Black Studies Course Offered," *Parson*, 28 August 1969, 3. One course offering, on pornography and obscenity, generated negative publicity in the Salt Lake community. According to Stephen R. Baar, then a nontenured faculty member in the Department of English, Shaw supported Baar's decision to teach the class but insisted that it be the most "academic, tough, above-board course" that had ever been offered at Westminster. "Dr. Manford A. Shaw," *Forum*, 2 February 1993, 1.

50. Dana Tumpowsky, "Westminster in the Seventies and All That Jazz," *Westminster Review* (spring 1991): 10–11. Although the jazz program was popular, it did not survive budgetary cuts necessitated by financial problems and was discontinued in 1978.

51. "Interim Report," 1975, 29.

52. WC Trustee Minutes, 25 September 1974 and 21 May 1975. See also "Interim Report," 1975, 26–27.

53. "Alternative Entry Assessment" (typescript, n.d.), WC Archives. Although some individuals attended classes on campus, others met with groups on the premises of participating companies or at other convenient locations. Faculty for this program came from Westminster staff or from other qualified teachers. One of the oldest alternative entry students, Dr. Keith Good, age 72, received a bachelor's degree in psychology in 1977, graduating with a straight A average. See "Naturopath," *Salt Lake Tribune*, 18 May 1977.

54. *Westminster Catalog*, 1977–78, 48–49. The placements in the Cooperative Education Program were as diversified as student interests. Mary Schurtyz, a behavioral science major, worked as an outpatient therapist trainee at the Human Resource Clinic. Brian Carsik served as a marketing director for the American Ski Association, and Kim Hansen, a nursing student, was placed with the personnel office at St. Mark's Hospital.

55. Random copies of these newspapers can be found in "College Publications," 1969–70, WC Archives.

56. "Vietnam Moratorium," *Parson*, 17 October 1969, 2; and "Westminster Joins Vietnam Talk-
Back," *Parson*, 24 October 1969, 1.

57. "Student Unrest," *Parson*, 24 April 1973, 1.

58. "Let's Re-examine Dorm Hours," *Parson*, 4 October 1967, 2.

59. "Into Women," *Parson*, 23 February 1972, 4.

60. WC Trustee Minutes, 30 March 1971. See also Peggy Beach, "I Remember," *Newscope* (spring 1984): 8. Coed dormitories were approved in 1977 but were not implemented because of the cost of renovating Ferry Hall. WC Trustee Minutes, 11 May 1977 and May 24, 1978.

61. "Dr. Manford A. Shaw," *Forum*, 2 February 1993, 1.

62. "Two Students on Board of Trustees—Yes or No?," *Parson*, 14 May 1969, 2.

63. "Trustees Put Two Students as Board Members," *Newscope* (winter 1972): 1.

64. WC Trustee Minutes, 28 September and 18 November 1971 and 19 September 1972. See also "Dr. Shaw Evaluates Faculty Evaluation," *Parson*, 27 February 1970, 1; "Westminster Moves Ahead," *Salt Lake Tribune*, 25 November 1971; and *Deseret News*, 23 November 1971. Trustees subsequently added two faculty members to the board and also elected Mrs. George S. Eccles, the first woman to be selected since the early 1940s. See Nyman, "A Short History of Westminster College," 67.

65. "Westminster Student Asks 'Why?'" *Salt Lake Tribune*, 1 October 1971. See also "Trustee Report," *Parson*, 23 February 1972, 4.

66. "Happenings," November 12, 1971, 1–2, WC Archives.

67. WC Trustee Minutes, 20 February 1973. A copy of the student code is included in the trustees' minutes.

68. "Are Traditional Freshmen Initiations Needed Now?" *Parson*, 9 September 1970, 2.

69. "Initiation Rites," *Parson*, 27 September 1967, 1.

70. *Etosian*, 1974, 147.

71. Student Greg Floor is credited with starting the new tradition in 1970. "Mayfest," *Parson*, 10 May 1974, 1.

72. "Steve Lewis Seeks 'Right to Choose' New Drinking Rule," and "Ridiculous Rules, Regulations, Lessen Homecoming Festivities," *Parson*, 14 October 1971, 2.

73. WC Trustee Minutes, 28 September 1971 and 18 November 1971. The policy went into effect February 1, 1972. See also "Alcohol Policy," *Parson*, 22 February 1974, 2; and "Abuse of the Few," 12 May 1978, 2.

74. "Keep the Spirit for the Keggers," *Parson*, 4 October 1967, 2; and "Hangin' Out Westminster Style," *Westminster Review* (summer 1994): 4–5. In 1986 trustees modified the policy to permit the use of alcohol in designated areas for special events. "College Establishes Two New Alcohol Policies," *Forum*, 1 December 1986, 5.

75. "Drug Questionnaire Produces Results," *Parson*, 11 April 1970, 1.

76. "Narcotics Agents Arrest Four," *Parson*, 15 November 1974, 1.

77. "New Drug Policy," *Parson*, 12 March 1968, 2.

78. WC Trustee Minutes, "President's Annual Report," 21 May 1975.

79. Ibid.

80. WC Trustee Minutes, 21 May and 19 November 1975.

81. WC Trustee Minutes, 24 September and 15 October 1975.

82. WC Trustee Minutes, 22 September 1976.

83. WC Trustee Minutes, 28 September 1977 and 24 May 1978. Without formally acknowledging the change, Westminster had shifted from a liberal arts emphasis toward career preparation and adult education. In 1968–69, twenty-seven of thirty-four full-time faculty were in the liberal arts. A decade later, the number was thirty-four out of sixty. Nursing staff numbered twelve, education nine, and business five.

84. "Academics Realize Major Reorganization," *Parson*, 11 March 1977, 1; and *Westminster Catalog 1978–79*, 56. See also WC Trustee Minutes, 8 April 1976 and 22 February 1977.

85. "Westminster's Women's Center: New Resource," *Parson*, 4 February 1977, 7; and "Terminations Announced," 25 January 1979, 7. Alumae Reva Beck Bosone was the guest at the center's dedication in February 1977. See "Campus Sees Close of Women's Center," *Parson*, 13 April 1979, 4. Pressure from female students for intercollegiate athletic program comparable to those available for males resulted in the introduction of women's sports in skiing, volleyball, and basketball in 1976. See "Plea Raised for Equality," *Parson*, 21 March 1975, 4; and "Women's Athletic Program Begins Second Season," *Parson*, 2 December 1977, 4.

86. Douglas W. Steeples, "Westminster College of Salt Lake City," 68, in Douglas W. Steeples, ed., *Successful Strategic Planning: Case Studies* (San Francisco and London, 1988).

87. "Business Office Operations Examined," *Parson*, 20 February 1976, 2.

88. "Westminster College Self Study Report, 1981," II-4. During the period 1977–79 the college "borrowed" approximately $250,000 of Title IV federal monies designated for student loans and grants and used them for operating expenses. As a result, Westminster was placed on probation until the funds were repaid and procedures in place to monitor money more accurately. WC Trustee Minutes, 20 July 1981; and Craig Green, interview by author, 1 June 1994.

89. "Letters to the Editor," *Parson*, 29 February 1980, 2.

90. WC Trustee Minutes, 22 September 1978; and Wilson, "The Process of Secularization at Westminster," 86–87.

91. Steeples, "Westminster College of Salt Lake City," 68–69; "State of the College," *Parson*, 25 January 1979, 3; and WC Trustee Minutes, 22 September 1978.

92. WC Trustee Minutes, 17 November 1977. The auditor from the accounting firm of Coopers & Lybrand, Stephen Morgan, said that records were in such disarray that his first audit took over ten months. Interview, Stephen Morgan with Keith Wilson, 18 March 1994, WC Archives.

93. WC Trustee Minutes, 26 January 1979.

9

Almost a Miracle

It is not hyperbole to suggest that these [financial] changes have been dramatic. The cumulative deficit in the current fund has been eradicated and now shows a positive balance. The endowment has grown from one to eighteen million dollars and a competent and stable financial management system is in place. There has been an extraordinary qualitative growth and improvement in the entire approach to fiscal management since the last full-scale review.
—Northwest Association of Schools and Colleges,
Evaluation Committee Report, 1993.

Many faculty and students learned about Westminster's declaration of financial exigency through the evening news or the morning newspaper. The chair of the board of trustees, Alonzo W. Watson Jr., reported that the school was $1.3 million in debt and that emergency measures would be taken to keep the institution functioning. He also announced that board member Robert Pratt, general manager of the Kennecott Copper Division, had offered the services of his company's industrial relations manager, James E. Petersen, to act as Westminster's interim president. The appointment of Petersen, a nonacademician known for closing a mining operation in his hometown of Lark, Utah, fueled rumors of impending closure; gallows humor around the campus claimed that rather than a rescue mission, Petersen was coming to Westminster "for a Lark."[1]

By his own admission, Petersen was an unlikely candidate for president. He lacked a baccalaureate degree, and his work experience as a miner, union leader, and industrial relations director was not that which is usually associated with college administration. While lacking traditional academic credentials, Petersen acknowledged other qualities that fitted him for the Westminster presidency. "I don't know a helluva lot about the education industry," he admitted to a reporter. "I wouldn't know how to be a good academic vice president or a vice president of financial affairs. But I do have good, practical common sense."[2]

Petersen's initial impression was that of Westminster as a campus dominated by dissension and strife. "There is a lot of division here," he told a student newspaper editor. "Everybody says they love Westminster, but they love *their* part of Westminster."[3] Although faculty were wary about someone who acted like a businessman and occasionally sounded like a miner, Petersen quickly gained the confidence and respect of the campus community. His first act was to call a convocation of faculty and students at which he described in broad lines a program of retrenchment designed to reduce college expenses by more than half a million dollars. The cutbacks included eliminating nine full-time equivalent (FTE) faculty positions and a number of administrative appointments, reducing student services and other support programs, dropping the physical education major, and eliminating all intercollegiate sports.[4] These actions, however, dealt only with Westminster's immediate financial problems.

Petersen believed that if the college were to survive, it needed clearly articulated institutional goals and the definite financial resources with which to implement them. Through the offices of board chair Watson, Petersen employed as a consultant Sterling McMurrin, the graduate dean of the University of Utah and a former U.S. commissioner of education. McMurrin was highly regarded for independent thinking and decisive leadership, and his Mormon upbringing also provided some linkages with church authorities and community leaders. McMurrin enlisted the support of his long-time friend, O. C. Tanner, a distinguished businessman, educator, and philanthropist, and together they devised a strategy that involved hiring a prestigious educational consulting team and seeking the support of the First Presidency of the Mormon Church.[5]

Convinced that the college had little likelihood of long-term success without Mormon support, McMurrin and Tanner contacted influential church leader N. Eldon Tanner. They emphasized the college's contribution to the educational diversity of Utah and its long history of service to the Salt Lake City community. The Mormon president responded favorably. He agreed to serve as the honorary chair of a financial campaign designed to raise $3 million for Westminster, offered an immediate $100,000 toward the project, and indicated that additional funds would be forthcoming. President Tanner's endorsement of Westminster College generated positive publicity and broad support from the Salt Lake City business community. In retrospect, McMurrin said, "They [O.C. and N. Eldon Tanner] saved Westminster College from the auction block during those cloudy days."[6]

With funds provided by O. C. Tanner, Westminster engaged the services of the Academy for Educational Development (AED) in Washington, D.C. Its vice president, Sidney Tickton, undertook a comprehensive review of Westminster's educational program during the summer of 1979. Compiling data on the college and placing it in the context of higher education in Utah and throughout the United States, Tickton concluded that Westminster would have to make radical changes in order to survive in the highly competitive educational market.[7] Tickton identified the personal commitment and dedication of college staff as one of Westminster's greatest assets: "The spirit of the Westminster family is pulling the college through what would otherwise be an impossible situation."[8] He recommended eight new educational objectives for the college. Heading the list was a change in its programmatic focus to transform Westminster into a career- and profession-oriented institution with a liberal arts core that would enroll two thousand FTE students, sixty percent of whom would be twenty-one years and older. To achieve this goal would require a new mission statement and new programs. Other recommendations specified tight control over spending, greater administrative and organizational efficiency, vigorous recruitment of students and funding, and expanded trustee participation in day-to-day operations of the college. He released a draft of his findings, referred to as the Tickton Report, on August 15 to Westminster trustees, administrators, faculty, and students.[9]

With the completion of the Tickton Report, Petersen ended his interim presidency. During the eight-month period of his presidency, he had implemented a major retrenchment, raised more than a million dollars, initiated a process of outside evaluation and self-study, and quelled rumors of imminent closure. As he returned to his position at Kennecott Copper, students and faculty placed a full-page advertisement in the school paper entitled "We Love You, Pete."[10] A student editorial in the *Parson* praised board chair Watson's leadership and complimented Petersen. "It is a rare combination to find a person that exudes so much sincerity and enthusiasm and has so effortlessly become an integral part of a previously unfamiliar community."[11] Trustees announced the appointment to the presidency of C. David Cornell, vice president of Wagner College in Staten Island, New York. Cornell had served previously as vice president of Wittenberg University in Ohio and Davidson College in North Carolina, director of federal and foundations relations at the University of Iowa, and in private industry. Hailed as a fund raiser and effective administrator, Cornell came to Salt Lake City with a mandate to expand the college's financial base and revamp its administrative and curricular policies.[12]

At the October board meeting, trustees took action on the Tickton Report. Through Vice President for Academic Affairs Dale Johnston, faculty presented concerns about proposals in the report, including quality control of off-campus programs and staff, subsuming student affairs under academic affairs, and dropping faculty representation on the board of trustees. Student representatives voiced fears that the college might become too career-oriented at the expense of liberal arts and deplored the absence of student representatives on the board of trustees. While acknowledging the legitimacy of these concerns, trustees unanimously voted to implement the Tickton Report "as rapidly as possible as good logic dictates." Cornell endorsed that decision, noting that he had accepted the presidency on the assumption that the AED report would be adopted in principle and form the blueprint for the college's future.[13]

To implement the Tickton Report, Cornell brought in a new administrative team to guide the college through major curricular changes, new recruitment programs, and revised financial policies and procedures. In 1980 he appointed Douglas W. Steeples as vice president for academic affairs. Steeples moved from a similar post at Wartburg College in Waverly, Iowa. A scholar in American history, Steeples previously had taught for sixteen years at Earlham College in Richmond, Indiana. Appointments the following year included Dean of Admissions and Records Craig A. Green, a colleague of Steeples's at Wartburg College, and Business Manager Stephen R. Morgan, a member of the staff of Coopers & Lybrand who audited Westminster's financial accounts in 1978–79. Supported by other new arrivals, this trio played a major role in shaping Westminster's institutional future.[14]

Under Cornell's leadership, Westminster instituted a ten-year plan in 1980 entitled "A Pursuit of Excellence: The Case for Westminster College" based on recommendations in the Tickton Report. Designed by a joint task force of students, administrators, and faculty members, the plan called for increased enrollment (seventeen hundred by 1990), expansion of adult education programs on and off campus, tuition increases to cover eighty percent of student educational expenses, a streamlined liberal arts core curriculum, and expanded career-oriented offerings, including a new master of management degree. Financial expectations would be annual giving of $1 to $1.5 million dollars to balance the operating budget, restoration of endowment assets, and retirement of obligations of a $1.7 million deficit. The plan also projected a capital fund program to increase the endowment by raising $10 to $12.5 million during the decade.[15]

Driven by the need for increased enrollment, the college implemented major curricular changes. The 4-1-4, which had an unprofitable January term, was replaced with a 4-4-1, with a May term that proved to be more attractive to local students. New offerings included the Legal Assistant Certificate Program, in which students learned basic legal principles under the guidance of local attorneys, judges, legal secretaries, and paralegal personnel, and the degree program in applied politics affiliated with the American Institute of Applied Politics, a private bipartisan organization. Students completed comprehensive liberal arts requirements, and, under the guidance of political professionals, studied campaign management techniques, such as fund raising, political research, and lobbying.[16] Courses in continuing education also proliferated. An article in *Newscope* noted that students could learn "to appreciate and identify red and white wines, design a newsletter on your kitchen table, trounce your neighbor in a fast-paced game of bridge, be a better step-parent, or overcome the guilt that so often accompanies divorce."[17]

Since declaring financial exigency in 1979, the college had been functioning without a formal operations manual to provide the faculty and staff with clear statements of conditions of employment. A committee headed by Vice President Steeples produced a *Faculty Handbook* that made distinctions between contractual matters and administrative aspects of college operations. After extended discussion and debate, the faculty overwhelmingly approved the new document, which gave the board of trustees more explicit control over conditions of faculty appointments, teaching loads, tenure, compensation, and personnel procedures.[18] Trustees also ratified a new mission statement that described the college as being dedicated "to the integration of liberal education with career and professional programs." Discussion centered around the reference to Westminster as a "church-related" college. By a vote of 21-18, the faculty recommended omitting the phrase, but President Cornell suggested that "church-related" be replaced by "Judeo-Christian," a phraseology approved by the board of trustees by a vote of 18-2.[19]

Rapprochement with the Latter-day Saints Church also reached a new level. President Cornell recommended to the board of trustees that Mormon leader N. Eldon Tanner be awarded an honorary degree at a special convocation on February 25, 1981. With the entire First Presidency of the Mormon Church in attendance and television cameras recording the event, Tanner received accolades from dignitaries, including Cornell, who said, "We salute you who has done so much for our

College and our students." O. C. Tanner, acknowledging the dramatic change in relations between the Latter-day Saints and Westminster College, stated "President Tanner, you have lighted a torch for an institution that would hardly have expected it."[20]

Despite the implementation of the Tickton Report, Westminster continued to experience financial difficulties. Cornell raised more than a million dollars during each of his three years as president, but he could not keep pace with a volatile economy and declining enrollment. Cash flow was so problematic that fiscal officers prepared a daily status sheet for Cornell showing the bank balance each morning, and local suppliers demanded payment in advance before making deliveries. By the fall of 1980 additional personnel cuts were required to avoid continuing deficits. The college announced in the spring of 1981 that majors in music, geology, and political science would be eliminated, resulting in the loss of six full-time faculty equivalents. Faculty and administrators clashed regarding these decisions, and campus morale plunged.[21]

In his zeal to present a positive image of Westminster, Cornell sometimes overestimated potential gains and understated actual problems. Downplaying the retrenchment, Cornell presented an optimistic financial report at a press conference with representatives from the *Deseret News* and *Salt Lake Tribune*. Announcing that Westminster would produce its first balanced budget since 1974, Cornell affirmed that the college was "turning the corner" and heading toward better days as an academic institution. When financial figures were released in July 1981, however, they revealed a deficit of $324,000 for the 1980–81 academic year.[22] When the Northwest Association of Schools and Colleges gave the college a qualified six-months' accreditation in 1981 and warned that Westminster was in danger of losing its accreditation unless it immediately rectified institutional finances, Cornell emphasized only the positive aspects of the report. A bold headline in the college newsletter proclaimed, "WE DID IT!" implying that Westminster had passed its accreditation visit with flying colors.[23]

In addition to the financial problems, Cornell experienced conflicts with staff, trustees, faculty, and students. In part due to conditions beyond his control, in other respects they were exacerbated by his administrative style and failure to establish rapport with the various constituencies. Some observers attributed these difficulties to Cornell's image as one who never really understood the unique cultural environment of the intermountain region. Others pointed to his outbreaks of temper that sometimes resulted in overreaction to incidental problems. Staff members reportedly were fired in the hallway when the president was upset over some aspect of work performance.[24] Cornell also clashed with key members of the board of trustees who thought that the president was not being entirely honest regarding Westminster's financial difficulties. Cornell's optimism in the face of mounting deficits and declining institutional support in the Salt Lake community caused some trustees to wonder aloud if Westminster needed a new leader. At a board meeting in February 1981, almost one-third of the thirty-six trustees resigned, citing "personal reasons" as the cause of their action. Others expressed their displeasure by erratic attendance. On a number of occasions, the board conducted business with only one-third of its membership.[25] Trustee Robert Weyher, a long-time board member and prominent supporter of the college, demonstrated his opposition to Cornell at a convocation at which the speaker, a protégé of Cornell, congratulated the president for his service to the college. Weyher rose from the podium and exited the meeting in full view of the audience. He did not attend another board meeting during the remainder of Cornell's leadership.[26]

During the spring of 1981, students organized a referendum concerning Cornell's administration. Disturbed over faculty terminations and conflicting stories regarding the future of college programs and the school's financial status, the students conducted an unscientific poll that indicated that nearly seventy percent of the student body disapproved of Cornell's leadership. The students released a statement in which they charged that the administration had made "false and/or misleading statements regarding the direction, program, and financial position of the college." They also challenged the administration to produce a "Constant Statement of Truth" to clear the air of rumors and conflicting reports that emerged almost daily from official and unofficial sources.[27] A contributor to the *Parson* described the administration as elusive and uncommunicative. Regarding Cornell, the writer said, "It's just too bad that a virtual unknown waltzes in here from Ulululand and seizes credit for saving the college, while relegating all of you to the relative anonymity known only as the faculty."[28]

When a team from the Northwest Association of Schools and Colleges visited Westminster in the fall of 1981, it found a campus on the verge of fiscal collapse. According to the accreditation report, campus morale was at a low ebb. Faculty were becoming increasingly fatalistic about the institution's future even though the many years of survival with constant losses had made it difficult for them to accept the seriousness of the present problems, an attitude the visitation committee termed "disastrous." The committee also perceived a "reservoir of fear" among faculty because of the rapid changes and hard decisions already made and those that might continue to be made without consultation with the college community. Cautioning administrators to be sensitive to this situation because uncertainty "quickly translates into a diminished educational project," visitation chairman James F. Bemis reaffirmed accreditation but called for a report on the financial condition of the college by May 1, 1982. Unless the college demonstrated progress in balancing its budget and ceasing interfund borrowing, the committee would recommend that Westminster's accreditation be revoked. Bemis informed Cornell, "The action is to be interpreted as a next to last chance for Westminster College to demonstrate that it continues to merit the confidence which accreditation implies."[29]

As financial conditions failed to improve and morale deteriorated, even Cornell's supporters recognized that change was both inevitable and desirable.[30] Acknowledging that he had done his best and that it was not good enough, Cornell submitted his resignation on January 26, 1982. In an interview with the *Salt Lake Tribune,* Cornell stated that his three years at Westminster constituted the most difficult period of his academic career. He attributed much of his administration's turmoil to the inevitable result of change and admitted that "many of these changes have left bruises, scars, anger and resentment." He remained convinced that actions he and his staff had taken to implement the Tickton Report had started Westminster on the road to recovery and that, despite its present institutional crisis, the future of the college remained bright.[31]

Trustees again turned to James Petersen for leadership, this time on a permanent rather than an interim basis. Returning to the office in February 1982, Petersen's agenda contained no academic subtleties or programmatic innovations. Addressing the college community, Petersen stated, "Let's eliminate the trauma of forced decisions dictated by economics. Let's place Westminster on the kind of secure economic foundation that will allow it to continue."[32] Even though some skeptics doubted that the blue collar president could accomplish the task, Westminster supporters hoped that the administrative change would prove beneficial, and indeed Petersen's informality and directness initially reduced tensions and stimulated confidence on campus. In a welcome letter to returning students he said, "I look forward to having an opportunity to greet each one of you personally as the semester goes by. As the President, I have an open door policy. I invite you to visit with me to get acquainted."[33] At the same time, he was refreshingly candid in his dealings with faculty, many of whom expressed dissatisfaction with working conditions at the financially strapped college. Informing a faculty member that she merited a promotion but would not receive increased compensation, Petersen bluntly told her, "A faculty member only days ago shouted at me, 'This contract is a blankety blank disgrace,' and I had to agree. The same statement can be made in far too many instances."[34]

Before Petersen had settled into an office routine, he was already working on damage control. An article in the *Salt Lake Tribune* by education editor Diane Cole cast the college in an unfavorable light and triggered a new round of closure rumors. Assuming that the college was on the verge of "becoming history" due to financial problems, Cole conducted interviews with LDS and University of Utah officials, soliciting their interest in taking over Westminster's assets. Neither organization expressed any intention to include the Westminster campus in their expansion plans. According to Cole, Westminster's future looked bleak.[35] Admitting that the article was damaging, Petersen called a town meeting to present a more positive portrait of Westminster's status. With local press and television reporters on hand, Petersen assured the audience that Westminster was not on a trajectory for absorption by other educational entities. He cited recent support from the LDS Church and indicated that he anticipated additional financial contributions from a variety of sources. Petersen also expressed confidence that Westminster would continue to provide a quality education for Salt Lake City residents and the intermountain region.[36]

Nevertheless, fiscal issues persisted. Fearing that Westminster would be priced out of the educational market, trustees rejected the administration's pleas to raise tuition by ten percent for the 1982–83 academic year. Even the low tuition rates, however, failed to attract students in sufficient numbers to provide the college with enough immediate cash to meet operating expenses. The public building inspector condemned and ordered closed Ferry Hall; other buildings badly needed major repairs. Plans to revitalize the Alternative Entry Program could not be made operative, and auditors warned that Westminster's debts and its need to address structural modifications of buildings indicated that the institution could not remain in existence much longer. Interfund borrowing stood at $1.2 million, most of which came from endowment funds. Without an immediate infusion of cash, it appeared that Westminster's treasury would run dry at the end of April 1983.[37]

Petersen hoped that a proposal submitted to a local foundation would result in a major contribution to the college and generate sufficient working capital to maintain day-to-day operations. That hope ended on November 24, 1982, when the foundation failed to deliver either endowment funds or a large cash subsidy. Instead, it awarded Westminster fifty new four-year merit scholarships worth nearly a quarter of a million dollars, but not enough to save the school. At this point, Petersen rallied his staff and the board of trustees to take charge of the institution's destiny. Describing Westminster as "a nice little college in a lot of trouble," Petersen said that the college was directionless and incapable of making important and difficult decisions, and a new strategy would have to be devised to save the college from perishing. In particular, Petersen thought that faculty leaders were too ambivalent regarding issues that called for immediate and decisive action. He felt that public confidence in the school had to be restored so that it could continue to attract students and secure financial support.[38]

At a special closed meeting of the trustee's executive committee on November 29, 1982, staff members requested permission to enact a radical reorganization plan that called for closing down the institution and reopening under a new name. This procedure, they reported, had been followed by several financially troubled small colleges with positive results. After much questioning and with considerable hesitancy, the committee agreed with one of the board members who said, "Why not? Nothing else has worked. This might."[39] During the following six weeks, key staff members, Steeples, Morgan, Green, and Dean of Students Deborah Jenkins, worked in strict secrecy, holding late evening or early morning meetings off campus in order not to arouse suspicion regarding their activities. Believing that prolonged debate would delay action until it was too late to save the college, they excluded the faculty from the deliberation process. They also wanted an element of surprise which they considered essential in order to capture public attention and rally enthusiasm for a revitalized college. Only with a new positive identity could public confidence in Westminster be restored.[40]

In preparation for reorganization, staff members visited the University of Charleston in West Virginia, which had experienced a successful reorganization. The Charleston president told them, "Plan to succeed, but be prepared to fail." Under advisement by Westminster trustees, the group also conferred with local attorneys and the state commissioner of higher education to explore questions of liability, contractual rights, and due process. Since concerns for creditors' rights precluded a full-scale bankruptcy organization, the group decided simply to transform the organization by rewriting the bylaws.[41] At a meeting on January 5, 1983, the executive committee of the board of trustees accepted the reorganization plan and called a meeting of the full board for January 17 in order to elect a new chair and vote on the plan. Petersen introduced the reorganization plan with a call for action. He told trustees that the faculty for the past twenty-five years had managed to tie the hands of the administration, making effective government impossible.

By approving this radical reorganization, the board could regain control of the college's destiny and lead it to recovery.[42]

The reorganization plan revolved around five resolutions. One reaffirmed financial exigency and a second revised articles of incorporation, changing the college's name and giving the board more flexibility by transferring most regulations to the bylaws where they could be modified or superseded by trustee vote. A third resolution provided for registration of the amended articles with Utah's secretary of state, and a fourth, through a twenty-page amendment, completely rewrote the bylaws. The new bylaws made college employees, including faculty and students, ineligible for membership on the board. Term limits for trustees and a new "necessary and proper" clause ensured continuity, provided for change in leadership, and enlarged the board's authority to take action. The fifth resolution described the internal organization of the new college, which featured a streamlined administration organized into three areas: education, support, and marketing. Academic programs were to be housed in four new schools: arts and science, nursing and health sciences, business, and professional studies, the latter designed to attract nontraditional adult students.[43]

The carefully orchestrated surprise culminated in an all-college convocation called for the morning of January 18, 1983, in the college gymnasium to which the local media had been invited. As the meeting convened, workers were hurriedly installing secretly prepared campus signs that proclaimed the creation of a new institution. The former Westminster College became Westminster College of Salt Lake City. At the meeting Petersen and trustee chairman Weyher informed the audience of the major features of reorganization, including the new name and administrative divisions. They also announced that letters were in the mail to all employees informing them that their positions with the current college would end at 11:59 P.M. on June 30, 1983. Everyone was invited to apply for available posts for the new college which would open on July 1, 1983. All faculty members, tenured and untenured, were invited to respond with letters of intent and updated credentials by February 7 if they desired to remain with the college after June 30. Tenure rights and eligibility for tenure of current faculty were to be maintained, but new faculty added after reorganization would receive multiple-year, renewable appointments rather than tenure.[44]

Immediately following the convocation, administrators held a press conference to elaborate on their actions and to invite questions. As anticipated, they received extensive coverage on television and in the press, much of it positive. The *Deseret News* and *Salt Lake Tribune* responded favorably to Westminster's dramatic reorganization announcement. Editorials in both papers acknowledged the difficulty of the decision but agreed that the school's survival depended on decisive action. The *News* called Westminster's action "a bold and critical step" and affirmed that "the educational and cultural climate of the state certainly would be poorer if the school succumbed."[45] *Tribune* education editor Diane Cole praised Westminster administrators for their innovative measures, but reported that while students and administrators seemed to support the new plan, faculty feelings were mixed.[46] Although most faculty agreed that Westminster's precarious financial status warranted immediate attention, many resented their exclusion from input into the process and questioned implementing such a sweeping institutional change in total secrecy. Long-time faculty member Barry Quinn, professor of biology and the faculty chair, publicly expressed his dismay regarding the nonparticipatory process and observed that "there is a very depressed air about the campus."[47] Others described the treatment of faculty and staff as demeaning and demoralizing and expressed their wish that the reorganization could have been conducted in a more humane manner. An observation about the reorganization attributed to Professor Jay Lees is still quoted. "Having tenure at Westminster College is like being strapped to a deck chair on the Titanic."[48]

Three weeks after the announcement, the newly constituted board named Petersen president, and he in turn reappointed his current staff as administrative officers of the college. A review of curriculum and staffing needs quickly followed. In a letter directed to the faculty Committees of Appointment and Rank, Academic Planning, and Curriculum, Petersen set forth a comprehensive cost-cutting program that reduced college expenses by more than half a million dollars. Included in the proposal were reductions in the size of traditional liberal arts programs and departments and the elimination of aviation and early childhood majors. Eight faculty positions were eliminated, including tenured posts in history and education, and staff cuts were made in all nonacademic areas except student services, which was still understaffed from previous cuts. Proposed additions to the curriculum included two humanities courses for first-year students, computer science instruction, an interdisciplinary capstone course, and comprehensive examinations for seniors, a device to gauge program and graduate quality in comparison with national performance measures. While Petersen's letter invited faculty committees to study the proposals and make suggestions, it did not ask for a formal vote or endorsement. Faculty who opposed the institution's underlying philosophy were advised to look elsewhere for employment.[49] Faculty members experienced another shock when Petersen informed them late in February that contrary to what had been previously stated about the continuance of tenure, all faculty appointments for the 1983–84 academic year would be for one year only. According to a decision reached by the board of trustees, "there would be no faculty appointments on continuous tenure." Initially, trustees opted to add thirty-day cancellation clauses to future faculty contracts, but rescinded that action when informed that accreditation would almost certainly be withdrawn if they followed that action.[50]

The dramatic reorganization of 1983 bought time and enhanced Westminster's image in the Salt Lake community, but it failed to alter the underlying problems of financial exigency and campus stability. A follow-up visitation by the Northwest Association accreditation team in May 1983 resulted in an extremely negative evaluation of the college's financial condition that concluded, "The well is nearly dry." The team was also critical of the secretive reorganization process, terming it "unwise if not inhumane," and stated that the means by which abrogation of tenure and rehiring were handled fostered suspicion, uncertainty, and distrust. Noting that one of the purposes of reorganization was to clarify the ultimate authority of the trustees and administration over the faculty, the visitation team highlighted a sentence in the revised *Faculty Handbook* that asserted, "It is the case that the Board of Trustees of Westminster College of Salt Lake City retains final authority in all matters." Acknowledging that this was not a new policy, the team nevertheless found it significant that trustees put it in writing.[51]

In a summary letter to Petersen, visitation chairman Bemis accused the school of moving backward rather than forward since 1981 and issued a "show-cause" ultimatum that unless Westminster could successfully document progress in eleven specified areas by the end of the year, he would recommend that the college's accreditation be withdrawn at the association's next annual meeting. The areas specified by Bemis included repayment of debts, increased enrollment, a balanced budget, a substantial increase in unrestricted gifts, and development of realistic plans for dealing with chronic financial problems. Bemis also required Westminster to decide whether it was to be a school of liberal arts or one of specialized education, to include faculty in decision making and improve communications between faculty and administration, and to remove trustees from involvement in decisions regarding curriculum that were normally the prerogative of faculty and administration.[52]

Anticipating such a response from the Northwest Association, Westminster officials had planned several fund-raising strategies to forestall loss of accreditation. Instead of depending on older adult enrollment, administrators decided to channel a disproportionate amount of money into efforts to attract traditional students, a concept that went counter to the Tickton Report. At the same time, the college announced that it would increase tuition fifteen percent for the 1983–84 academic year. Critics questioned whether Westminster could afford to invest so heavily in recruitment at a time when finances were scarce and doubted the wisdom of raising tuition when attendance at the college had been on a downward trend for several years. The new strategy, however, paid dividends, led by Allan Kuusisto, who had replaced Steeples in 1983 as vice president for academic affairs. A combination of tactics, including economy measures, renewal of public confidence, and aggressive marketing, triggered a turn-around. Because the University of Utah placed caps on enrollment and Brigham Young University filled to capacity, Westminster was able to attract many LDS students. As a result, the number of incoming first-year students increased more than fifty percent, from 86 in 1982 to 133 in 1983, and the fall semester head count went up 5.5 percent to 1,255.[53]

Yet even these positive signs could not stabilize Westminster's tenu-ous financial condition. Unless the college could raise a significant sum of money before the end of the year, its accreditation remained in jeopardy. Some trustees reportedly said that only a miracle could save the college from extinction. Apparently that miracle came about as the result of a tragedy that took the life of a Westminster aviation student during the spring of 1983. On a foggy morning in April, Louis Merz crashed his res-cue helicopter into the nearby Wasatch Mountains while traveling from the University of Utah Hospital to pick up a young child who was sched-uled for surgery. Westminster students initiated a $40,000 scholarship fund drive in Merz's name and requested donations from Salt Lake City citizens. Touched by the tragic loss of life, Berenice Jewett Bradshaw appeared unannounced at Petersen's office and informed the president that she would fund the balance of the Merz scholarship, which amounted to approximately $20,000. Learning from Petersen of the college's des-perate financial status, Bradshaw said she would consider another gift to the college in the range of half a million dollars.[54]

Bradshaw had the means and the motivation to support Westminster College. She had attended Westminster as a high school student in 1922 with fond memories of her educational experience on the Presbyterian campus. Her recently deceased husband, Franklin Bradshaw, who forged an automotive parts and gas and oil enterprise in the intermountain west, left her a considerable fortune. Bradshaw's initial gift of $300,000 infused cash at a crucial moment and turned out to be only the beginning of con-tributions that in fewer than twenty months would amount to $800,000.

She was honored in 1985 as the college's largest single benefactor with gifts in excess of $2 million.[55]

Additional gifts followed Bradshaw's beneficence, including substantial contributions from the Wilbert (Bill) Gore family, long-time supporters of Westminster, and other individuals and local foundations.[56] The Northwest Association voted to withdraw its show-cause warning in December 1983 with the stipulation that Westminster produce a satisfactory progress report one year from that date. Business Manager Morgan reported to the board of trustees in September 1984 that Westminster's fiscal year had ended with an operating surplus of $503,000, with record gift receipts of $1.57 million. The college had made it through the summer without borrowing money, and revenue from tuition increases covered sixty-five percent of operating expenses compared to forty-six percent in recent years. When Northwest Association representative Leonard Rice visited the campus in October 1984, he concluded that the school had "recovered well and is now in a reasonably sound fiscal and academic condition." A balanced budget, deficit reduction, growing endowment, and increased enrollment featured prominently in his report. Moreover, he indicated that faculty morale had significantly improved, that their role in the governance of the college had been clarified in the revised *Faculty Handbook*, and that the role of the board of trustees in everyday college operations had considerably diminished. In summary, Rice concluded that 1983–84 was, as asserted by the college, a "turnaround year" and that conditions looked favorable for the coming year.[57]

Westminster nevertheless found itself embroiled in a prolonged tenure dispute initiated by Jack J. Gifford, a professor of history, who took his case to the American Association of University Professors (AAUP), charging that administrative officials had not followed proper procedures in terminating his contract. An AAUP visitation team determined that Westminster officials were unable to demonstrate that the college's financial exigency required the termination of faculty appointments and that it operated against Gifford contrary to principles of academic tenure that were generally accepted at American institutions of higher learning. Affirming that Westminster trustees and administrators had imperiled academic freedom by removing the safeguards of tenure, the committee called for Gifford's restoration to his professorial position and for the reinstitution of tenure. When President Petersen declined to reverse Gifford's dismissal, the AAUP in 1985 placed Westminster on a list of censured administrations and recommended that members of faculty associations not accept appointments at the college. These sanctions remain in effect to the present day.[58]

During the summer of 1984, Petersen informed trustees that the coming academic year would be his last at Westminster. In making his decision public, Petersen stated, "I think that the College has been turned around and the foundation for continuing progress has been laid. It is a good time to move on."[59] His three and one-half years at Westminster had been pivotal ones for the college, with Petersen presiding over the rescue of a floundering institution. Despite a residue of faculty resentment, he managed to restore the sense of community that had been eroded. During the extended reorganization campus morale reached a nadir, but a climate of cautious optimism was emerging.[60] One trustee observed, "He had the courage to make the hard decisions to get the college where it is today." Another said that Petersen had a genuine concern for people and an uncanny ability to relate to them. "Despite his rough side, Pete is one of the great intellectuals I've known."[61] Prior to his retirement, Petersen was awarded an honorary doctor of laws degree from the University of Utah in recognition of his accomplishments in business and college administration.

In preparation for a national search for a president, committee members developed a profile for screening potential candidates. Mindful of Westminster's previous decade of monetary crises, they placed "fund raiser" and "ability to deal with large donors" at the top of their list. But the committee also wanted a multitalented individual to lead Westminster: an educator and an administrator with a demand for excellence and a forceful personality who could deal with people. Only one interviewee—Charles H. Dick—scored high in all categories.[62] Dick was an experienced academician whose previous positions included president of Centenary College in New Jersey, vice president for development and public affairs at Cornell University Medical Center in New York, and deputy assistant secretary for health in Washington, D.C., during the Nixon administration. A graduate of the University of Kansas in biological sciences and communication, the fifty-five-year-old president-elect also held a master's degree from California State University and a Ph.D. in marketing and management from Northwestern University. An accomplished flutist and avid jogger, Dick brought a combination of energy, enthusiasm, and experience to Westminster at a crucial period in its history.[63]

Dick accepted the presidency on March 26 and assumed office on July 1, 1985, marking the beginning of ten years of service to Westminster College. A senior faculty member asked Dick, "Why would you want to be president of a college like this?" Dick responded, "I like challenges, and this certainly is a unique one."[64] In a more formal setting, Dick replied to the same question, "I accepted the job because the institution has taken a good look at itself and can move ahead. It is ready to build on the solid foundation established in the last several years."[65] A self-acknowledged pragmatist, Dick felt that Westminster's future lay in its ability to meet the educational needs of Salt Lake City and the wider Utah community.

In his opening address to the Westminster faculty, Dick articulated a vision for Westminster in the coming years. Calling for "innovative, quality education" in a rapidly changing educational environment, Dick praised the faculty for past accomplishments and challenged it to lead Westminster into a new era of service. He assured the audience of his commitment to academic freedom and promised to involve faculty in decision-making procedures, although Dick reminded them that he and the board of trustees would make the final decisions. "I know that some of my decisions may not be popular," he said, "but I hope that you will be able to say, 'It didn't happen the way I wanted it to, but I did have input into the decision.'"[66]

Early in his presidency, Dick appointed a representative Strategic Planning Committee, chaired by Executive Vice President Stephen R. Morgan, to identify approaches to ensure the continued success of Westminster College. From its research and consultation, the committee developed twelve goals that would strengthen the educational enterprise, and, with input from other administrative and faculty officers, means by which the goals could be accomplished. The objectives included the integration of a broad liberal education, with a balance among the liberal arts and the professional programs, support for professional development for teaching faculty, increased enrollment and less dependence on unrestricted private gifts for daily operations, sensitivity to changing educational patterns and flexibility in responding to student demands for new courses and programs, and more emphasis on placement services. Specifically, the committee recommended that Westminster should plan on an enrollment of approximately two thousand five hundred, maintain a balance of students at about seventy-five percent undergraduates and twenty-five percent graduates, place greater emphasis on attracting and retaining full-time students, broaden the constituency of the student body and increase the ratio of international students, and raise the academic quality of entering students.[67]

Dick needed to identify the sources of fiscal resources to implement this program. Three families played prominent roles in Westminster's renaissance during the late 1980s and the early 1990s. Berenice Bradshaw continued to support the college as she had done during Petersen's administration. Wilbert L. (Bill) and Vieve Gore and their daughter Ginger Gore Giovale extended their family's commitment to Westminster with major contributions to endowment and campus expansion, and George S. Eccles, Dolores Doré Eccles, and their foundation, whose gifts to Westminster dated back to the 1960s, also played an important role in the dramatic increase of endowment income and scholarship aid. Eccles personal and foundation-related donations included a $4 million grant in 1993.[68] By 1991 Bradshaw's donations had exceeded $4 million, and, before her death in 1996, she had contributed more than $8 million to various campus projects and programs. Most prominent was for the Jewett Center for the Arts and Humanities that consisted of a modern performing arts center and renovated and refurbished Converse and Foster Halls. The $2.5 million Jewett Center for the Performing Arts, dedicated on April 13, 1991, contained rehearsal rooms, faculty offices, a 267-seat theater, and a 100-seat conservatory.[69]

Following Bill Gore's death in 1986, Vieve Gore and Ginger Gore Giovale underwrote the $1.7 million Bill and Vieve Gore School of Business Building, which was dedicated in October 1988. Shortly thereafter, Giovale, who had been a trustee since the early 1970s, became chair of the board, the first woman in Westminster's history to so serve, and announced a Challenge of Freedom Campaign that rallied Westminster supporters to raise $1.5 million with a pledge that the Gore-Giovale family would match that amount, the total $3 million designated for endowment. Within four months the campaign reached its goal.[70] When Giovale announced the successful completion in October 1989, she also informed the board of trustees that the operating deficit had been eliminated for the first time in nearly forty years and that the operating fund balance had reached half a million dollars. She made the motion that the stigma of financial exigency under which Westminster had labored for nearly a decade be removed; it was greeted by standing applause.[71]

But the Gore-Giovale family were only beginning their philanthropic contributions to Westminster College. As honorary chair of a new $25 million Challenge of Freedom campaign, Vieve Gore announced her intention to give $7 million dollars for the endowment, at the time the single largest gift made to any Utah college or university. As a result, by the end of 1991 the endowment fund exceeded $14 million dollars and continued to grow as support for the college increased. In 1995 trustees displayed plans for a new forty-seven thousand square foot three-level library named for Ginger Gore Giovale and John Giovale, its primary donors. The $14 million edifice, which takes its architectural cues from Westminster's stately Converse Hall, opened for campus use in the fall of 1997. New state-of-the-art computing centers connect library users with access to the latest in information technology, library databases, and bibliographic tools.[72]

Indicative of the deep-rooted community loyalty to the college is the Woman's Board of Westminster College, which has raised funds annually for specific campus needs. Organized in 1911 in conjunction with the opening of Ferry Hall, the Woman's Board held its first silver tea benefit in 1916 and raised $53. Between 1916 and 1983 the board contributed almost $150,000 for scholarships, landscaping, building restoration, library books, and audiovisual and computing equipment. It has also provided countless hours of volunteer work in preparation for fund raising events and has provided hostesses at college receptions. Today the organization continues among Westminster College's most loyal and active supporters. In the past ten years, the Woman's Board has contributed $64,055 to a scholarship program; it annually awards to students four $1,500 and five $2,000 scholarships.[73]

Undergirded by improved financial conditions, the Dick administration implemented the college's strategic planning goals. Two vice presidents for academic affairs, Michael Gershowitz and Stephen R. Baar, developed programs and courses to attract a diverse student body. Baar, whose experience at Westminster as an English professor and divisional dean dated back to 1971, assumed the senior academic post in 1988 and remains in that position today. His extended service to the college provides continuity, and his openness to change facilitates innovative programming.[74] One of the most successful curricular experiments has been a diversified and upgraded graduate education emphasis. New programs including the Master of Business Administration (M.B.A.), Master of Professional Communication (M.P.C.), and Master of Nursing (M.S.N.) joined with the Master of Education (M.Ed.) emphasize Westminster's business and professional orientation.[75] One of the unique features of the programs is that graduate students are encouraged to take some electives from another program area. M.S.N. students can take an M.B.A. class in health care administration, and M.B.A.s can take an M.P.C. business writing course or one in visual communication. The graduate programs also have strong clinical or experiential components. M.Ed. students must be currently teaching or training, M.B.A. candidates engage in internships, M.P.C. students complete a field project, and M.S.N. students train to become nurse practitioners.[76]

In undergraduate education, the Department of History announced a new history major in 1989 that includes field studies and internships. A few years later the Business School introduced a bachelor of arts degree in business and international business. The 3-2 engineering program features three years at Westminster during which students gain a strong liberal arts foundation and two years of specialization at either the

University of Southern California or Washington University in St. Louis. Through seminars and small classes in the Westminster honors program, fifty-two select students study humanities, social sciences, fine arts, mathematics, and natural sciences. This program uses team-teaching in which faculty members from different disciplines interact and involve students in discussions of important issues. A four-year honors degree program, limited to twenty-five students, requires the completion of a sequence of interdisciplinary, team-taught honors courses. Another Westminster innovation was the establishment of the Tanner-McMurrin Lecture in 1987, based on an endowment from Obert C. and Grace Adams Tanner. Named in honor of the Tanners and Sterling McMurrin, the lecture series brings to campus major scholars in the history and philosophy of religion to give public addresses and conduct seminars. Speakers have included E. E. Eriksen, Jaroslav Pelikan, Martin Marty, Harvey Cox, and Rosemary Radford Ruether.[77]

As curricular offerings expanded and enrollment reached the two thousand mark, Westminster became more selective in its admissions process and improved working conditions for faculty. Faculty teaching loads were reduced to twenty-four hours per academic year, and salaries increased to near the national norms for private colleges. By the 1987–88 academic year a contractual review process had been established, and contracts extending up to five years were being issued. Creation of a Faculty Senate in 1987 allowed faculty participation in curricular decisions and provided a forum for discussion of a variety of issues related to the institutional mission. Presently one faculty representative sits as an observer at meetings of the board of trustees, and faculty serve on several trustee committees. Other indications of faculty support include summer research grants, travel funds, and faculty training and development workshops. An Excellence in Teaching Award has been inaugurated, and Westminster's first endowed faculty chair has been established.[78]

Visiting team reports from the Northwest Association in 1988 and 1993 confirmed that Westminster was shedding its image as a financially troubled institution in search of an educational mission. When Francis J. Kerins visited campus in May 1988 to verify an interim progress report previously submitted by the college, he found it to be accurate and complete and noted that there had been "a remarkable turnaround" at Westminster bringing it from "a condition of hazard to a very healthy state." In an accompanying letter to Dick, he stated that what had transpired since 1983 was "just short of a miracle."[79] In 1993 the Northwest Association conducted a comprehensive accreditation evaluation under the leadership of Patrick J. Ford, academic vice president of

Gonzaga University. From beginning to end, the accreditation report had complimentary remarks, such as "dramatic," "extraordinary," and "remarkable," to describe Westminster's financial, academic, and attitudinal status. The accreditation team found a competent and stable financial management system in place and a coherent master plan for the development and renovation of the campus in process. It observed that the college had received an unqualified opinion by independent auditors since 1984, had accumulated an endowment in excess of $18 million, and had eradicated the cumulative deficit in the current fund. With a balance of more than $1 million in place, the college no longer faced the threat of closure. In summarizing Westminster's financial status, the committee noted "an extraordinary qualitative growth and improvement in the entire approach to fiscal management since the last full scale review."[80]

The committee also gave high marks to Westminster's expanded educational program both in terms of its organizational structure and its outcomes assessment. The new programs were drawing students and also helping them to find jobs in a variety of fields. Students reported high satisfaction with the quality of academic offerings and the supportiveness of faculty. They ranked faculty availability and concern for individuals as one of the most important parts of their Westminster experience. While the committee expressed concern about heavy reliance on part-time and adjunct faculty, inadequate library facilities, and ambiguities in the institutional mission statement, the overall assessment of Westminster's academic achievements was very positive.[81] In the important area of campus attitudes, the evaluation committee reported considerable improvement. During the 1970s and 1980s, Northwest Association teams frequently commented on low morale among faculty and students and high tension among administrators, trustees, and faculty. In 1993 team members discovered an atmosphere characterized by cooperation and a common quest for the fulfillment of educational goals. They noted no unwarranted intrusion of trustees into administrative spheres and saw increased involvement of faculty in curricular decisions at all levels of college operations. With minor exceptions, they found a lack of the "we-they divisions" once so prevalent.[82]

During Dick's tenure as president, marginal relationships with the Presbyterian, Methodist, and United Church of Christ denominations ended. Dick continued to attend meetings of Presbyterian college presidents and maintained contacts with the Synod of Rocky Mountains, but he referred to Westminster's religious orientation as ecumenical rather than denominational. Dick explained his position to United Church of

Christ officials in 1986. Noting that nearly half of Westminster's student body came from LDS families, he said that if a private college is to be successful in the midst of a Latter-day Saint community, it *"must* take the position of nonspecific alliance with *any* denomination."[83]

Subsequent actions by the Westminster board of trustees in 1993 and 1995 clarified policies regarding the college's historic church relationships. Urged by the Northwest Association to align its mission statement with its current academic programs, the college reviewed its mission, beginning with faculty committee recommendations and concluding with trustee modification and endorsement. The existing statement included a phrase, "As an institution rooted in the Judeo-Christian tradition," which became the focal point of considerable discussion. A substantial majority of the faculty favored deleting the phrase because they thought it no longer accurately represented the institutional ethos. After extended discussion, the board of trustees by a vote of 14-2 sustained the faculty, and the phrase was removed and inserted in a brief historical statement in the college catalog.[84] In 1995 the trustees amended its bylaws to remove the requirement of guaranteed representation on the board, an action that ended the right of the Synod of Rocky Mountains of the Presbyterian Church (U.S.A.) to nominate one trustee and that removed the last formal connection between the denomination and the college.[85]

The college has maintained an active intramural sports program with a variety of team and individual sports that provide recreational opportunities for students, faculty, and staff. Westminster ceased its intercollegiate athletics program in 1979, although in response to student interest, Westminster reinstated varsity men's soccer in 1982 and initiated women's volleyball in 1995. Despite their low-budget operations, the Parsons compete effectively with peer institutions in the NAIA Cascade Conference.[86] In 1988 Westminster entered into a formal relationship with the Utah Jazz of the National Basketball Association, granting the team limited use of Payne Gymnasium and the weight room facilities. The presence of the Jazz on campus attracted media and heightened public awareness of Westminster. As part of the agreement, the Jazz provided the college with season tickets for home games, distributed to faculty and staff by means of a monthly drawing.[87]

Student life changed dramatically during the 1980s and 1990s. In the past, social activities and the campus were inextricably intertwined. As the number of resident students dwindled and the social groups separated by fields of study, ages, life styles, and family responsibilities, no identifiable unified center of campus life emerged. Events such as the Spring Fling, the Tanner-McMurrin lectures, soccer games, and the Poetry Series have drawn crowds of students from different segments of the campus community. No longer is it possible to gather the entire student body for one event, a feature that contributed to a closeness among previous student generations. Current leaders of the Associated Students of Westminster College (ASWC) are challenged to plan functions that appeal to a diverse student body, most of whom spend only a few hours a day on campus.[88]

Early in April 1994 Dick announced his intention to retire on June 30, 1995, after a decade of service to Westminster College. The accomplishments of his tenure were impressive: endowment increased from $1.7 million to $21 million; a $25 million capital campaign successfully completed; enrollment doubled; three new buildings erected and three others completely renovated; new graduate and undergraduate degree programs launched; and increases in faculty and staff salaries. Perhaps Dick's most important achievement, however, was the improved image of Westminster in the Salt Lake City community. During his tenure, the college acquired stability and a reputation for offering caring and quality education.[89] Westminster recognized the leadership and service of the Dicks with a farewell dinner in the grand ballroom of the Red Lion Hotel. In addition to renaming the Science Building in Dick's honor, trustees announced that $20,000 had been raised to name a room for Charles and Barbara Dick in the new Giovale Library. Dick's parting message to the college community contained a challenge for future leaders. "Westminster College is at a pivotal point in its history. While we can justifiably celebrate our accomplishments, we must take bold steps to insure its future. The college must build on its strengths if it is to remain a quality institution."[90]

NOTES

1. "Debt Puts School in Jeopardy," *Salt Lake Tribune*, 27 January 1970; and "Westminster President Quits," *Deseret News*, 27 January 1979. For student response, see "Academic Council Talks Retrenchment," *Parson*, 23 February 1979, 1–2.

2. "Westminster President Hopes to Solve Institution's Crisis," *Salt Lake Tribune*, 1 April 1979; and "President Pete Responsible for Turnaround at Westminster," *Daily Utah Chronicle*, 28 September 1984.

3. "Petersen Urges Internal Communication," *Parson*, 16 March 1979, 11.

4. "Retrenchment," *Parson*, 2 March 1979, 1; and WC Trustee Minutes, 28 February 1979.

5. Sterling McMurrin, interview by author, 1 June 1994. See also WC Trustee Minutes, 19 March and 23 April 1979.

6. "Community Leaders Meet in Support of Westminster College," *Parson*, 18 May 1979, 1; "Westminster Gears Up for Fund Raising," *Deseret News*, 25 August 1979; and Sterling McMurrin, interview by Keith Wilson, 17 February 1994, WC Archives.

7. *Westminster College Looks to the Future: A Report to the President and the Board of Trustees* (Washington and New York, November 1979), 17–35. See also Sidney G. Tickton to James E. Petersen, 20 April 1979, WC Archives.

8. Tickton, "Westminster College Looks to the Future," 53.

9. Ibid., 81–116. See also "Study Plots School's Future," *Parson*, 14 September 1979, 1–2.

10. "We Love You Pete," *Parson*, 18 May 1979, 4.

11. "Thanks to All," *Parson*, 13 April 1979, 2.

12. "New College President Takes Office," *Parson*, 14 September 1979, 1; and "New Westminster President," *Deseret News*, 1 August 1979. According to Cornell, he was told "save it or close it." C. David Cornell, interview by author, 16 May 1995.

13. WC Trustee Minutes, 15 October 1979; and "Tickton Report Draws Student Response," *Parson*, 12 October 1979, 1.

14. WC Trustee Minutes, 28 January 1980, 23 February and 21 December 1981; and "Vice Presidential Resignations Announced," *Parson*, 15 February 1980, 1.

15. "Westminster College Self-Study Report, October 1981," III-7, WC Archives.

16. "Westminster Gains New Program in Applied Politics," *Newscope* (spring 1980): 2; and WC Trustee Minutes, 19 November 1979.

17. "Everything from Wine to Bridge," *Newscope* (fall 1980): 19; and "Curriculum Changes Necessary," *Parson*, 27 October 1980, 1.

18. WC Trustee Minutes, 23 February and 16 March 1981.

19. WC Trustee Minutes, 19 May 1980.

20. "President N. Eldon Tanner Honored in Impressive Ceremony," *Newscope* (spring 1981): 2; and "LDS Apostle to Receive Honorary Doctorate," *Parson*, 23 February 1981, 1. The special convocation was held because of Tanner's health.

21. "Changes Due to Programs Not Performances," *Parson*, 27 April 1981, 1.

22. WC Trustee Minutes, 15 December and 20 July 1981; and C. David Cornell, Memo to Faculty and Staff, 21 January 1981, WC Archives.

23. "We Did It!," *Newscope* (spring 1982): 1.

24. Wilson, "The Process of Secularization at Westminster College," 96–97. Wilson's observations are based on interviews with various Westminster administrators from this time period. One secretary related that she had been dismissed because her home telephone line was busy for an extended period when Cornell was trying to reach her.

25. WC Trustee Minutes, 20 July 1981. In February, Cornell described campus conditions to a friend. "Things are tense here. We are in the process of eliminating non-productive academic programs: geology, most of political science, and music. This is not a happy assignment. And, as you might suspect, some faculty members are firing away at me and my new Academic Vice President and Dean. The faculty members are going directly to the trustees. Now we'll find out how strong the latter really are." C. David Cornell to Richard Armour, 9 February 1981, WC Archives.

26. Stephen R. Morgan, interview by Keith Wilson, 18 March 1994; and Alonzo Watson, interview by Keith Wilson, 7 March 1994, WC Archives.

27. WC Trustee Minutes, 18 May 1981; and "To Confide or Not to Confide," *Parson*, 17 April 1981, 1.

28. "Letters to the Editor," *Parson*, 6 October 1980, 2.

29. James F. Bemis to C. David Cornell, 10 December 1981, WC Archives.

30. One campus observer wrote Cornell, "The morale among faculty and staff is at an all time low. Having very limited opportunity to participate in decisions, feeling alienated

and insecure, there is fear and resentment. Such feelings are not confined to a few malcontents. They are widespread." Horace M. McMullen to David C. Cornell, 17 July 1981, WC Archives.

31. WC Trustee Minutes, 22 February 1992; and "Westminster President Resigns," *Salt Lake Tribune*, 23 February 1982.

32. "Board of Trustees Appoints New President," *Newscope* (winter–spring 1982): 9.

33. James E. Petersen to returning students, 30 July 1982, WC Archives.

34. James E. Petersen to Deborah M. Jenkins, 30 June 1982, WC Archives.

35. Diane Cole, "Neither Church nor State Eager to Aid Westminster," *Salt Lake Tribune,* 23 February 1982; and WC Trustee Minutes, 5 April 1982.

36. "Community Expresses Confidence," *Parson*, 2 April 1982, 1.

37. Steeples, "Westminster College of Salt Lake City," 72–73.

38. WC Trustee Minutes, 15 November 1982. According to one faculty member, Petersen boasted that his greatest accomplishment at Westminster was "beating the faculty." Interview, Barry Quinn with author, 27 May 1994, WC Archives.

39. Steeples, "Westminster College of Salt Lake City," 73–74.

40. Ibid., 74.

41. Ibid., 74–75.

42. WC Trustee Minutes, 17 January 1983.

43. Steeples, "Westminster College of Salt Lake City," 74–75. The revised bylaws also removed language indicating any connection with the Presbyterian Church. If the college were to be dissolved, then assets could be distributed to any nonprofit organization.

44. "Trustees Inaugurate a New Era in History of Westminster College," *Newscope* (spring 1983): 1.

45. "Bold Move by Westminster," *Deseret News*, 19 January 1983.

46. "Westminster to Streamline Operations, Save Money," *Salt Lake Tribune*, 19 January 1983.

47. Karen J. Winkler, "Faculty Wary of Plan to Close Utah College," *Chronicle of Higher Education* 32 (February 1983): 11.

48. Robert Warnock, interview by author, 27 May 1994. A number of faculty members resigned in the wake of reorganization. One professor said, "The personal trauma suffered by my family, due to the College's financial instability and organizational flux, in many respects is irreparable and unwarranted. We, as a family, can no longer justify the personal and professional sacrifices we have been forced to make because of the College's inability to become fiscally and organizationally sound." Douglas F. Kennard to Douglas Steeples, 6 May 1983, WC Archives.

49. James E. Petersen to Faculty Colleagues, letter with attachment, 14 February 1983.

50. WC Trustee Minutes, 25 February 1983; and Douglas W. Steeples to James F. Bemis, 17 June 1983, WC Archives. The Westminster faculty passed a resolution favoring the retention of tenure "because it protects faculty members against pressure from inside and outside the academic community and protects academic freedom which, in turn, maintains the college's dedication to the search for truth." Minutes of the Westminster Faculty, 6 April 1983, WC Archives.

51. "Interim Evaluation Committee Report, May 17–19, 1983," 5–26, WC Archives.

52. James F. Bemis to James E. Petersen, 21 June 1983, WC Archives.

53. Steeples, "Westminster College of Salt Lake City," 77.

54. Stephen R. Morgan, interview by author, 17 October 1996, WC Archives.

55. "Dr. Bradshaw Exclusive," *Newscope* (summer 1985): 1–2.

56. WC Trustee Minutes, 19 August 1983.

57. "Report of Interim Visit to Westminster College of Salt Lake City," 30 October 1984, 1–15, WC Archives; and Elaine Jarvik, "Westminster—The Turn Around Year," *Newscope* (spring 1984): 1–3.

58. "Academic Freedom and Tenure at Westminster College of Salt Lake City," *Academe* (November–December 1984): 1-a-10a. According to current Westminster administrators, the AAUP censure neither has impacted negatively on faculty recruitment nor created problems for Westminster's national or regional reputation.

59. "President Announces Anticipated Resignation," *Newscope* (fall 1984): 1.

60. "Death of James E. Petersen," *Salt Lake Tribune*, 20 April 1996.

61. Petersen died on April 18, 1996, age seventy-seven, in Phoenix, Arizona.

62. "Board of Trustees Selects New President," *Forum*, 5 April 1984, 1. In announcing the appointment of Westminster's fourteenth president, search committee chairman Robert Pratt said, "We were looking for a superman, and we found one."

63. Dana Tumpowsky, "Westminster College's Renaissance Man," *Westminster Review* (summer 1995): 6–7; and Christopher Thomas, "The Legacies of Leadership," 13.

64. Robert Warnock, interview by author, 27 May 1994.

65. "Westminster's New President," *Newscope* (spring 1985): 1–2.

66. Charles H. Dick, "President's Address to the Faculty," 3 September 1985, WC Archives.

67. "Westminster College Salt Lake City Strategic Plan," 1989, 1–6, WC Archives.

68. "George Stoddard Eccles—The Man, The Legend," *Parson*, 26 February 1982, 1.

69. "Jewett Center for the Arts and Humanities," *Westminster Review* (winter 1989): 4.

70. WC Trustee Minutes, 15 December 1988, 22 March 1989, and 19 October 1989. See also "Challenge of Freedom," *Westminster Review* (spring 1989): 2–3.

71. "Capital Campaign Announced," *Westminster Review* (winter 1989): 3.

72. "Library to Become Center of Campus," *Westminster Review* (fall 1995): 4–5; and "Cornerstone Placed for the Giovale Library," *Connections*, Inaugural Edition (fall 1996): 5; and "Westminster's Latest Victory: New Library," *Salt Lake Tribune*, 13 September 1997, D1.

73. *Forum*, 19 April 88, 6; "72 Years of Support for the College" and "Woman's Board Continues to Play Significant Role," *Newscope* (winter 1983): 7. Also Noreen C. Rouillard to author, 6 May 1997. The four endowed scholarships (Helen Koch Memorial, Ruth Skeeters Memorial, Wheatlake Memorial, and Katherine Rouillard Memorial) have a market value exceeding $135,000.

74. Britt Fekete, "The Baar Necessities," *Forum*, 11 October 1995, 1.

75. "Westminster to Establish School of Education," *Forum*, 29 March 1995.

76. "Graduate Students Lead Double Lives," *Westminster Review* (winter 1989): 5–6; and Dana Tumpowsky, "Masters Degree Programs at Westminster," *Westminster Review* (summer 1995): 25. Presently Westminster has three professional schools: education, nursing, and business, in addition to a fourth school of arts and sciences.

77. *Westminster College Academic Catalog 1996–97*, 98–104, 134–35, 147–150, 151–53; "Tanner McMurrin Lecture," *Newscope* (spring 1991): 9; and "Westminster Scholars: A Program Whose Time Has Come," *Newscope* (spring 1988): 10–11.

78. "Westminster Self-Study Report," 1993, 353–58, 372–73. See also WC Trustee Minutes, 19 October 1989 and 29 May 1992; and "Westminster's Adamson Chair," *Westminster Review* (winter 1994): 9. The teaching award, bearing a $5,000 stipend, was

first presented in 1992 to Shirley Knox of the School of Nursing. Subsequent recipients have included Bruce Bemis, mathematics; Suzan Cottler, history; Alan Rogers, accounting; and Diane Van Os, nursing. The Kim T. Adamson Chair in International Studies, funded in 1993, is presently held by Professor Robert Ford, whose research specialty is cultural ecology.

79. "Report to the Commission on Colleges, Northwest Association of Schools and Colleges on Interim Visit to Westminster College of Salt Lake City," 11 May 1988, n.p., WC Archives. See also "Accreditation Visit," *Forum*, 1 October 1991, 1, where the Kerin's letter is quoted. In October 1988, *U.S. News and World Report* listed Westminster among the top twenty-five regional liberal arts colleges. See WC Trustee Minutes, 20 October 1988.

80. "Northwest Association of Schools and Colleges, Evaluation Committee Report of Westminster College," 5–7 April 1993, 4.

81. Ibid., 1–25. A University of Utah survey on in-state public and private educational institutions and five peer institutions conducted in 1991 gave Westminster positive evaluations. In the survey Westminster ranked first in student employment and vocational preparation, second in concern for students, and fourth in general reputation. WC Trustee Minutes, 19 March 1991.

82. "Northwest Association Evaluation Report," 1993, 28–30.

83. Charles Dick to Joseph T. McMillan, Jr., 2 August 1985, WC Archives. In 1986 Westminster's trustees voted unanimously to remain an ecumenical institution with no specific religious affiliation. Charles Dick to Roy B. Shilling Jr., 7 October 1986 and 23 October 1987, WC Archives.

84. WC Trustees Minutes, 13 October 1993.

85. WC Trustee Minutes, 18 October 1995. See also Stuart M. Hanson, Jr., and Kelly De Hill, "Report to the Board of Trustees: Westminster College and Its Current Connection with the Presbyterian Church U.S.A," WC Trustee Minutes, 15 March 1996. The college continues to employ a part-time chaplain who coordinates religious activities on campus.

86. Christopher Thomas, "Parsons Kick-Off New Season," *Westminster Review* (summer 1995): 28; and "Lady Parsons Take to the Net," *Westminster Review* (summer 1995): 29.

87. "Westminster: Home of the Utah Jazz," *Westminster Review* (spring 1989): 10–11.

88. Elizabeth Peterson, "Hangin' Out Westminster Style," *Westminster Review* (summer 1994): 4–6.

89. Dana Tumpowsky, "Westminster College's Renaissance Man," *Westminster Review* (summer 1995): 6–8.

90. Carli Dixon, "Westminster Says Goodbye to Dr. Charles and Barbara Dick," *Westminster Review* (summer 1995): 9; and Charles Dick, "President's Message," *Westminster Review*, (winter 1993): 17.

Epilogue

Into the New Century

*The future belongs to those who believe in the beauty of their
dreams.*
—Eleanor Roosevelt, inscribed on the Giovale Library.

In the summer of 1995 Peggy A. Stock was named president of
Westminster College. Based on experience, credentials, and demonstrated
ability, she was chosen to lead Westminster College into the next century.
She also became Utah's first female college president, an item that the
Utah news media highlighted in their reports. In an interview with the *Salt
Lake Tribune*, Stock did not dwell on a discussion of gender. "It is not an
issue for me. Being competent is the issue."[1]

Stock received her bachelor of science degree at St. Lawrence
University in Canton, New York, and earned a master's degree and doctor
of education in counseling psychology from the University of Kentucky.
Prior to her ten-year tenure as president of Colby-Sawyer College, Stock
held several administrative posts at the University of Hartford. She gained
some familiarity with the western United States during three years at
Montana State University, at which she served as assistant dean in the
Office of Student Services.[2]

Stock was inaugurated as Westminster's fifteenth president on
October 19, 1996, in the state capital rotunda. Attended by a large assem-
blage of Westminster faculty and staff, representatives from other colleges and universities, townspeople, and guests, Utah Governor Michael
Leavitt and Senator Orrin Hatch were among the featured speakers. Other
participants included Richard O. Wyatt, executive of the Synod of Rocky
Mountains, Presbyterian Church (U.S.A.), Keith Christensen, chair of the

Salt Lake City Council, and Merrill Bateman, president of Brigham Young University. Also invited to make remarks were Cecilia Foxley, commissioner of higher education in Utah, Spencer Eccles, chief executive officer of First Security Corporation, and Ginger Giovale, chair of Westminster College's board of trustees.

In her inaugural address, Stock charted a course for Westminster College as it approaches its 125-year anniversary in the year 2000. Recognizing the dramatic changes taking place in higher education, Stock asked, "Why shouldn't Westminster College lead the transformation of higher education in the Intermountain West?" She offered her response: "Our size, our mission, and our governance structure make it much easier for us to try new things. We do have the opportunity and the flexibility. The question is, do we have the courage and the gumption? I think we do. Why not?" Using the theme of change, Stock challenged the institution to reevaluate assumptions about educational process and provide leadership for a revitalized and renewed curriculum that would address the needs of a new century. "It is our responsibility to those we serve to lead educational reform. It is, in fact, our duty."[3]

In keeping with her call for innovation and flexibility at Westminster, Stock is pursuing plans that include a weekend college program for adults whose responsibilities preclude the traditional weekday and evening pattern, an enlarged residential student body of five hundred that will require the acquisition of more acreage as well as additional dormitory and parking facilities, a computerized campus that will provide every student with access to the latest information technology resources, and a fully equipped health-wellness center that will serve the academic and wider community. In addition she anticipates inaugurating an academic honor code, establishing closer working alliances with other state and private institutions of higher education in Utah, and increasing faculty salaries to make Westminster competitive with its peer institutions. Because these plans require substantial funding, Stock also is attempting to increase Westminster's endowment so that the college can keep pace with anticipated growth and development.[4]

Predictions about Westminster's future lie beyond the bounds of this institutional history. Rather than engage in speculation then, this narrative will reflect on questions that have emerged during the research. Even though such questions can appear myopic in retrospect, they also can summarize historical accomplishments and foreshadow future issues. Not unlike other private institutions of higher education, the college faces challenges involving the cost of the growth and development of facilities and programs in an environment of widening distance between the price of private education and the ability or willingness of a large enough constituency to pay for it. With information technology influencing the entire spectrum of education, from the primary to the graduate level, needs will escalate for the purchase and replacement of current equipment, the education and training of faculty, staff, and students in its use, the development of strategic planning and costs analysis for its integration into the institution, and the implementation of a plan for outcomes assessment of technology in the educational program. Westminster surely will engage in discussions of the appropriate curricular changes that might be required in a world using technology in different and innovative ways. It also will deal with the development of its faculty and the composition of its student body, its admissions recruitment strategy and entrance standards as well as the issues regarding the rising needs for student financial aid.

Westminster has always been an institution in search of an identity. Initially a minority Presbyterian college in tension with the dominant Mormon culture, Westminster has evolved into a private independent institution with no religious affiliation. As it enters a new period, the history uncovered by this document suggests three issues that might warrant a continuing discussion among the college community. First, without suggesting that past church relationships be restored, the administration and faculty might debate the value of the college's incorporating in some way the rich religious traditions that have gone into its creation and sustentation. Second, rooted in the liberal arts tradition, Westminster has introduced a variety of professional courses and programs into its curriculum. How these two different educational philosophies can be integrated while maintaining the academic integrity of both could lead to stimulating, frank, and instructive conversations. Third, throughout its history Westminster has been noted for its personalized education and campus community. The changing enrollment patterns, the increasing emphasis on information technology, and the use of part-time and adjunct faculty might lead to dialogues on ways in which the institution can sustain and strengthen individual attention and community spirit, whether by a return to a more traditional residential campus or the creation of a new kind of campus community, or both.

One hundred years ago, Westminster approached the new century housed in rented rooms with two faculty members and no educational support services, such as a library, laboratory instrumentation, or classroom equipment. Nevertheless, the founders persevered to establish an institution that through the years has produced quality, diversity, and innovation in the area of higher education in Utah. Today Westminster stands on the threshold of another century, having a modern and well-equipped campus with a hundred full-time faculty and an equal number of part-time instructors. While its situation may be different from that of 1897, the future is equally challenging and calls for prudent and daring responses. In 1938, near the end of his quarter-century presidency and in the midst of a debilitating economic depression, Herbert W. Reherd expressed hope for Westminster's future in words that still seem appropriate. "Let me express my faith that Westminster has a real future. I am convinced that Utah and this intermountain country need Westminster, and that enough men and women of vision and generous spirit will be found to build here a college of growing influence and abiding strength."[5]

NOTES

1. Joan O'Brian, "Westminster Names Woman as President," *Salt Lake Tribune*, 9 April 1995. Stock left a similar position at Colby-Sawyer College in New Hampshire to assume the new post in Salt Lake City.

2. Carli Dixon, "Dr. Peggy Stock Accepts Position as New Westminster President," *Westminster Review* (summer 1995): 4–5. At the University of Hartford, her positions included vice president, executive associate in development, and special assistant to the president. An avid outdoors person, Stock and her husband, Robert, also an educator, own six Arabian horses and share common interests in gardening and antique collecting.

3. "The Inaugural Address," *Westminster College Connections* (fall 1996): 3–4.

4. Peggy Stock, interview by author, 10 March 1997, WC Archives.

5. WC Trustee Minutes, 15 September 1938.

Selected Bibliography

ARCHIVAL MATERIALS
This history relies heavily on archival materials such as minutes, committee reports, memoranda, narratives, correspondence, and various
denominational and college publications. Although most of these materials
can be found in the Westminster College archives, some are located in
regional and national archival depositories, including the Presbyterian
Historical Society and the University of Utah. Other collections relating to
Utah Presbyterianism and Latter-day Saints (LDS) are located in the LDS
Historical Department, the Utah State Historical Society, the University of
Utah, Utah State University, Brigham Young University, Wasatch Academy,
and San Anselmo Presbyterian Theological Seminary in California. The
sources of archival materials cited are indicated in the endnote references.
Presently, the Westminster archives are in the process of relocation to a new
library facility and will not be readily accessible to researchers for some
time. There are also documents stored in the Robinson Room of Walker
Hall that will eventually be integrated into the present archival collection.
In the Westminster archives are annual academic catalogs that date back to
1875 and the founding of the Salt Lake Collegiate Institute. Although a few
issues are missing from the period 1878–1895, the collection is otherwise
complete. Catalogs from the period 1914–1969 are numbered as volumes
of the *Utah Westminster*, a monthly college newsletter that contains photographs and information about campus activities. Minutes of the Board of
Trustees along with related papers and correspondence provide the best
continuous narrative of administrative policies, curricular changes, and
financial developments. Accreditation Self-Study Reports dating back to

1947 offer unique perspectives on institutional history because they contain both internal and external evaluations of college operations. The collections of presidential papers and photographs are stored in metal filing cabinets along with other biographical data, including John Coyner's handwritten "History of the Salt Lake Collegiate Institute" and the correspondence of Robert Caskey, Robert McNiece, George Sweazey, Robert Stevenson, Herbert W. Reherd, and Robert D. Steele. With correspondence in the Sheldon Jackson Papers and the College Board Record Group in the Presbyterian Historical Archives, this material sheds light on the origins and early history of Westminster. More recent presidential papers and related academic and financial records are stored in the Robinson Room in Walker Hall. With these papers are some correspondence, reports, publications, and photographs from the era 1920–1950. A filing cabinet presently in the library work area contains correspondence, scrapbooks, photographs, and copies of various Presbyterian periodicals donated by William Peden, former minister of First Presbyterian Church in Salt Lake City and trustee of Westminster College.

INSTITUTIONAL MINUTES, REPORTS AND PAPERS

Presbyterian Historical Society Archives

Annual Report of the Board of Christian Education, 1923–1972.

Annual Report of the Board of College Aid, later Board of General Education, 1884–1923.

Annual Report of the Board of Home Missions, 1870–1910.

Annual Report of the Woman's Executive Committee, later Woman's Board of Home Missions, 1880–1910.

Board of National Missions—Reports and Histories. Record Group 111 (reprocessed).

College Board Records (Presbyterian Church in the U.S.A.), 1883–1948. Record Group 32.

Minutes of the General Assembly of the Presbyterian Church in the U.S.A., later United Presbyterian Church of the United States of America, 1870–1983.

Minutes of the General Assembly of the Presbyterian Church (U.S.A.), 1983–1997.

Minutes of the Presbytery of Utah, 1874–1900.

Minutes of the Synod of Utah, 1884–1945.

Reeves, Kenneth. "Survey Report on Expressions of Religious Life: Westminster College, Salt Lake City, Utah." 12 February 1952.

Sheldon Jackson Papers, 1855–1909. Record Group 239.

Winters, C. L. "Survey Report: Westminster College, Salt Lake City, Utah." 6 May 1951.
Woman's Executive Committee of Home Missions/Woman's Board of Home Missions, 1866–1958. Record Group 305.

Westminster College Archives
Briscoe, Raymond G. "Westminster College and Other Institutions of Higher Learning: A Specified Utah Market Survey." Spring 1980.
Coyner, John M., "A History of the Salt Lake Collegiate Institute," 1875–1899.
Kelly, Robert L. *Cooperation in Education in Utah: Report on Westminster College.* New York, 1922.
Martin, Theodore D. and Marian E., "Presbyterian Work in Utah 1869–1969," typescript, 1970.
Minutes of Board of Trustees of Sheldon Jackson College, later Westminster College, and related papers, 1892–1997.
Minutes of the Student Association of Salt Lake Collegiate Institute and Westminster College, 1910–1926.
Minutes of the Woman's Board of Westminster College, 1905–1985.
Minutes of the Westminster Student Council, 1948–1955.
"A Pursuit of Excellence: The Case for Westminster College 1980–1990."
Reherd, Herbert W., "A History of Westminster College," complied by Emil Nyman, n.d.
Self-Study Accreditation Reports and Evaluations, Northwest Association of Schools and Colleges, 1947–1993.
"Westminster College Looks to the Future: A Report to the President and Board of Trustees," Academy for Educational Development, Washington and New York, 1979.
Works, George A. and H. M. Gage, "Statement on Westminster College," 20 January 1944.

University of Utah Archives
Minutes of the Board of Directors of the Salt Lake Collegiate Institute, 1875–1896.
Minutes of the First Presbyterian Church of Salt Lake City, 1872–1900.
Addresses at the Tenth Anniversary of the First Presbyterian Church, 1882.

NEWSPAPERS AND PERIODICALS

Presbyterian Historical Society Archives
Assembly Herald, 1900–1910
Continent, 1890–1926

The Church at Home and Abroad, 1887–1898
Home Mission Monthly, 1886–1923
Presbyterian Advance, 1910–1934
Presbyterian Home Missions, 1882–1883
Presbyterian Home Missionary, 1883–1886
Herald and Presbyter, 1897–1915
Interior, 1890–1910
Our Mission Field, 1871–1885
Rocky Mountain Presbyterian, 1872–1882
United Presbyterian, 1920–1922

University of Utah Archives
Church Review, 1894–1895
Deseret Evening News, 1868–1910
Deseret News, 1910–1997
Salt Lake Herald, 1890–1900
Salt Lake Tribune, 1870–1997
Utah Educational Journal, 1875–1876

Westminster College Archives
Collegiate Life, 1912–1913
Campus Crier, 1945–1953
Etosian, 1919–1977
Parson, 1953–1982
Forum, 1982–1997
Kinsman, 1897–1901
Newscope, 1972–1995
Utah Evangelist, 1883–1884
Utah Westminster, 1914–1972
Westminster Connections, 1996–1997
Westminster Herald, 1903–1904
Westminster Review, 1988–1997

Books

Alexander, Thomas G. *Mormonism in Transition: A History of the Latter-day Saints, 1890–1930*. Urbana and Chicago, 1986.

Alexander, Thomas G., and James B. Allen. *Mormons and Gentiles: A History of Salt Lake City*. Boulder, Colorado, 1984.

Antrei, Albert C., and Ruth D. Scow, editors. *The Other Forty-Niners: A Topical History of Sanpete County, Utah 1849–1983*. Salt Lake City, 1982.

Arrington, Leonard J, and Davis Bitton. *The Mormon Experience.* New York, 1979.

Balmer, Randall and J. Fitzmier. *The Presbyterians.* Westport, Connecticut, 1994.

Banker, Mark T. *Presbyterian Missions and Cultural Interaction in the Far Southwest.* Urbana and Chicago, 1993.

Bender, Norman. *Winning the West for Christ: Sheldon Jackson and Presbyterianism on the Rocky Mountain Frontier.* Albuquerque, 1996.

Buchanan, Frederick S. *Culture Clash and Accommodation: Public Schooling in Salt Lake City, 1890–1994.* San Francisco and Salt Lake City, 1996.

Bushman, Richard L. *Joseph Smith and the Beginnings of Mormonism.* Urbana and Chicago, 1984.

Clarke, James E. *Presbyterian Colleges.* New York, 1913.

————. *General Education in the Presbyterian Church in the U. S. A.* New York, n.d.

Cuninggim, Merriman. *Church-Related Higher Education.* Valley Forge, Pennsylvania, 1978.

Drury, Clifford. *Presbyterian Panorama.* Philadelphia, 1950.

Dwyer, Robert J. *The Gentile Comes to Utah: A Study in Religion and Social Conflict.* Second edition. Salt Lake City, 1971.

Geiger, C. Harve. *The Program of Higher Education of the Presbyterian Church in the United States of America.* Cedar Rapids, Iowa, 1940.

Grueningen, John Paul. *Toward a Christian Philosophy of Higher Education.* Philadelphia, 1958.

Horowitz, Irving L., and William H. Friedland. *The Knowledge Factory: Student Power and Academic Politics in America.* Chicago, 1970.

Kelly, Robert L. *The American Colleges and the Social Order.* New York, 1940.

Leslie, W. Bruce. *Gentlemen and Scholars: College and Community in the 'Age of the University,' 1865–1917.* University Park, Pennsylvania, 1992.

Marsden, George. *The Secularization of the Academy.* New York and Oxford, 1992.

————. *The Soul of the American University.* New York and Oxford, 1994.

May, Dean. *Utah: A People's History.* Salt Lake City, 1987.

McNeil, John T. *The History and Character of Calvinism.* Philadelphia, 1967.

Miller, Howard. *The Revolutionary College: American Presbyterian Higher Education 1707–1837.* New York, 1976.

Murray, Andrew. *The Skyline Synod: Presbyterianism in Colorado and Utah*. Denver, 1981.

Nyman, Emil. *A Short History of Westminster College Salt Lake City*. Salt Lake City, 1975.

Parker, T. H. L. *John Calvin: A Biography*. Philadelphia, 1975.

Patillo, Manning M., Jr. and Donald M. Mackenzie. *Church-Sponsored Higher Education in the United States*. Washington, D.C., 1966.

Poll, Richard D., editor. *Utah's History*. Logan, Utah, 1989.

Reherd, Herbert W. "An Outline History of Protestant Churches of Utah." In *Utah A Centennial History*, edited by Wain Sutton. 2 vols. New York, 1949.

Ringenberg, William C. *The Christian College: A History of Protestant Higher Education in America*. Grand Rapids, 1984.

Sherrill, Lewis J. *Presbyterian Parochial Schools*. New Haven, 1932.

Shipps, Jan. *Mormonism: The Story of a New Religious Tradition*. Urbana and Chicago, 1985.

Simmonds, A. J. *The Gentile Comes to Cache Valley*. Logan, Utah, 1976.

Snavely, Guy E. *The Church and the Four-Year College*. New York, 1955.

Steeples, Douglas W. "Westminster College of Salt Lake City." In *Successful Strategic Planning: Case Studies*, edited by Douglas W. Steeples. San Francisco and London, 1988.

Stewart, Robert Laird. *Sheldon Jackson*. New York, Chicago, and Toronto, 1908.

Szasz, Ferenc M. *The Protestant Clergy in the Great Plains and Rocky Mountain West 1865–1915*. Albuquerque, 1988.

Tewksbury, D. *The Founding of American Colleges and Universities before the Civil War*. New York, 1966.

ARTICLES

Brackenridge, R. Douglas. "The Evolution of an Anti-Mormon Story." *Journal of Mormon History* 21 (spring 1995): 80–105.

Buchanan, Frederick S. "Education among the Mormons: Brigham Young and the Schools of Utah." *History of Education Quarterly* 22 (winter 1982): 435–59.

Davies, George K. "History of the Presbyterian Church in Utah." *Journal of Presbyterian History* 23 (December 1945): 228–48, 24 (March 1946): 44–68, 24 (September 1946): 147–51, and 25 (March 1947): 46–63.

Fisher, John H. "Primary and Secondary Education and the Presbyterian Church in the United States of America." *Journal of Presbyterian History* 24 (March 1946): 13–43.

Goslin, Thomas S. "Henry Kendall: Missionary Statesman." *Journal of Presbyterian History* 27 (June 1949): 70–85.

Hinckley, Ted C. "Sheldon Jackson: Gilden Age Apostle." *Journal of the West* 23 (January 1984): 16–25.

Hollis, Frances L. "The Church's Mission in Higher Education." *Journal of Presbyterian History* 59 (fall 1981): 440–61.

Hough, C. Merrill. "Two School Systems in Conflict: 1867–1890." *Utah Historical Quarterly* 28 (spring 1983):113–28.

Ivins, Stanley. "Free Schools Come to Utah." *Utah Historical Quarterly* 22 (July 1954): 321–42.

Lyon, Thomas E. "Religious Activities and Development in Utah, 1847–1910," *Utah Historical Quarterly* 35 (fall 1967): 292–306.

Vinatori, Joseph A. "The Growing Years: Westminster College from Birth to Adolescence." *Utah Historical Quarterly* 43 (fall 1975): 344–51.

DISSERTATIONS AND THESES

Baird, Paul. "A Critique of Presbyterian Ministry in the Great Basin 1897–1931." Doctor of Theology dissertation, San Fransisco Theological Seminary, 1977.

Buzza, David E. "Contributions to a History of Utah's Westminster College." Master's thesis, Presbyterian Theological Seminary of Chicago, 1939.

Davies, George K. "A History of the Presbyterian Church in Utah." Ph.D. dissertation, University of Pittsburgh, 1942.

Hodges, Muriel Lee Hurtt. "Perception of Westminster College by Selected Constituent Groups." Ph.D. dissertation, University of Utah, 1972.

Lyon, Thomas. E. "Evangelical Protestant Missionary Activities in Mormon Dominated Areas." Ph.D. dissertation, University of Utah, 1962.

Wankier, Carl. "History of Presbyterian Schools in Utah." Master's thesis, University of Utah, 1968.

Webster, Lewis G. "A History of Westminster College of Salt Lake City, Utah, 1875–1969." Master's thesis, Utah State University, 1970.

Wilson, Keith J. "The Process of Secularization at Westminster College of Salt Lake City: A Case Study," Ph. D. dissertation, The University of Utah, 1995.

INTERVIEWS

Westminster College Archives
By Author
Stephen R. Baar, 26 May 1994 and numerous occasions
Bruce Bemis, 23 May 1994

Alice and James Boyack, 27 May 1994
Lucille Bywater, 31 May 1994
Haydon Calvert, 23 May 1994
Miriam Cooper, 8 August 1995
C. David Cornell (telephone), 16 May 1995
Arthur T. Cox, 23 May 1994
Stephen Crane, 24 May 1994
Charles Dick, 18 May 1994
Virginia Frobes-Wetzel, 24 May 1994
Vieve Gore (telephone), 15 May 1995
Craig Green, 1 June 1994
Kay Hammill, 25 May 1994
Pat Lees, 26 May 1994
Calvin Lum (telephone), 10 November 1995
Coleen Malouf, 8 August 1995
Sterling McMurrin, 1 June 1994
Stephen R. Morgan, 2 June 1994 and numerous occasions.
Lorraine Nickerson, 26 May 1994
Ray Ownbey, 26 May 1994
Janet Booth Palmer, 1 June 1994
Barry Quinn, 27 May 1994
Don and Noreen Rouillard, 1 June 1994
June Shaw, 25 May 1994
Byron Sims, 15 May 1994
Mansel Smith, 7 August 1995
Beverly Snodgress, 24 May 1994
David Steele (telephone), 15 June 1995
Douglas W. Steeples (telephone), 24 May 1994
Thomas Steinke, 21 May 1996
Harold Viehman (telephone), 8 October 1996
Frances Wahlberg, 15 May 1995
Robert Warnock, 27 May 1994
Alonzo Watson, Jr., 16 May 1994
Burton Wheatlake, 18 October 1996
Richard Wunder, 24 May 1994
John Young, 23 May 1994

Index